TSBA

$6.95

THE SMALL BUSINESS ADMINISTRATION

ADDISON W. PARRIS

The Small Business Administration (SBA), an independent agency of the U.S. Government, was created in 1953 and made permanent in 1958 out of concern for that independent businessman described by the author as being typically "impatient, contrary, and unpredictable."

It is estimated that there are today about 4.8 million small business firms out of a total of slightly more than 5 million businesses in the United States. No one can give an exact figure for the number of small firms, nor precisely define what "small" means. The Small Business Act calls for the preservation and expansion of full and free economic competition; under its provisions, in 1966, it was determined that American Motors, one of the 200 biggest corporations in the United States, would henceforth be considered "small" for purposes of competing in government procurement. Generally, however, it is the truly small, independently owned business that is served by the SBA through its four principal functions: financial assistance, procurement assistance, management assistance, and assistance in providing venture capital.

Mr. Parris describes how the agency's 4,000 employees work in Washington and in more than seventy field offices across the country. Their job is to give advice and direct help to eligible small businesses. This book explains the details of their criteria for giving assistance: To be eligible for regular business loans (up to now, the most important program of the SBA), a small manufacturing firm is defined as one with 500 or fewer employees; a small wholesale business is one with annual sales or receipts of less than $5 million; a small retail sales or servive firm is one with annual sales or receipts of less than $1 million.

In addition to its regular business loans, the SBA gives disaster and displaced-business loans, economic-opportunity loans (under legislation that was part of the Johnson Administration's War on Poverty), and development-company loans (intended primarily to help rural and small-town areas).

Mr. Parris shows how the government procurement assistance program seeks to assure that small businesses receive their fair share of U.S. Government procurement and surplus property contracts. In the management assistance program, "how-to" publications, seminars, and personal counseling by SBA staff and retired business executives aim at reducing the number of business failures due to bad management. The complex —and controversial—SBA investment program is designed to help firms that are handicapped competitively by their inability to get long-term loans or equity capital from conventional sources.

Like other volumes in the Praeger Library of U.S. Government Departments and Agencies, this book covers the legislative history of the agency and treats its often stormy relations with Congress. Also treated in full, and with the insider's sense of controversy and compromise, are the agency's relationships with other sectors of the government, with the public, and with developing trends in American and international business life.

THE AUTHOR: Addison W. Parris joined the Small Business Administration in 1963 as Director, Office of Economic Adviser. Subsequently, he has served as Deputy Assistant Administrator for Management Assistance and Director, Office of Economic Opportunity Assistance. He has also been SBA Director, Office of Research and Policy Analysis. His many publications on economic and foreign policy include *The European Common Market and Its Meaning to the United States*.

FREDERICK A. PRAEGER, *Publishers*
New York • Washington • London

PRAEGER LIBRARY OF U.S. GOVERNMENT DEPARTMENTS
AND AGENCIES

Consulting Editors

ERNEST S. GRIFFITH

Former University Professor and Dean Emeritus, School of International Service, American University; former Director, Legislative Reference Service, Library of Congress; and author of *The American System of Government* and *The Modern Government in Action.*

HUGH LANGDON ELSBREE

Former Chairman, Department of Political Science, Dartmouth College; former Managing Editor, *American Political Science Review;* former Director, Legislative Reference Service, Library of Congress.

The
Small Business
Administration

Addison W. Parris

FREDERICK A. PRAEGER, *Publishers*

New York • Washington • London

In memory of my father,
PAUL SOUTHERLAND PARRIS

———————

FREDERICK A. PRAEGER, PUBLISHERS
111 Fourth Avenue, New York, N.Y. 10003, U.S.A.
5, Cromwell Place, London S.W.7, England

Published in the United States of America in 1968
by Frederick A. Praeger, Inc., Publishers

Library of Congress Catalog Card Number: 68–30938

This book is No. 15 in the series
Praeger Library of U.S. Government Departments and Agencies

Printed in the United States of America

Preface

The small businessman the world over is impatient, contrary, and unpredictable, seemingly an unlikely person to have a government agency devoted to his affairs. Yet that is exactly the job of one of the newer agencies of the U.S. Government: the Small Business Administration (SBA), created in 1953 and made permanent in 1958.

The SBA grew out of a series of agencies beginning with the Reconstruction Finance Corporation (RFC), born of the Great Depression. Then came the Smaller War Plants Corporation, established in 1942; the Office of Small Business in the Department of Commerce, which followed in 1946; and the Small Defense Plants Administration, set up in 1951. Although the other agencies bore something of a family name, the RFC was the real father of the present-day Small Business Administration.

Concern for the small businessman, however, is not a recent phenomenon in American society. The writers of the Constitution created a government of checks and balances in order to prevent the concentration of political power by dividing it among many individuals and groups. The fear of centralization has recurred throughout our history, and there has long been a suspicion among many Americans that economic power is political power. Hence, there have always been voices inveighing against great interests and championing diffusion. For example, Judge Learned Hand wrote in *United States* vs. *Aluminum Company of America,* "It is possible, because of its indirect social or moral effect, to prefer a system of small producers, each dependent for his success upon his own skill and character, to one in which the great mass of those engaged must accept the direction of a few."

This widely accepted view of our economic and political system involves the proposition that one of the basic requisites of the good society is numerous and economically significant and effective small businesses.

Sprung from the theories of the Founding Fathers, this conviction remains a basic American principle. The constitutional framework has had to be buttressed over the years by laws designed to meet changing economic and social conditions and massive alterations in our economic structure. Thus, in 1890, Congress passed the Sherman Antitrust Act and, in 1914, the Clayton Act. More recently, Congress has given greater attention to fair trade laws of various kinds, notably the Robinson-Patman Act, and favored small businesses on some federal purchases and sales of goods and services. In addition, special programs have been designed to help small firms overcome their short- and long-term credit problems.

Small business is a powerful political and economic stabilizer in a free society, but it has far more than intellectual interest to Americans. It strikes an emotional chord with many. From our earliest beginnings, the small businessman—like the yeoman farmer—has been and remains symbolic of our traditional aspirations. As he tends to pass somewhat from view, the American feeling about him is probably more, rather than less, emotional.

Ours is a society where everyone dreams, and believes, that he can be his own boss. Who does not know a friend who has his heart set on opening his own hardware store, insurance agency, motel, or boat marina? Horatio Alger is a peculiarly

American hero, and in our society one can still achieve the modern-day equivalent of going from a log cabin to the White House or from obscurity to fame or fortune. Small business is often the vehicle for the realization of these American dreams. During the years immediately following World War II, however, there was a growing uneasiness in Congress about the future of small business. The big firms were getting bigger, and it appeared that the small ones were not keeping pace. In some circles, there was a feeling that "small" business was a synonym for "inefficient" business and that large-scale enterprise was needed for efficiency in production, distribution, and finance. Many in Congress felt that small business was threatened and the laws passed previously to preserve competition were inadequate to deal with the threat. What was needed was an agency that would be active in promoting and protecting the interests of the small businessman. As a result of this thinking, the SBA was established.

This book will try to set forth as clearly as possible the major programs and policies of the SBA and describe the events leading up to the establishment of the agency. Particular attention will also be paid to developments on Capitol Hill. But the book will attempt to be much more than a simple history. It will be a chronicle of one instance of the way government works. As such, it will also seek to identify the economic and social elements underlying many of the policies, programs, and problems of the agency and to show the ways in which our political system handles these fundamental issues.

Why was the SBA created? What does it do? What does it fail to do? What could it do? How well does it do its job? And in what ways can we seek to measure its effectiveness politically, socially, and economically? These are certain of the questions with which we shall be concerned.

In a way, I suppose, everyone should write a book about something in which he has a keen interest, even if the book is only for his personal files. Not only will the author learn a lot that he already thought he knew; probably more importantly, he will become more aware of how little he actually does know or ever will know.

I undertook this assignment about the time I went to Somalia as economic adviser to that remote land. I had not thought at the time of returning to the SBA, for which I had worked from 1963 to 1967. Now I find myself in the somewhat embarrassing position of being at the agency while this book is being published.

Recently I told a friend of mine, not in government, that I had just finished a book on the SBA. He inquired whether the government was instituting a "publish or perish" policy, which, of course, is widely regarded as characterizing academic institutions today. I said that the opposite was more likely to be the case—that I might publish and perish. For the sake of my dependents, I hope not.

I cannot honestly say I enjoyed writing the book. Writing is a painful process, and one comes to the end of the task, uneasy, filled with nagging doubts and uncertainties about the adequacy of the effort.

But I am glad someone wrote this book. To my knowledge, it is the first to be published on the SBA, an institution I regard with affection. Many hours of my life have been spent there, and it is also there that I have formed some of my closest and most lasting friendships and associations.

So many people who work at the SBA have helped in the preparation of this volume that I am unable to single out any names for special thanks. I do wish to mention a former SBA colleague, Dr. Judith Ann Heimlich, now of the Brookings Institution. Dr. Heimlich wrote chapters IV, VIII, IX, and X and reviewed the entire manuscript.

ADDISON W. PARRIS

Washington, D.C.
July, 1968

Contents

List of Tables

xi

The Small Business
Administration

I

The SBA Is Born

The Small Business Administration was officially launched by Congress on July 30, 1953. Its basic charter is the Small Business Act of 1953, as amended, which states:

> It is the declared policy of the Congress that the Government should aid, counsel, assist, and protect, insofar as is possible, the interests of small-business concerns in order to preserve free competitive enterprise, to insure that a fair proportion of the total purchases and contracts or subcontracts for property and services for the Government (including but not limited to subcontracts for maintenance, repair and construction) be placed with small-business enterprises to ensure that a fair proportion of the total sales of Government property be made to such enterprises, and to maintain and strengthen the overall economy of the Nation.

As this is written, the SBA is but one of forty-six independent agencies of the federal government. In size and importance, it stands somewhere between such agencies as the National Aeronautics and Space Administration or the Atomic Energy Commission on the one hand and the American Battle Monuments Commission or the Commission on the Fine Arts on the other. At the end of 1965, the SBA had 3,785 employees, over three-fourths of them working outside Washington, D.C.

From its inception, in 1953, through 1965, the SBA had invested over $2.4 billion of the public's money in financial and development assistance to small firms. Of this amount, over $1.2 billion was outstanding at the end of 1965.

FORERUNNERS OF THE SBA

Before going into the Small Business Administration's past and present policies and operations, it is well to tell the story of the agency's predecessors. There were four: the Smaller War Plants Corporation; the Office of Small Business, within the United States Department of Commerce; the Small Defense Plants Administration; and the Reconstruction Finance Corporation.

These agencies have had a considerable bearing on what the SBA does and how it does it. The procurement policies and programs of the SBA were actually developed, for example, by the Smaller War Plants Corporation and the Small Defense Plants Administration. Again, the business lending programs were formulated and carried out previously by the Reconstruction Finance Corporation. And the management assistance and information services of the SBA closely parallel those formerly provided by the Office of Small Business at the Department of Commerce.

Perhaps more important is the fact that significant numbers of key SBA personnel are graduates of these predecessor organizations. Thus, many veterans of the older agencies can be found in SBA procurement assistance activities and many old Commerce hands in the management assistance activities. The financial assistance division has been characterized by at least one SBA administrator as being "imbued with the RFC mentality" and—perhaps more crudely—by the same SBA head as "being loaded with RFC types."

SMALLER WAR PLANTS CORPORATION (SWPC)

The Smaller War Plants Corporation was established on July 11, 1942. Small in scope and rather pedestrian in its functions, it was nonetheless important because it was the first government agency created for the purpose of helping small business meet the rigors of competition.

The SWPC was set up during the early days of America's involvement in World War II. At that time, many large manufacturers had been awarded prime military contracts, which absorbed nearly all the productive capacity of these big firms. This pattern had a considerable impact on small business. Small manufacturers were caught in a squeeze. Material was very scarce, and nearly all of it was going into the war effort. But neither the government nor the big war contractors really knew what small business firms could do for war production; they tended to be skeptical of the potential of small business. Thus, the small manufacturer faced a rather bleak prospect in both the civilian and military markets.

Sensitive to the complaints of small businessmen, Congress unanimously passed Public Law 603, of 1942, which created the Smaller War Plants Corporation. The law gave the new agency authority to make loans for war and essential civilian production to small firms and to undertake prime contracts from government procurement agencies for the purpose of awarding subcontracts to small concerns. In addition to these two major programs, the SWPC was also directed by the chairman of the War Production Board to make inventories of the productive facilities of the smaller manufacturers, to direct the attention of procurement officers at government contracting agencies to small plants, to help small businesses obtain subcontracts from big companies with war contracts, and to make various business studies.

During its lifetime, from November, 1942, to November, 1945, some 58,385 prime government contracts valued at more than $5.7 billion were awarded to small plants with the assistance of the SWPC. In addition, the agency helped obtain more than 52,000 subcontracts valued at $30.6 million. This modest figure was due primarily to the fact that subcontractors were able to contract business directly with the prime contractor or through the procurement agency. This became more and more the case as the war went on, and the need for SWPC's help dropped sharply in time. Subcontracting has been, after all, a traditional role for smaller concerns in the American industrial complex.

The SWPC made very little use of its authority to act as the prime contractor for government procurements. It took twelve prime contracts involving only $35.5 million. About 260 subcontracts were awarded by the SWPC to carry out these contracts. Nine of the twelve contracts were satisfactorily completed; two were terminated at the war's end; and one was inactive during this period.

Production pools, covering more than 2,000 small companies employing over 140,000 workers, obtained more than $600 million in war contracts. There were 32 formally certified production pools and nearly 100 in existence at the end of 1945.

On the financial side, the SWPC made some 5,808 loans and leases to small firms. This financial assistance was valued at $504 million. Banks participated with the agency in about a quarter of these loans and lent about $191 million in private funds under this program during the course of the war.

OFFICE OF SMALL BUSINESS, U.S. DEPARTMENT OF
    COMMERCE

After the war, the SWPC—always considered a temporary agency designed to expedite military production—was abolished. At that time, its lending, prime contract, and surplus property disposal powers were transferred to the Reconstruction Finance Corporation. Its remaining functions were given to the Department of Commerce.

Commerce Department officials who became responsible for the old SWPC operations were convinced that the predecessor agency had been too concerned with day-to-day projects for individual small businessmen and insufficiently involved in the more theoretical aspects of small business problems. The real need, the Commerce officials believed, was for general understanding of the unique problems of small business and the development and implementation of sound policies to deal with these special problems.

And, of course, there was a great need to educate the small businessman. The reason why many remained small and relatively unsuccessful rather than commercial Horatio Algers was, in the opinion of the Commerce Department, simply the fact that many small businessmen were not well educated. They had not kept pace with the rapid and ever accelerating developments in the art of management. Some did not even know the most rudimentary management principles and techniques.

This view had merit. Many students of small business today, in fact, would focus their primary attention upon management training and counseling and the necessity of specific legislation to assist small business with its particularly acute competitive problems.

But the view was also in line with bureaucratic realities. The Commerce Department had been given no operating responsibilities. The RFC got them. As a result, Commerce had to content itself with producing brochures and information and counseling those occasional small businessmen or would-be entrepreneurs who happened to wander into its offices.

THE SMALL DEFENSE PLANTS ADMINISTRATION (SDPA)

The Small Defense Plants Administration was created in October, 1951, with very limited functions. Congressional pressure for a new small business agency and the special urgency of the Korean War situation were responsible for its creation. It was given all the powers of the old Smaller War Plants Corporation except for the most important, the small business lending authority, which was kept by the RFC.

The SDPA had five principal functions. It issued certificates of competency regarding the ability of specific small firms to carry out government contracts. The agency claimed that this activity resulted in awards of $54 million in business to small firms during the nearly two years it was in existence. The SDPA also counseled small businessmen interested in obtaining defense business. Further, the agency itself took some seven military prime contracts with a total worth of $2.3 million and subcontracted the work. Moreover, SDPA offered materials and equipment aid programs for managers of small concerns. Finally, the agency carried on a modest information service dealing with its own programs and small business problems generally.

Essentially, the SDPA was not as effective an agency as many friends of small business would have liked. It wanted a direct voice in the process by which government contracts were placed with small businesses; it failed to get this power, receiving only a rather vague advisory role. Perhaps more significantly, it could not claim to be a true spokesman for small business because its authority was limited to defense production. It could not function in the civilian realm. The SDPA was also sharply constrained by budget and staff limitations, the red tape situation being such that its first administrator resigned in despair at the slow pace with which its key procurement assistance program got under way. In all, the SDPA never quite got off the ground.

The Reconstruction Finance Corporation (RFC)

The RFC is the real father of the SBA. Even today, the SBA bears the indelible stamp of the RFC on its policies and procedures and—most importantly—in the thought processes and style of many of its senior civil servants.

The RFC was created in January, 1932, during the depths of the Great Depression. It was actually established by President Herbert Hoover, although it later was anathema to many Republicans. It became the official residence of Thomas ("Tommy the Cork") Corcoran, Oscar Cox, and many other bright young men of President Franklin Roosevelt's New Deal —the "brain trusters"—and was a live-wire agency, reputed to have the best switchboard in the capital, the prettiest and most efficient secretaries, and, above all, enormous talent.

The RFC was also Jesse Jones, a giant of a man, a big hulking Texan, who had made a fortune in publishing, cattle, oil, real estate, and finance. Jones never went past the third grade and is reputed never to have read a book after his rather limited schooling. But he was shrewd and intelligent, and he had the burning ambition and indefatigability of the poor boy determined to make good. After he had made his millions, Jones became a power in Texas and national politics. It was Jones who brought the Democratic National Convention to Houston in 1928 and in large part arranged for its financing.

After Franklin Delano Roosevelt was inaugurated, in March, 1933, Jones was asked to head the RFC. He accepted and plunged into a job of monumental proportions, for Jesse Jones's assignment was to bail out the economy. Many firms, large and small, faced insolvency; the banking system was shattered. Even insurance companies were having a hard time. Manufacturers and retailers saw their sales shrink and their books became daubed in red ink. Many of their costs were fixed and could not be readily adjusted to changes in demand.

Jones and the RFC must receive a large part of the credit for saving our banking system from ruin, and many insurance companies, as well. Some of our largest corporations were kept afloat by the RFC during the 1930's, and the over-all image of the RFC was extremely favorable then. It was highly regarded by most businessmen, only the crustiest of conservatives opposing it because they believed that the government had no business being in business.

Jesse Jones was "Mr. Finance" and "Mr. Credit," in Washington, with no one comparable to him before or since. To list just a few of the present-day agencies created by Jones as part of his RFC empire will give an idea of the scope of his activities and imagination: the Federal Housing Administration, the Federal National Mortgage Association, the Export-Import Bank of Washington, and the Federal Home Loan Bank Board.

As hostility to President Roosevelt grew during his second term, he decided to appoint Jones Secretary of Commerce. Jones, a businessman and one of the few Roosevelt appointees respected by business and bankers, had helped many of them through the Depression, and his courage and sound business judgment were greatly admired. The Department of Commerce had deteriorated since the halcyon days of Secretary Herbert Hoover. It was generally believed to be one of President Roosevelt's bureaucratic objectives to reduce the Republican citadel to a department of impotence and insignificance. And he succeeded. The roster of the secretaries of Commerce in the days of the New Deal, up to the appointment of Jesse Jones, is one of either improbable candidates or near nonentities.

President Roosevelt hoped, of course, to win back part of the business community with this new appointment. At first, Jesse Jones demurred at the offer of the Commerce post. His love and his life had become the RFC. But after much prodding he accepted—with one important condition. He wanted also to retain his post as RFC chairman. From that time on, Jones made no bones about the fact that he was interested primarily in the RFC and not the Department of Commerce. Wayne Chatfield Taylor, the able under secretary of Commerce, actually ran that department during Jones's period in office. Jones did not try to conceal this, but repeatedly made public statements that this was the case.

During World War II, the RFC grew even more important than it had been during the 1930's. In effect, it helped the nation's financial institutions finance the war. New subsidiary agencies were created for this purpose: the Defense Supplies Corporation, the Defense Plants Corporations, the Rubber Reserve Company, and the Metals Reserve Company. The RFC's activities were global, and its personnel were scattered all around the world looking for strategic minerals and materials. It brought the raw materials needed for the war effort, stockpiled them, and built the plants needed for war production. One of its most amazing feats was the creation of a synthetic rubber corporation in the midst of the war, to fulfill our rubber needs because the world's distant plantations were either under enemy control or their produce was a prey to his fleet.

At war's end, the RFC had over 15,000 employees and was apparently at the height of its power. But dark days were ahead. Most significant, perhaps, was the resignation of Jesse Jones in protest at President Roosevelt's appointment of former Vice President Henry A. Wallace as Secretary of Commerce, in 1945.

Wallace, it will be recalled, had been dumped from the 1944 ticket by the Democratic Party in favor of an obscure Senator from Missouri, Harry S. Truman, whose associates were soon to have an adverse effect on the RFC. As regards Wallace, many in the party and, of course, FDR himself had become convinced that the quixotic Iowan was a liability to the national ticket and that he should be replaced.

President Roosevelt, often ruthless in making key decisions but also remorseful for their effects on the people concerned, felt he had to "do something for Henry." He decided to make him a cabinet officer once again (he had previously been a vigorous but controversial Secretary of Agriculture). It was merely a sop. Commerce was commonly regarded as being one of the least influential departments in the federal establishment.

In January, 1945, the President told Jesse Jones, the incumbent Commerce Secretary, of his plans. He knew that Jones was not interested in being Secretary of Commerce and thought that he would go along with the scheme as a good party man. But the forceful Texan protested vigorously. He thought Wallace "unfit for the job," "incompetent," and "an incredible appointment." Jones knew that the Wallace appointment would be resented by the American business community and would be pointed to as another example of Roosevelt's duplicity and cynicism.

But Roosevelt persisted, and Wallace was nominated for the position. In one of the most candid letters ever written by a public official, Jesse Jones resigned. He said in public precisely what he had told the President and others privately. This was hardly the customary Washington style. A storm of protest followed, but after several weeks of discussion, Wallace's nomination was finally accepted by the Senate on March 1, 1945, by the unusually close vote for a Presidential nomination of 56 to 32.

In April, Roosevelt died and Truman became President. Secretary Wallace did not last long in the Truman Administration, although his passing from the Commerce Department was of scant comfort to those in the RFC.

As V-J Day neared, the prevailing mood of the country's leading economists was one of deep pessimism. Reconversion from a wartime to a peacetime economy threatened to be a vast and extremely complicated undertaking, fraught with danger. A deep, severe, and prolonged recession was predicted by most American economists.

Reconversion went far more smoothly than predicted. American industry, and in particular the Committee for Economic Development, did a remarkable job of seeing to it that the transformation from wartime to peacetime was solidly based and carried out with efficiency. But fear of massive unemployment and a profound and long-lasting recession persisted. Memories of the Great Depression were still vivid. There was a widespread belief that high employment could only be attained within a wartime economy. Although the New Deal had continued to pull the economy upward from the dark days of 1930–32, its peacetime efforts in the economic area could hardly be described as successful. In 1940, for example, on the eve of America's entry into World War II, over 8 million people were unemployed and they constituted 14.6 per cent of the civilian labor force.

Many American leaders in business and government feared a return to these levels of unemployment. The Employment Act of 1946 was passed, stating that one of the principal objectives of government was to attain and sustain high employment. It has long been believed by economists that a state of high employment exists in the American economy when unemployment is at a level of 4 or 5 per cent. Higher rates of unemployment call for the adoption of countercyclical monetary and fiscal policies designed to raise effective demand.

While there was grave concern about an imminent but unpredictable recession and a return to the unsatisfactory pattern of the 1930's, the economic problems of the Truman Administration were for the most part—and particularly during the immediate postwar period—exactly the opposite. Except for the minor recession of 1949–50, just prior to the Korean War, the country was beset with problems arising out of a huge backlog of demand. At the end of World War II, personal savings were at an all-time high. And the people, denied many of the things they had wanted during the war, went on a buying binge. New houses, new cars, new consumer durables, such as washing machines and refrigerators, were eagerly sought and for a long period in short supply.

The problems and policies of the Truman Administration

were those of price control, shortages, and inflation. While it might have been expected that the government would seek to restrain credit, this surely was not the case with the RFC. More and more loans were made in each succeeding year and the levels of lending reached unprecedented heights. This was partly because of the inept—some might say "corrupt"— leadership of the RFC during much of this period. But it also appears to have been a product of the administration's fear of recession. The period might be depicted as one of economic schizophrenia.

Jules Abels has described this early postwar era well in his book *The Truman Scandals:*

> The years had rolled by and the RFC was now in a new era. It was postwar inflation. Price and materials controls had to be retained for a long time after V-J Day; materials had to be conserved for housing; the President campaigned in 1948 on a platform which demanded stand-by price controls to fight inflation. It would be expected that in this climate RFC loans would diminish. Instead they soared. In 1940, the RFC had made 1,125 business loans totaling $68,803,000. In 1947, it made 10,551 loans for a total of $393,000,000. In 1948, the 80th Congress, in renewing the charter of the agency, gave it a set of directions, the Buck Report, of which Senator Fulbright heartily approved. It also instructed the RFC to put emphasis on small business loans. The plain intent of the instructions was to restrict loans, not to expand them. Instead, the RFC quickened its loan activity. For the year ending June 30, 1950, the loan figure was well over $500,000,000.

Sardonically, Abels added:

> The agency which had been born to "reconstruct" was now making loans to concerns vital to our economy, such as a gambling casino, a rainbow trout fishery, night clubs, snake farms, swank resort hotels in Miami Beach, movie houses, and a grower of cactus plants for sale in dime stores.

In 1950, an investigation of the RFC was launched by a subcommittee of the Senate Committee on Banking and Currency. This special subcommittee was headed by the Democratic Senator J. William Fulbright of Arkansas. The hearings proved a disaster for both the RFC and the Truman Administration.

Senator Fulbright was a quiet, scholarly, contemplative man. At a young age, he had been appointed president of the University of Arkansas. He was a man of conviction but not sufficiently pliable politically to remain president for long. He was unceremoniously fired by the governor after a series of clashes that were fully reported in the Arkansas press. He then entered politics actively and won election to the House of Representatives in 1946. In 1948, he won his campaign for the Senate.

Fulbright was no maverick intent on destroying his party. The RFC had received a lot of bad publicity in 1949 and early 1950 because of some rather dubious loans it had made. Fulbright and his colleagues started out as investigators of the policies of the RFC to see why certain loans had been made. Before the Fulbright subcommittee was through, however, it unearthed some truly scandalous information, leading to the Republican battle cry of 1952: "Let's clean up the mess in Washington!"

In September, 1949, the RFC lent over $10 million to Texmass Petroleum to bail out some Massachusetts investors, including the Massachusetts Mutual Life Insurance Company and the John Hancock Life Insurance Company, which had made bad investments in oil properties in Texas. The taxpayers' money was in effect used to pay for the poor judgment of seasoned and wealthy investors. In October, 1949, the RFC voted to lend Kaiser-Frazer $34 million, although it was obvious to most observers that the company could not compete successfully with the big automobile manufacturers. Later that month came word of the most celebrated RFC loan of them all

—$37.5 million lent three years previously to the prefabricated home builder, Lustron. This was probably the most ill-starred of all RFC ventures. The whole Lustron case smelled of old-style back-room politics at its worst. In February, 1950, the RFC voted to foreclose and filed suit against the company.

These events led to the investigation by Senator Fulbright and his subcommittee. It soon became apparent to Fulbright and others like Senators Paul H. Douglas, of Illinois, and Charles Tobey, of New Hampshire, that the "fixers" and "influence peddlers" were having a field day. A particular power at the RFC was Donald Dawson, the President's administrative assistant and one of his principal dispensers of patronage. Before moving to the White House, Dawson had been chief of personnel at the RFC and was familiar with the agency and its key officials. In fact, Dawson's wife was in charge of the RFC's central files during his tenure at both the RFC and the White House.

At the outset, Senator Fulbright treated the whole business with kid gloves. He did not wish to damage the Democratic Party. He handled the witnesses deferentially and at times sounded like a pedantic professor of finance. In July, however, the Fulbright subcommittee went into closed session. There it took over 1,250 pages of testimony. The testimony contained evidence of wrongdoing, wire-pulling, and influence-peddling.

Wishing to avoid a scandal that would seriously injure the Truman Administration and the RFC, Fulbright arranged an interview with the President about the matter, toward the end of the year. He took Senators Douglas and Tobey, both widely respected for their ethical standards, along with him. According to Abels, "Mr. Truman listened to their tale, told them not to worry and showed them to the door."

The senators were furious at being brushed off in this manner, and decided that they had no choice but to publish their report. In February, 1951, the subcommittee's report, "Favoritism and Influence," was issued. It was front-page news, disclosing the operations of an influence ring. It named names and cited case after case of dubious RFC dealings. The report was juicy stuff for the Washington press corps.

Now it was the President's turn to become furious. He labeled the report "asinine." Perhaps the following words of Senator Fulbright stung Truman in particular:

Scandals in Government are not a new phenomenon. What seems to be new about these scandals is the moral blindness or callousness which allows those in responsible position to accept the practices which the facts reveal. It is bad enough to have corruption in our midst, but it is worse if it is to be condoned and accepted as inevitable.

Responding at a news conference in March, 1951, to questions concerning the scandals, the President blurted out: "My people are all honorable—all of them are. My house is always clean, what are you talking about?" In the months to come, these words were to haunt the harried but fiercely independent and loyal President. And they were to help the Republicans return to power in 1953 after twenty years of Democratic rule.

The Truman Administration attempted to discredit the Fulbright subcommittee and other members of Congress. Stung, Senator Fulbright announced new RFC hearings. These were to be public sessions, not closed as the previous ones had been. In announcing the hearings, Fulbright stated: "These hearings have a limited objective—that is to demonstrate, I hope, to the Congress and the people that the report that we issued in the early part of February was not an asinine report."

The new Fulbright hearings sounded the death knell of the RFC. The testimony before the subcommittee was far more damaging than its February report. The second set of Fulbright hearings ended in May; at that time, there was still at least a chance that the RFC could reform and survive as an agency. However, in October the investigations subcommittee of the House Committee on Expenditures, chaired by Congressman

Clyde R. Hoey, of North Carolina, investigated the American Lithofold Company case. It turned out that American Lithofold had received three RFC loans for over $600,000, through what appeared to be a questionable use of influence.

ESTABLISHMENT OF THE SMALL BUSINESS ADMINSTRATION

After the Fulbright and Hoey inquiries, the RFC was to all intents and purposes a dead agency. Morale had been shattered and personnel left in droves. The return of the Republicans, determined to "clean up the mess in Washington," meant that the RFC would soon be scuttled. For the RFC had been a prime Republican target during the 1952 campaign. Besides, the RFC was an example of the government's being in business, and the Republicans had pledged themselves to taking it out.

On May 14, 1953, the House Committee on Banking and Currency began its hearings on a bill to establish a Small Business Administration that had been prepared and unanimously approved by the House Select Committee on Small Business, under the chairmanship of Congressman William S. Hill.

On May 20, the Senate Committee on Banking and Currency started hearings. Their principal intent was to consider measures calling for the abolition of the RFC. At the same time, bills to create the SBA had been sent to the committee. Eventually, the two ideas were fused. The Senate bill, introduced by Senator Edward J. Thye, of Minnesota, chairman of the Senate Small Business Committee, was the key measure calling for establishment of the SBA. Small business organizations and the Small Business Committee had for many years been urging such a significant, permanent agency. They noted that the Smaller War Plants Corporation and the Small Defense Plants Administration were limited to defense production, with small staffs and budget and generally sluggish operations.

Meanwhile, the new Republican administration was primarily interested in dissolving the RFC. Because they had only a slim majority in the Congress, the Republicans apparently thought that they had to create a small business agency, preferably weak, in order to get the necessary votes to slay their bête noire, the RFC.

Coming as it did from the House Select Committee on Small Business, the House bill was entitled the Small Business Act of 1953, and described as "a bill to create the Small Business Administration and to preserve small business institutions and free, competitive enterprise." The main features of the legislation appeared in eight principal provisions. These provided for the agency's establishment; authorized it to borrow through a revolving fund set up in the Treasury; provided funds for small business loans; provided funds for a small business procurement program; empowered the agency to provide technical assistance to small firms; defined "small business"; empowered the SBA to make an inventory of small business production facilities, and also authorized the agency to analyze how those facilities could be most productively used.

Under the pending bill, the SBA was to be established as an independent federal agency "under the general direction and supervision of the President." In other words, it was to have a direct pipeline to the White House and was not to be controlled by any other agency or department. Congress frequently calls for such independent agencies in hopes of strengthening its own hand in dealing with them, since it is assumed that the President is generally too busy elsewhere to pay much attention to a small agency's day-to-day operations.

Second, the SBA was to be authorized to obtain money from the Treasury. The total was not to exceed $500 million, and this sum was to be appropriated and put into a revolving fund within the Treasury Department. Considering the scope of RFC operations, the SBA lending effort was to be a relatively modest one, at least initially.

Of the $500 million revolving fund, up to $400 million could be used to make loans or advances under general policy guidelines to be laid down by a Small Business Loan Policy Board. The board was to be composed of the secretaries of the Treasury and Commerce and the SBA administrator. This provision meant coordination of SBA lending policies with other government loan policies. It also assured influence of two conservative incumbent secretaries over SBA operations.

The bill also spelled out the uses to which SBA loan money could be put. These included plant construction or expansion, acquisition of necessary materials, financing of research and development operations, and as working capital for worthwhile projects. Loans could be made either directly by the SBA or in cooperation with a commercial lending institution. No loans were to be provided unless the prospective borrower offered proof that he was unable to obtain such financing elsewhere. And loans were to be sufficiently sound as to offer reasonable assurance of repayment.

The remaining $100 million of the SBA revolving fund was to be used to help small business concerns get contracts or subcontracts for government business.

In addition, the SBA was authorized under the bill to provide technical and managerial aids to small business. This advice was to deal primarily with the means by which the small businessmen could get government contracts and general counseling on the principles of good business management. The general feeling was that small businessmen did not know their way around Washington or a balance sheet as well as their big business competitors.

Under the pending bill, a small business concern was defined as any business that is independently owned and operated and that is not dominant in its field of operation. Beyond that general definition specific size standards would be up to the SBA.

The SBA was also empowered under the bill to make a thorough inventory of the productive facilities of small busi-

ness concerns. And, finally, the agency was authorized to coordinate and ascertain the most effective means of using small
business capabilities.

Hearings on the House bill were brief. They were held on
May 14, 15, and 18, 1953. There were only fourteen statements presented to the House Banking and Currency Committee. In addition to five administration witnesses, one Republican member of the House, William S. Hill, of Colorado,
chairman of the House Small Business Committee, offered
testimony.

Establishment of the SBA was not considered at the time a
matter of great moment. Only one federal department, the
Department of Commerce, testified from a policy standpoint.
Commerce Department spokesmen said they believed that it
might be a good idea to have an independent agency, but that
for the moment, "in the interest of good Government organization and economy, there should be an integration of this program into a regular continuing agency of the Government."
The Department of Commerce claimed that the Department
of Commerce, "with . . . responsibility for fostering and promoting commerce and industry, would appear to be the appropriate agency to take up this job . . . and to devote its many
resources to this task."

Only one well-known trade association, the American
Bankers Association, offered testimony. The American Bankers
Association was flatly opposed to the creation of the SBA but
was in favor of liquidating the RFC. It announced that it was
fundamentally against government lending, direct or indirect.
The two spokesmen of the commercial bankers of America
were attacked during the course of the hearings by Democratic
Representative Wright Patman, of Texas. Patman has made a
career out of dissecting and attacking bankers and the Federal
Reserve System.

The only other issue brought out in the open in the hearing
was the question of whether the SBA should be an independ-

ent agency or made a part of the Department of Commerce. There was little real support expressed for putting small business affairs in the Commerce Department. George Burger, of the National Federation of Independent Business, put the case against Commerce this way: "We have respect for the Department of Commerce, but when it comes to small business, by past performances, we are a little bit doubtful as to their sympathetic feeling to small business."

Congress Patman later said on the House floor that putting the SBA in the Department of Commerce would be "just like sending a rabbit for a head of lettuce."

The Senate hearings on the bill to establish the SBA were far more extensive than the House sessions. The Banking and Currency Committee met in open session May 20 through May 22, May 25 through May 27, and July 13 and 14. In contrast to the House's rather routine sessions, some twenty-seven people testified before the Senate committee, including Senator Harry F. Byrd, of Virginia; George M. Humphrey, Secretary of the Treasury; Treasury Under Secretary W. Randolph Burgess, for many years the senior vice president of the National City Bank of New York; William McChesney Martin, Chairman of the Board, Federal Reserve System; Senator John J. Sparkman, of Alabama; and Senator Edward J. Thye, of Minnesota, the chairman of the Senate Small Business Committee. In addition, many statements, letters, and views on the various bills were submitted for the formal record.

By the time of the Senate hearings, something new had been added: the administration had decided to kill the RFC. Senator Thye's and several of the other bills, as originally introduced, were similar in form and scope to the House-approved bill. They dealt only with the creation of the SBA. The sole mention of the RFC was that that agency should refer small business loans to the new agency.

The RFC's authority, if not renewed, was due to expire on

June 30, 1954. Now the timetable was to be moved up. The administration wanted the RFC to expire by June 30, 1953, if possible. Senator Byrd, a fiscal conservative and close to the Treasury as chairman of the Senate Finance Committee, was for liquidation of the RFC. He wanted the liquidation to begin within sixty days after enactment of the bill. Part of his urgency arose from the fact that a deficit was anticipated for Fiscal Year 1954, and liquidation of the RFC would help considerably in reducing the expected deficit. The Republicans had hoped to balance the budget but found it a more formidable task than they had supposed during the campaign.

Senator Byrd saw no need for a small business agency. Administration stalwarts, such as Burgess and Humphrey, did not go so far. The House bill had provided for a revolving fund of $500 million for the new small business agency. This had been cut in half by the House when it passed the measure. Senator Thye's bill provided for a revolving fund of only $150 million.

Treasury Secretary Humphrey set the tone of the administration line:

> I personally think in theory there should be no difference between lending money to a large business or lending money to a small business. In theory, small business should get its money from banks and lending institutions. I cannot quarrel with the theory of the American Bankers Association's representatives who appeared before you. But, in practice, in just good common sense, I think, there should be some additional body arranged to assist small business, and I think that when the RFC goes out some other suitable arrangement should be in force to attempt to help small business.

In his testimony, the Secretary of the Treasury kept referring to loans to small business as being in "the twilight zone" and saying he wanted to cut government loans to business back to size. In fact, he went on, if the Congress decided merely to liquidate the RFC and get the government out of the lending business, the Treasury would not object. Obviously, Humphrey felt uncomfortable in "twilight zones."

Meanwhile, as the Senate hearings were in progress, the House Banking and Currency Committee reported its bill favorably, on May 28. The major change was a cut in the revolving fund authority from $500 million to $250 million. There was no provision calling for liquidation of the RFC. The bill was called up on a special order on June 4 and passed by a House voice vote the next day. On June 8, the proposal was referred to the Senate Banking and Currency Committee.

The Senate committee instead reported its bill favorably on July 18. The measure was brought to the Senate floor on July 20. In the course of debate, the Senate, in response to the administration's wishes, postponed its bill indefinitely, and by a voice vote passed an amended House bill as a substitute.

There were three principal changes in the bill as approved by the Senate. First, Title I provided for liquidation of the RFC through June 30, 1954, at which time liquidation would be taken over by the Treasury. The RFC, however, was empowered to make loans for only sixty days after enactment of the new legislation. In the second place, the SBA was to be a temporary agency with a two-year life. Finally, the SBA revolving fund was to be $275 million.

A conference committee to resolve differences between the House and Senate bills was agreed to on July 21. Its report was submitted three days later. In essence, this report had gone the way of the Senate. The RFC was to be liquidated, a revolving fund of $275 million was to be authorized, and the SBA was to be a temporary agency.

On the House floor, Congressmen Wright Patman and Abraham J. Multer, of New York, fought the proposed liquidation of the RFC and the cut in the SBA revolving fund from the original $500 to $275 million. But nonetheless the House approved the conference report by a voice vote on July 27.

On the Senate side, J. William Fulbright announced that he was opposed to liquidation of the RFC. But the die was cast. The Senate by voice vote approved the conference report on July 29. On July 30, 1953, President Eisenhower signed the enrolled bill, the RFC expired, and the SBA was born.

II

What Is Small Business?

The SBA was established in order to carry out the declared policy of Congress, "to aid, counsel, assist, and protect, insofar as is possible, the interests of small-business concerns in order to preserve free competitive enterprise." But how important is American small business? What are the economic merits of the case for such an agency? How extensive is the small business community? And how does one go about defining "small business"?

These questions and others of an economic character have been matters of great concern to the SBA and its predecessor institutions. One might be tempted to say that these questions have long plagued these agencies. The answers to most of the questions are matters of opinion, indeed controversy. And they are imprecise and incomplete, subject to considerable qualification and interpretation. Let us first turn to such matters as the business population, the concept of size and the related subject of the structure of industry, certain national economic aggregates, the concept of economic competition, and trends in small business activity and in economic concentration.

Today there are about 4.8 million small business firms out of a total of slightly more than 5 million businesses in the United States. These 5 million firms serve a population of roughly 200 million citizens. The number of business firms—the business population—has grown steadily with the increase over the years in the total population of our country. A century ago, there were 300,000 business firms serving a population of 29 million. Put another way, there was about one business establishment for each ninety-seven Americans 100 years ago, whereas today there is one firm for every forty people.

In part, these figures illustrate the vast transformation of the American economy over the past century or so. In 1879, over 48 per cent of our population was engaged in farming and 19 per cent of our national income originated in the agricultural sector. As Table I shows, agriculture was then our leading occupation. In 1965, however, farming contributed only 3.8 per cent of the national income and a mere 5.7 per cent of the labor force in the United States was engaged in tilling the soil.

The business population and broad changes and trends in economic activity will be examined in greater detail. But first, let us look at the matter of defining small business.

WHAT IS A SMALL BUSINESS?

The Small Business Act has this to say:

For the purposes of this Act, a small-business concern shall be deemed to be one which is independently owned and operated and which is not dominant in its field of operations. In addition to the foregoing criteria, the [SBA] Administrator, in making a detailed definition, may use these criteria, among others: Number of employees and dollar volume of business. Where the number of employees is used as one of the criteria in making such definition for any of the purposes of this Act, the maximum number of employees which a small-business concern may have under the definition shall vary from industry to industry to the extent necessary to reflect differing characteristics of such industries and to take proper account of other relevant factors.

TABLE I

National Income and Persons Engaged in Production

Year or Period	Total	Agriculture	Mining	Construction	Manufacturing	Transportation, Communications, Public Utilities	Trade	Finance, Insurance, and real Estate	Services	Government Federal	Government State and Local
	Millions of Dollars					PER CENT DISTRIBUTION					
1879	10,701	19.0	2.1	5.0	13.3	12.9	16.1	12.0	15.2	4.2	}
1929–37	58,763	9.3	2.1	3.1	22.8	11.2	16.1	12.9	11.4	3.7	6.6
1937–44	108,684	8.4	2.0	3.5	30.6	9.2	15.8	8.6	8.4	8.9	4.3
1944–48	191,442	9.2	1.9	3.5	29.4	8.3	17.5	7.8	8.5	10.1	3.6
1948–53	258,476	7.2	2.0	5.0	31.6	8.5	16.7	9.0	8.8	6.2	4.5
1953–57	330,092	4.8	1.8	5.2	32.1	8.5	15.7	10.3	9.4	6.4	5.3
1957–60	386,032	4.3	1.5	5.1	30.5	8.4	15.7	10.9	10.4	6.2	6.2
1960–65	474,201	3.9	1.2	5.0	29.9	8.3	15.3	11.9	11.2	6.2	7.2
1965	559,020	3.8	1.2	5.1	30.5	8.2	15.0	10.9	11.3	6.0	7.5
	Thousands of Persons					PERSONS ENGAGED IN PRODUCTION					
1879	15,639	48.9	1.8	4.1	18.0	5.2	7.9	0.4	9.9	3.9	}
1929–37	42,214	12.3	2.0	4.1	20.5	7.5	16.9	3.5	13.9	3.7	6.4
1937–44	53,002	15.1	1.8	4.0	24.4	6.3	16.3	3.0	12.4	11.4	5.4
1944–48	59,952	11.8	1.5	4.0	25.9	6.8	16.7	2.9	(NA)	13.5	3.9
1948–53	61,110	10.6	1.6	5.6	26.7	6.9	18.1	3.4	13.1	7.7	6.2
1953–57	64,496	8.8	1.3	5.6	27.0	6.5	18.0	3.8	13.5	8.4	6.9
1957–60	64,798	7.6	1.2	5.5	26.1	6.3	18.6	4.1	15.0	7.6	8.0
1960–65	67,620	6.6	1.0	5.5	25.6	5.7	18.4	4.3	16.1	7.6	9.1
1965	71,248	5.7	0.9	5.6	25.9	5.6	18.4	4.3	16.5	7.4	9.6

Source: *Long Term Economic Growth, 1860–1965: A Statistical Compendium* (Washington: Bureau of the Census, October, 1966).

Size is a relative concept. What is big in one line of endeavor in terms of employees or sales is small in another industry. This was clearly recognized by the Congress in creating the SBA in 1953. At the time, Congressman Wright Patman had this to say:

> The steel business is very big, like the automobile business. I suspect a small steel plant, to start an operation, would have to use at least four or five thousand people. And yet it would be small. It would be a small business, because small business is a relative term. It depends upon the business you are in.
>
> In the case of a peanut stand, of course, there are big ones and little ones. Kaiser was a little business when he started in the automobile business. Even Studebaker is little business compared to General Motors, Chrysler, and Ford.
>
> So whenever you use the term it is relative in the particular type of business.[1]

SBA SIZE STANDARDS

To carry out the intent of Congress, the SBA has developed a complex set of size standards indicating what is considered small. Definitions are developed on an industry-by-industry basis. Within the SBA, this work has been carried out by economists and lawyers.

The Standard Industrial Classification (SIC) system provides the framework for SBA size standards. The SIC is an industry system of classification developed under the supervision of the Office of Statistical Standards of the Bureau of the Budget. The SIC is used by all federal statistical units and many state agencies and private organizations.

The SIC is organized in such a way as to provide various degrees of detail. To illustrate, let us look at Table II, which

---

[1] U.S. House Committee on Banking and Currency, *Creation of Small Business Administration* (83rd Cong., 1st Sess.) (Washington: Government Printing Office, 1953), p. 20.

TABLE II

Value of Shipments of Selected Classes of Products
for the United States and Per Cent of Value
of Shipments by Employment Size of Company
1958

Class of Product (SIC No.)	Value of Shipments (In Thousands of Dollars)	Percentage Distribution of Shipments by 4 Employment Size Classes of Companies			
		Less than 250 Employees	250–499 Employees	500–999 Employees	1,000 Employees and Over
Surgical Appliances and Supplies (3842): Surgical, orthopedic, and prosthetic appliances and supplies (38421)	256,573	30	5	5	60
Personal industrial safety devices (38423)	56,365	35	5	10	55
Electrical hearing aids (38424)	39,517	25	35	—	40
Photographic Equipment (3861): Still picture equipment (38611)	179,448	25	10	5	65
Photocopying, etc., equipment (38612)	57,668	20	(NA)	(NA)	50
Motion picture equipment (38613)	147,969	15	5	15	65
Photographic sensitized film and plates (38615)	396,014	—	(NA)	(NA)	100

Source: U.S. Small Business Administration, *Opportunities for Smaller Manufacturers* (Washington: Small Business Administration, 1963), p. 30. NA: Not available.

shows the value of shipments of selected classes of products for the United States in 1958, the per cent of value of shipments by the employment size of companies cited, and the number of companies in each size class.

Under a broad heading come industry groups, such as SIC Code Number 3842, Surgical Appliances and Supplies, and SIC Code Number 3861, Photographic Equipment. These *industry groupings* are usually referred to by size specialists as being "four-digit SIC's." A finer or *product* breakdown, is provided by the five-digit SIC's. Thus, under the SIC industry Number 3841, Photographic Equipment, come several classes of products, including SIC product number 38613, Motion picture equipment, and SIC product Number 384615, Photographic sensitized film and plates.

With only a couple of minor exceptions, the SBA has, since its inception, used the four-digit—or industry—SIC classifications as the basis for its size standards. This has long been a bone of contention within the agency. Some believe that the five-digit classification would be more appropriate since individual companies compete on a product basis. In the main, however, the four-digit classification is more useful. The five-digit product classification is too detailed for practical use. In addition, use of the five-digit categories would bring about more inequities because many firms within an industry make two or more products. Still, it should be kept in mind that any statistical classification system is essentially arbitrary. Hence, there should be, and have been, some departures from the basic use of four-digit SIC's by the SBA. So although the four-digit SIC system provides the framework for the orderly conduct of this important work, it should never become an administrative straightjacket.

SMALL BUSINESS AS DEFINED BY THE SBA

To be eligible to receive an SBA loan (from the Financial Assistance Division), generally speaking, the size standards of the SBA are as follows:

For manufacturing: In a few cases, small manufacturers are defined as those having 250 or fewer employees. In the majority of cases, however, a manufacturer is considered small if he employs 500 or fewer people.

For the wholesale trades: A business is generally considered small if on the average over the last three years its annual sales or receipts have not exceeded $5 million.

For the retail trades and services: In most instances, a business is considered small if on the average during the past three years its annual sales or receipts have not exceeded $1 million.

To be eligible to bid on government contracts set aside for small business firms (handled by the Procurement and Management Assistance Division):

For manufacturing: Generally, the size standard is 500 or fewer employees. There are more exceptions to this rule, however, than is the case with the size standard for manufacturers seeking financial assistance from the SBA. The more glaring exception has been the 1966 determination that American Motors, one of the 200 biggest U.S. corporations, was henceforth to be considered "small" for purposes of government procurement.

The American Motors decision was based on the provisions of Section 2 of the Small Business Act, which call for the preservation and expansion of full and free economic competition. At the time of the decision, American Motors accounted for less than 5 per cent of the U.S. market for passenger cars. Its share of the market was declining, and it was losing money. In the market sense, American Motors is "small." It is very small compared to General Motors, Ford, or Chrysler—just as Congressman Patman pointed out that the Studebaker Company was small compared to the big three, in 1953.

But compared to almost any other company in the United States, American Motors is extremely big. Where does one draw the line between small and big? Or, as wags put it at the time, how big is small?

Although there was a logical basis for determining that American Motors was a small business, it was a poor decision. It was a poor decision because it violated the spirit and general intent of the Small Business Act. In a broad economic sense, American Motors was not a small company. Furthermore, the decision probably contravened Section 3 of the act, which states that to be deemed small, a concern must be "independently owned and operated." American Motors has thousands of stockholders; it is hardly the type of family business that Congressman Patman and other framers of the Small Business Act had in mind.

For the wholesale trades: In general, the same rules apply as those for financial assistance—i.e., a maximum of $5 million in sales or receipts.

For the retail trades and services: Essentially, the standard parallels that for financial assistance—up to $1 million in sales or receipts.

Eligibility for assistance under the Small Business Investment Act of 1958 (handled by the Investment Division) is covered in Section 103 (5), which declared that "the term 'small business concern' shall have the same meaning as in the Small Business Act."

The SBA has given an extremely liberal interpretation of Section 103(5). The definition of small business for investment purposes differs completely from the definitions used by the SBA for the financial assistance and procurement assistance programs.

The present definition is as follows:

A small business concern for the purpose of receiving financial or other assistance from small business investment companies is a concern which:

(a) Together with its affiliates, is independently owned and operated, is not dominant in its field of operation, does not have assets exceeding $5 million, does not have net worth in excess of $2½ million, and does not have an average net income, after federal income taxes, for the preceding two years in excess of $250,000 (average net income to be computed without benefit of any carry-over loss); or

(b) Qualifies as a small business concern under Section 121.3-10 (definition of small business for SBA business loans).

In explaining the thinking that lay behind this great departure from the existing SBA definitions of small business, the SBA administrator who made the decision explained it in the following way:

We felt we should approach it from the standpoint of defining the gap in financing, if that was the purpose of this Act, and, therefore, we assumed that companies . . . [that] had obtained public financing during the past three years and were listed on any of the Nation's exchanges . . . would be *prima facie* ineligible. . . .

In addition, we felt that there is a correlation between the amount of funds invested in a company and the number of employees it has. We all know that in order to operate particularly a manufacturing company that it takes $10,000 to $15,000 investment for each employee to provide him the tools with which to work. So that if we take the 500 employees and apply $10,000 in invested capital for each employee, you have a company with assets of $5 million.

So we said that companies having $5 million or more in assets were *prima facie* ineligible.

We felt that companies that were not listed on the exchange but which had a good local market for their securities, across-the-counter market, were obtaining financing and thus would not be eligible on a *prima facie* basis.

Using these criteria, we formulated what we think is a relatively simple definition that a clerk working for an investment company could as a *prima facie* matter tell whether or not a borrower would be eligible for their financing.

Beyond that, we however permitted any of these companies to come in and ask for a certificate and make a showing that in fact they were small and that these principles did not apply to them.

Thus, we achieved flexibility in connection with the definition.

The upshot of the preceding explanation is that the SBA size standard for its Investment Division operations includes many far larger firms than its size standards for financial and procurement assistance.

To many observers, the other size standards might appear quite large enough. Although the investment program's size standard for manufacturing may be approximately the same as the standards of the financial and procurement programs, it is far larger for all other types of business activity.

Thus, the size standard for wholesaling may be three times as large for the investment program as the SBA wholesaling size standard for procurement and financial assistance. The latter is annual *sales* of $5 million. On the other hand, many wholesalers with total *assets* of $5 million—top of the investment program size standard—have annual *sales* of more than $15 million, well beyond the size limits of the other SBA divisions.

In even greater disparity, the investment program size standards for retailing and services may be as much as twelve times as large as for the other SBA programs. For most retail and service industries, the SBA size standard, other than for the investment program, is $1 million of sales. However, many retailers with total assets of $5 million, although "small" by Investment Division standards, have sales of $12 million or more.

THE BUSINESS POPULATION

No one knows precisely how many small businesses there are in the United States. Nor, for that matter, does anyone have an accurate count of how many businesses of all sizes there are in this country. Estimates of the business population made by several federal agencies vary considerably, as can be seen in Table III. According to the Bureau of Employment Security, there were 2,147,000 business firms in operation in the first quarter of 1959. However, the Internal Revenue Service said that there were 6,371,900 business firms in operation dur-

TABLE III

Business Population Statistics
of Various Government Agencies

Major Division of Industry and Trade	Office of Business Economics[a]	Internal Revenue Service[b]	Bureau of the Census[c]	Bureau of Employment Security[d]
Total	4,589,200	6,371,900	3,151,600	2,147,000
Mining and quarrying	42,000	65,600	30,100	27,000
Contract construction	475,900	725,700	—	257,000
Manufacturing	331,000	381,400	269,800	259,000
Transportation, communication, and other public utilities	211,800	345,300	—	85,000
Wholesale trade	317,000	406,700	213,100	
Public warehousing			7,500	897,000
Retail trade	1,956,300	1,989,600	1,688,300	
Wholesale and retail trade not allocable	—	113,000	—	—
Finance, insurance, and real estate	403,300	899,200	—	160,000
Services	851,900	1,362,100	942,800	431,000
All other	—	—	—	30,000
Nature of business not allocable	—	83,300	—	—

Source: Adapted from James Ira Mills, *A Study of Small Business and Federal Government Programs to Assist Small Business* (unpublished doctoral dissertation, George Washington University, 1965), 17.

[a] As of January 1, 1959. Cf. Betty C. Churchill, "Rise in the Business Population," *Survey of Current Business*, XXXIX, 5 (May, 1959), 15.

[b] Figures for 1958–59. Cf. U.S. Treasury Department, Internal Revenue Service, *U.S. Business Tax Returns, Statistics of Income, 1958–1959.*

[c] U.S. Department of Commerce, Bureau of the Census, *Enterprise Statistics: 1958.*

[d] Figures for first quarter of 1959. U.S. Department of Labor, Bureau of Employment Security, *Employment and Wages, First Quarter, 1959.*

ing 1958–59. The Commerce Department's Office of Business Economics declared officially that there were some 4,589,200 businesses. And so it goes.

How can these figures be so different? There are several reasons. Statistics are not usually gathered in a vacuum. They are compiled by different agencies with different needs and purposes. There are two principal explanations for these disparities: one is the definition of a business firm; the other, the kinds of business activity covered by the statistics. Thus, for its purposes, the Bureau of Employment Security defines a business firm as a company having one or more employees. The Internal Revenue Service, however, includes within its definition every taxpayer who turns in a business tax form. Because sole proprietors have no employees, obviously, the business population figures of the Internal Revenue Service turn out to be considerably larger than the total estimated by the Bureau of Employment Security, which is interested only in businessmen who must contribute to Social Security funds.

All business population statistics exclude agriculture, forestry, and fisheries. Other than this common ground, however, the agencies vary considerably in what types of business activities are included in their statistics. For example, the number of enterprises included in *Economic Statistics: 1958,* published by the Bureau of the Census, was estimated to be 3,151,600 in 1958. On the other hand, the estimate of the Office of Business Economics was 4,589,200 for 1959. The major reason that the numbers fail to agree is that the Census figures exclude contract construction, public utilities, finance, insurance, and real estate. All are included in the Office of Business Economics data. In addition, only manufacturers with one or more paid employees and nonmanufacturers with a specified amount of sales or receipts were within the scope of the 1958 Census.

For most purposes, the business population statistics of the Office of Business Economics are considered to be the most useful in analyzing business enterprise in the United States. In recent years, however, the work of the Office of Business Economics (OBE) has been drastically curtailed for budgetary reasons. Other OBE work has been given a higher priority. As a result, less attention has been paid to accurate measurement of the business population.

Table IV depicts the business population by major industry

TABLE IV

Business Population, by Major Industry Division for Selected Years
(In Thousands)

Year[a]	All Industries	Contract Construction	Manu-facturing	Service Industries	Retail Trade	Wholesale Trade	All Other[b]
1929	3,029.0	233.8	257.0	590.9	1,327.0	148.1	472.0
1935	2,991.9	180.2	205.0	615.8	1,387.2	157.0	446.5
1940	3,318.9	202.3	222.9	639.1	1,580.4	183.6	490.5
1943	3,030.0	164.4	242.9	579.1	1,401.4	181.8	460.4
1945	2,995.4	160.1	253.1	567.6	1,356.2	186.0	472.4
1950	4,008.7	352.5	317.6	735.3	1,802.8	263.3	537.2
1953	4,187.7	405.3	330.7	749.9	1,846.1	283.1	572.6
1956	4,381.2	451.7	327.3	789.6	1,903.2	296.9	612.5
1959	4,583.0	464.0	323.0	848.0	1,977.0	312.0	658.0
1960	4,658.0	476.0	323.0	872.0	1,997.0	317.0	674.0
1961	4,713.0	477.0	322.0	895.0	2,011.0	322.0	686.0
1962	4,755.0	473.0	317.0	918.0	2,022.0	327.0	698.0
1963	4,797.0	470.0	313.0	942.0	2,032.0	332.0	708.0
Projected							
1966	5,086.2	491.8	325.4	1,044.6	2,115.5	354.2	754.7
1970	5,335.7	517.2	339.5	1,101.6	2,189.1	375.2	813.1
1976	5,655.8	547.3	353.4	1,194.3	2,267.1	403.9	889.8

Source: Small Business Administration, *Small Business Administration and Small Business . . . A Partnership* (1967), Table I (unpaged).

[a] Figures for years prior to 1940 are average number; for years after 1940, number as of January 1 is given.
[b] Includes mining, finance, and transportation divisions.

for selected years from 1929 to 1963. Also included are projections for the years 1966, 1970, and 1976 made by the National Planning Association, a private research organization.

As Table IV shows, the growth and composition of business enterprises has been affected by economic fluctuations and by wars. Effects of the Great Depression are readily apparent. From 1929 through 1933, the number of firms fell every year. Attrition took place in most of the major divisions. During World War II, the number of firms once again dropped. Most of the major groups showed intermittent or consistent declines, with the exception of one important sector—manufacturing. The increase in manufacturing was, of course, the result of the sharp jump in demand for military hardware and supplies.

Since the end of the war, fluctuations in the size of the business population have been moderate. The total number of firms has increased every year. However, in the rather stagnant 1950's, the *rate* of growth of the business population dropped off. Furthermore, significant shifts in economic activity became apparent as the United States passed through the immediate postwar era. The annual rate of growth in the service industries increased, while that in manufacturing declined. In all other industrial sectors, the number of business concerns continued to grow, although at a slower pace.

BUSINESS POPULATION CHANGE, 1952–66

The period taken for illustrative purposes here roughly coincides with the life span of the SBA. Tables V and VI show that from the time the SBA was established, in 1953, the number of business firms has grown at an average annual rate of 1.6 per cent. The total number has climbed from 4.1 million to 5.1 million. Small businesses, in turn, are estimated to have increased from 3.9 million to 4.8 million.

During the time period studied, the construction industry

TABLE V

Average Annual Rate of Growth or Decline in Business Population,
by Major Industry Division
1952–66 and 1966–67

	Number of Firms (In Thousands)			Per Cent of Average Annual Rate of Growth	
Industry Division	1952	1966	1967 (est.)	1952–68	1966–76
All industries	4,118	5,086	5,656	1.6	1.1
Contract construction	387	492	547	1.7	1.1
Manufacturing	328	325	353	—.07	.83
Retail trade	1,831	2,115	2,267	1.0	.69
Wholesale trade	276	354	404	1.9	1.3
Services	739	1,045	1,195	2.5	1.4
Other	557	755	890	2.4	1.7

Source: Small Business Administration, *Small Business Administration and Small Business . . . A Partnership,* Table II.

and the wholesale trades grew at about the over-all average annual rate of 1.6 per cent. Services and miscellaneous industries—finance, real estate, insurance, transportation, communications, and mining—grew more rapidly than the average. In manufacturing, the number of firms actually declined.

TABLE VI

Average Annual Rate of Growth or Decline in Business Population,
by Industry Division for Five Periods:
1929–39, 1947–52, 1953–59, 1960–62, 1963–66

Industry Division	1929–39	1947–52	1953–59	1960–62	1963–66
All industries	0.6	2.2	1.5	0.9	1.7
Contract construction	—1.6	7.0	2.2	—0.4	(NA)
Manufacturing	—1.5	1.5	—0.35	—1.0	(NA)
Service industries	0.3	1.5	2.2	2.6	(NA)
Retail trade	1.5	2.1	0.9	0.8	(NA)
Wholesale trade	1.7	2.6	1.6	1.6	(NA)

Source: *Small Business Administration and Small Business . . . ,* Table IV.
NA: Not available.

THE RELATIVE IMPORTANCE OF SMALL BUSINESS
IN THE ECONOMY

These business population figures, of course, are merely an enumeration of the businesses in this country. Thus, by count, the SBA economists have estimated that 4,750,000 businesses out of a total of 5,086,000 existing in the United States in 1966 were small businesses. This is an important statistic. But it tells us nothing about the importance of small business in American life. How much do small business concerns produce? How many people do they employ? Is their economic significance rising or falling, or is it staying about the same?

In 1963, the SBA's Office of Economic Adviser estimated that small business—as defined by the SBA—employed about 40 per cent of the nation's labor force and accounted for roughly one-third of the gross national product. After a careful study of the facts at their disposal, these economists also concluded that there had been little or no change in the overall position of the small business community in the American economy during the past half-century. They also found that there have been significant changes in the importance of small business on a sector-by-sector basis.

In manufacturing, for instance, there has undoubtedly been a drop in the relative importance of small business. Significantly, manufacturing is the area most prominent in the minds of those discussing the economy of the United States. Ask almost any informed foreigner or nearly any knowledgeable American what the U.S. economy is all about, and he will be certain to say something about mass production, the division of labor, and giant corporations.

The power of the giant corporations is in fact truly staggering. There were about 360,000 industrial corporations in 1963. In 1964, the 500 largest in the United States had sales of $266.5 billion, total assets of $244.7 billion, invested capital of $142.4 billion, and net profits of $17.2 billion. The 100 biggest corporations had $172.6 billion in sales, $150.3 billion in assets, invested capital of $96.4 billion, and $12.2 billion in net profits. This is an economy with a Gross National Product totaling $628.7 billion. As one widely read economist has recently written, "the 500 largest corporations produce close to half of all the goods and services produced in the United States."[2] This is somewhat exaggerated but not too far off target.

MANUFACTURING

Let us look at the situation in manufacturing. In 1958, there were 298,000 manufacturing establishments in this country, having 15,394,000 employees, total payrolls of $73.8 billion, and whose value added by manufacture was some $141.3 billion.

Where did small business fit in this picture? It accounted for upwards of 98 per cent of all establishments. Less than 2 per cent of the manufacturing firms in the United States employed 500 or more people. But this 2 per cent employed 42.8 per cent of the total number of manufacturing workers, accounted for 48.9 per cent of the payrolls and 48.5 per cent of the value added by manufacturing.

These data are, of course, all aggregates. When one looks at the underlying detail, he finds the situation far more complex and diverse. One of the main statistical series that clarifies the situation are the so-called "concentration ratios," which are published regularly by the Antitrust and Monopoly Subcommittee of the Senate Committee on the Judiciary. They are based on information supplied by the Bureau of the Census and the Federal Trade Commission. Certain of the concentration ratios for 1958 are shown in Table VII.

Examination of this table tells a lot about the structure of

[2] John K. Galbraith, *The New Industrial State* (Boston: Houghton Mifflin Co., 1967), pp. 1–2.

industry in the United States. At one end of the spectrum are such industries as cigarettes, synthetic fibers, motor vehicles and parts, and aluminum rolling and drawing, where concentration is very high. In the cigarette industry, for example, the four largest companies in 1958 accounted for 79 per cent of the total value of shipments and the eight largest companies were responsible for over 99 per cent. At the other end of the spectrum are such industries as machine shops, ready-mixed concrete, and dresses, where concentration is very low. For instance, only 4 per cent of the ready-mixed concrete industry's shipments came from the four largest companies, and the eight largest accounted for only 7 per cent in 1958.

These data are published every five years. They are derived from the Commerce Department's Census of Manufactures, which is conducted every five years. Some economists are intrigued by these figures. They try to read all sorts of meanings into them. The concentration ratios for the various years are analyzed and re-analyzed to see what the trends are. One noted economist then says that concentration is increasing; another equally distinguished economist says it is decreasing. Then, still another says concentration is neither increasing nor decreasing. Much effort has been fruitlessly expended in this sort of exercise. There are just too many complexities involved to unravel the threads successfully or authoritatively. But these varying and contradictory conclusions provide fertile material for polemicists.

However, this is not to debunk concentration ratios. They are useful. But as with all statistics, it is important to know their limitations and their usefulness—their meaning. For example, the ratios *do* show in which industries there is a high degree of concentration and where concentration is low. If one compares the various years, *by industry,* one *may* find those where concentration is clearly on the increase or the decrease. But that is about all that can be done with them.

Although there has been a decline in the number of manu-

TABLE VII

Per Cent of Shipments and Employment Accounted for by
Large Manufacturing Companies, Selected Industries
1947 (or 1950), 1954, and 1958

Industry and Year	Number of Companies	Value of Shipments			Employment		
		Total (In Millions of Dollars)	Per Cent Made by		Total (In Millions of Dollars)	Per Cent in	
			4 Largest Companies	8 Largest Companies		4 Largest Firms	8 Largest Firms
Petroleum refining							
1947/1950[a]	277	6,624	37	59	(NA)	(NA)	(NA)
1954	253	11,757	33	56	153	39	61
1958	289	14,106	32	55	146	36	59
Motor vehicles and parts							
1947/1950[a]	779	3,545	56	64	721	59	69
1954	991	6,111	75	80	649	69	75
1958	989	6,419	75	81	531	70	74
Newspapers							
1947/1950[a]	8,115	1,891	21	26	267	16	20
1954	8,445	3,091	18	24	282	14	19
1958	7,947	3,616	17	24	294	15	20
Aircraft engines							
1947/1950[a]	54	465	72	88	67	54	79
1954	202	3,189	62	81	167	51	75
1958	186	3,359	56	77	159	48	69

Cigarettes	1947/1950[a]	19	1,132	90	99+	28	81	99
	1954	12	1,641	82	99+	30	75	99
	1958	12	2,159	79	99+	34	73	99+
Dresses, unit price	1947/1950[a]	4,165	1,359	3	5	(NA)	(NA)	(NA)
	1954	4,072	1,455	4	7	143	2	3
	1958	3,606	1,627	4	7	136	2	3
Ready-mixed concrete	1947/1950[a]	3,104	1,559	4	7	61	3	6
Machine shops	1947/1950[a]	(NA)	440	(NA)	(NA)	52	12	17
	1954	6,795	1,108	8	13	104	8	12
	1958	10,482	1,544	7	12	123	5	10
Synthetic fibers	1947/1950[a]	22	705	78	94	72	76	94
	1954	20	1,241	80	97	61	73	97
	1958	17	1,419	78	96	61	69	96
Aluminum rolling and drawing	1947/1950[a]	15	405	94	99	27	89	3
	1954	77	874	88	92	37	84	90
	1958	139	1,347	78	85	42	76	84

Source: U.S. Bureau of the Census, *Statistical Abstracts of the United States: 1966*, 778–80.

NA: Not available.

[a] For value of shipments, 1947; for employment, 1950.

facturers and certainly a decline in the percentage of output produced by small business in recent years, this does not mean that the small manufacturer is dead or, for that matter, that the small businessman is fading away. One thing that should be kept in mind is the fact that manufacturing is beginning to lose its relative pre-eminence in the American economy. Some economists, such as Walt W. Rostow and Colin Clark, have an explanation for this. They say that as an economy develops, it goes through a phase when agriculture is paramount; then, manufacturing becomes more and more important. Later, as the society becomes increasingly affluent, services of all kinds become increasingly significant relative to the other sectors. In fact, the United States has in recent years been described by some economists and business writers as the first of the "service economies."

SERVICE INDUSTRIES

Just what are the service industries? One way of defining them is to say what they are not. They are not agriculture—which includes fishing and forestry—nor are they manufacturing or mining. But they are just about everything else. Many service enterprises require much less capital equipment than is required for manufacturing or agriculture. But there are some, like railroads, air transport, shipping, and telephone services, that demand huge amounts of capital.

Table VIII depicts the national income originating in the major sectors of the economy for selected years from 1929–65. Most recently, there has been very little growth in agriculture and mining as compared with other major sectors of the economy. From 1950 through 1965, manufacturing has risen greatly, but services have risen more. Agriculture, in these years, increased by 19 per cent, and mining by 23 per cent, but manufacturing more than doubled its contribution to the national income—it rose by 124 per cent—and services leaped

TABLE VIII

National Income, by Sectors, for Selected Years
(In Millions of Dollars)

Sector	1929	1939	1945	1950	1955	1960	1965
Manufacturing	21,945	18,094	52,186	76,223	107,868	125,822	170,408
Agriculture	8,473	6,026	15,204	17,601	15,430	16,852	21,028
Mining	2,101	1,633	2,794	5,249	5,881	5,732	6,432
Contract construction	3,835	2,342	4,292	11,901	16,640	20,810	28,328
Government	5,093	8,523	36,764	23,602	38,087	52,891	75,243
Total services	44,538	35,633	69,876	105,334	145,316	190,055	253,315
Transportation	6,605	4,643	10,536	13,362	15,935	18,177	22,926
Communication	1,128	1,075	1,929	3,346	5,657	8,237	11,152
Electricity, gas, sanitation	1,638	1,766	2,290	3,910	6,218	8,934	11,605
Wholesale and retail	13,511	12,604	28,010	40,943	52,270	64,396	83,600
Finance, insurance, real estate	12,813	7,991	12,983	22,005	34,105	45,940	61,019
Other services	8,843	7,554	14,128	21,768	31,131	44,371	63,013

Source: U.S. Bureau of the Census, *Long-Term Economic Growth, 1875–1965* (Washington: Government Printing Office, 1966), pp. 228–35.

from $105.3 billion in 1950 to $253.3 billion in 1965, a rise of 141 per cent. Of particular interest to students of small business are the columns headed wholesale trade, retail trade, and other services (Table IX gives a more detailed breakdown of "other services" in the American economy.) In the main these are the traditional strongholds of small business. During this period, wholesale trade increased by 129 per cent and retail trade by 92 per cent, both hefty upswings. But "other services"—hotels, motels, personal services, repairs of various kinds, movies, and different forms of entertainment—nearly tripled, rising by 189 per cent.

THE CONCEPT OF SIZE

Many people, including some well-known economists, assume that in business to be big is to be efficient; to be small is to be inefficient or "marginal." Although there are certainly important areas where huge amounts of capital equipment are required for successful business operation, such as the production of passenger cars and the making of steel, this view is too simplistic. There are types of economic activity where bigness is a handicap. This is particularly true where the success of a product is determined by the whims of the consumer, as with stylish dresses or such crazes as Hoola-Hoops or Davy Crockett caps. What economists call "the economies of scale," or large-scale operation, can reach the point of diminishing returns. Costs at a certain stage begin to increase instead of decrease as an operation expands; more and more overhead is incurred, staff increases more than productivity, and so on.

The large firm is at a disadvantage where the pace is swift and the market always changing. It is not able to shift as swiftly and as well as its smaller competitors; its decision-making process is slower and more halting. The management of the large firm becomes more and more "muscle-bound" compared to its more flexible small competitors. Problems of

TABLE IX

National Income, "Other Services" for Selected Years
(In Millions of Dollars)

Other Services	1929	1939	1945	1950	1955	1960	1965
Hotels and other lodging places	623	485	1,087	1,388	1,717	2,111	2,785
Personal services	1,287	1,053	2,121	3,021	3,661	4,608	6,012
Miscellaneous business services	—	—	—	1,684	3,011	5,093	8,343
Automotive repair, services, garages	—	—	—	864	1,172	1,762	2,535
Miscellaneous repair services	—	—	—	665	873	1,105	1,482
Motion pictures	440	434	929	866	979	894	1,205
Other amusement and recreation services	379	288	613	788	1,196	1,661	2,237
Medical and other health services	1,536	1,381	2,459	4,412	7,097	10,724	15,562
Legal services	689	692	930	1,344	1,926	2,636	3,881
Educational services	442	449	641	1,109	1,524	2,402	4,137
Nonprofit membership organizations	640	556	983	1,803	2,675	3,815	5,291
Miscellaneous professional services	206	181	335	1,252	2,324	3,761	5,579
Services—private households	1,718	1,132	2,145	2,572	3,051	3,799	3,964
Totals	8,843	7,554	14,128	21,768	31,131	44,371	63,013

Source: *Long-Term Economic Growth*, pp. 233–35.

internal communications take up more time of top and middle management as the giant firm continues to grow. Because its capital commitments are so huge, it is usually much slower making fundamental changes in its product lines.

Nor are either the production costs or the productivity (output per man-hour) of the giant firm necessarily lower. Comparisons between firms of different sizes within an industry yield surprisingly inconclusive results. As Colin Clark has put it:

> The 1930 census of production of Great Britain provided material for such analysis, and it was found that only in a few industries was there a marked positive correlation between size of firm and output per person employed. In some cases, the results give a 'bell'-shaped curve with productivity highest in the middle range of size, lowest for unusually large or unusually small businesses, but in other cases the opposite result, or U-shaped curve, was obtained, where productivity was highest in large and small businesses and less in the middle ranges.[3]

There is the same mixed pattern in services. For example, when standardized goods are merchandized, costs fall as the size of the operation expands. A classic example here is in food retailing. It is virtually impossible for the small grocer to compete with the prices of the A&P's, the Krogers, or the Safeways.

On the other hand, there are many areas in retailing where the small firm excels. Fruits and vegetables, for instance, are often distributed more efficiently by small shops and hucksters than by the supermarkets. Another example is department stores. There is very little evidence that sales per employee increase as the size of business increases.

[3] Colin Clark, *The Conditions of Economic Progress* (London: Macmillan & Co., 1960), p. 347.

BUSINESS SUCCESS AND FAILURE

Every year in the United States about 500,000 brave souls venture forth into business. And every year about 350,000 firms go out of business for various reasons. Table X shows the number of new businesses and discontinued businesses for selected years, 1940 through 1962. There is no statistical series that gives the causes for discontinuance of businesses,

TABLE X

Number of Business Firms in Operation on January 1, and Number of New, Discontinued, and Transferred Businesses, Selected Years, 1940–62
(In Thousands)

Year	All Industries	New Businesses	Discontinued Businesses	Net Change	Transferred Businesses
1940	3,318.9	275.2	318.1	—42.9	(NA)
1944	2,839.1	330.9	174.6	156.3	359.4
1948	3,872.9	393.3	282.0	111.3	501.3
1950	4,008.7	348.2	289.6	58.6	419.4
1955	4,286.8	408.2	313.8	94.4	384.3
1960	4,658.0	438.0	384.0	54.0	(NA)
1962	4,755.0	430.0	387.0	42.0	(NA)

Source: James Ira Mills, *A Study of Small Business and Federal Government Programs To Assist Small Business*, p. 27.
NA: Not available.

but several studies have been made which give us some idea of why businesses die. In 1946, the Department of Commerce surveyed 1,650 businessmen who had either sold or liquidated their businesses in April through June of that year. It was found that 34 per cent of them did so in order to avoid loss. Other reasons included, "disposed of business at a profit," "alternative opportunity," "lost lease," "retired," and "became ill."[4]

An interesting study of the subject was carried out a few years ago for the SBA by a pair of sociologists at Brown Uni-

[4] Melville J. Ulmer and Alice Neilson, "Business Turnover and Causes of Failure," *Survey of Current Business*, XXVII, 4 (April, 1947), 10–16.

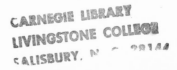

versity.[5] The study was a detailed investigation of eighty-one small retail and service firms in Rhode Island over a two-year period. The operations of each enterprise were systematically followed from the time of launching the venture through the end of its second year. Some of the firms did not last two years, and others were operated for such a brief period that they never appeared as mortalities in public or private tabulations. Others, of course, came through the period with satisfactory records and good profit potentialities. In all, at the end of the two-year period, forty-one of the eighty-one firms survived.

The report revealed that the decision to start a business is more often than not a spur-of-the-moment decision, not the result of careful planning and investigation. Thirty-five of the firms were previously established businesses that had been purchased by new owners. Only two of the thirty-five new "entrepreneurs" had checked the books or talked to accountants and suppliers about the profitability of the business. But both, ironically, had been unable to evaluate properly the financial statements which they had examined. They had failed to realize that evaluation of financial statements requires expert advice.

An interesting observation of the Brown researchers was that very few of the eighty-one new business owners conformed to the stereotype of the capitalistic entrepreneur who sets out to make a maximum profit. Only six of new owners could be said to have started their ventures with money primarily in mind.

Another finding was that the majority of the proprietors went into business for one of three reasons: (1) to make a living through self-employment, (2) to escape from unemployment, actual or expected, and (3) to build up a business as supplementary current income or as a resource for the future.

[5] Kurt B. Mayer and Sidney Goldstein, *The First Two Years: Problems of Small Firm Growth and Survival* (Washington: Small Business Administration, 1961) (Small Business Research Series No. 2).

Another rather surprising result of the Brown study was how little most of the new businessmen knew about the capital or the financial requirements for successful conduct of their businesses. As the authors wrote:

> The great majority of the owners in the sample had given little, if any, consideration to the minimum investment needed for the successful operation of a new business. Generally, they had only very hazy notions about the amounts of cash, stock, and credit required to maintain operations until the business could carry itself. Most of the owners committed all their liquid resources at the beginning of the venture. Coupled with the difficulty of obtaining loans, this commitment left them without reserves on which to draw when unexpected obstacles or emergencies arose. Moreover, most of the owners apparently did not separate their business and personal finances. Although direct access to the financial records was not available in most cases, it was clear from the answers given in the interviews that many owners used the same bank account for their personal expenditures as for their business operations. They would dip into the cash register whenever they needed personal spending money. By the same token, owners of grocery stores and spas would use the stock on their shelves for family consumption without appropriate notation in the records. As a result, the owners themselves in many cases were unable to determine whether the business was operating at a profit or loss. Furthermore, as later experience in several bases showed, this initial failure to distinguish clearly between business capital and personal finances resulted in financial disaster for the individual and his family. On the whole, the data suggest that the entire capitalization process of newly established retail and service enterprises is largely based on trial and error.[6]

The Brown study indicates once again how very small most businesses are in the United States. Only 31.2 per cent of the businesses had an initial capital investment of $5,000 or more.

[6] *Ibid.,* p. 55.

Gross sales of most of the firms were extremely modest. Only 2 of the 81 firms in the sample had 4 or more employees: a restaurant with 7 employees and a vacuum cleaner distributor with an office staff of 5, in addition to 100 door-to-door salesmen working on a commission basis.

On the national scene the figures are approximately the same. Most businesses in America are very small family-owned businesses. About 3 out of every 4 have 3 or fewer employees. Even in manufacturing, about 2 out of every 5 have 3 or fewer employees.

Some economists have decried this "economic waste," over 350,000 firms going out of existence every year and literally millions of very small "marginal" firms struggling for survival. Except for certain types of businesses, where minimum professional training, apprenticeship, certification, and licenses are required by law, just about anyone can go into business in America—in contrast to many European countries where entry into most businesses, including retailing, is carefully controlled. It is debatable, however, whether the European method is superior; indeed, it is probably inferior. For the persons excluded might well be just those active and enterprising people who could vigorously compete. Indeed, the relative ease of entry into an industry is usually the way American economists gauge the competitiveness of an industry: The easier the entry, the more competitive the field.

Nor is the American system as "wasteful" as it may appear on the surface. Certainly it is far preferable for a man to be earning his own living, however "marginal" that living might be, than for the man to be on the relief rolls, which is often his alternative.

Very few of the American business discontinuances are outright failures. In 1965, for example, only 13,514 business concerns failed, a rate of 53 out of every 10,000 concerns.[7]

[7] Dun & Bradstreet, *The Failure Record Through 1964*. The data is based on the 2,527,000 names listed in the Dun & Bradstreet *Reference Book*.

Also, in that year, 180,323 petitions for bankruptcy were filed in the U.S. District Courts. Of this number, however, only 14,208 were businesses, a mere 7.9 per cent of the total.[8] Most of the bankruptcies were employees of various firms whose personal finances had gotten out of manageable control.

COMPETITION AND ANTITRUST

Although one of the central purposes of the SBA is to maintain and increase economic competition, it has done surprisingly little in keeping abreast of the great wave of mergers that have been taking place in the business world for the past decade or so. It has left this field to the Antitrust Division of the Department of Justice and the Federal Trade Commission. Even though the SBA has the authority to act as the advocate of small business within the government, it has made little use of this power. Contacts with both Justice and the Federal Trade Commission, over the years, have been cordial but sporadic and unproductive. It would seem that the SBA could do far more than it has in bringing to the attention of these agencies the effects of specific mergers and acquisitions on small business concerns. But the SBA has done very little research on the subject and has paid scant attention to this important problem.

Similarly, other than the unfortunate American Motors decision, there is little if any indication that financial assistance or procurement assistance programs at the SBA have ever been specifically aimed at those industries where competition appeared to be declining. It may well be that the SBA had overlooked one of the most important factors affecting small business men today in the era of conglomerate mergers.

[8] U.S. Bureau of the Census, *Statistical Abstract of the U.S.: 1966,* p. 506.

III

Principal Functions of the SBA

The SBA has four principal activities: (1) financial assistance, (2) procurement assistance, (3) management assistance, and (4) assistance in providing venture capital. The first three have always been important and, indeed, were functions that were discharged by various agencies prior to the founding of the SBA in 1953. Responsibility for providing equity capital and long-term financing for small business firms through Small Business Investment Companies (SBIC's) was given the SBA in 1958 with the passage of the Small Business Investment Act.

FINANCING SMALL BUSINESS

Ask any small businessman what his principal problem is, and he will invariably say "Money," or the lack thereof. If he only had some more money he could renovate his store, do some effective advertising, and add to inventory. After a while the profits would start to roll in. Or, if he is a manufacturer, if he could only modernize his antiquated plant or could buy new machines, then he could really compete with the "big boys."

Who has not heard stories like these? Certainly the congressmen have, because the principal reason for creating the SBA was to see to it that small business was not discriminated against in seeking credit. If a small businessman is not able to obtain credit from private financial institutions on "reasonable terms," he is urged to go to his nearest SBA office and apply for a loan. That is the intent of Congress.

Financial assistance is the most important function of the SBA, whether measured in terms of money or SBA personnel engaged in lending. As of December 31, 1965, the SBA had over $1 billion outstanding in loans made to small businessmen. The breakdown by major purpose was:

"Regular" business loans	$724,494,326
Economic Opportunity ("poverty") loans	5,472,349
Disaster Loans	230,506,684
Development company loans	60,413,607

The financial assistance activities accounted for 81 per cent of total loans and investments of the SBA; investment company loans and investment company debentures constituted 19 per cent. In 1965, administrative expenses of the SBA were $40.1 million. Of this amount $29.9 million, or just about three-fourths of the total, was spent on the agency's financial assistance activities. At the end of 1965, the SBA had 3,785 employees. Of these, 3,016 were in the field, and 769 were stationed in Washington. Out of the total payroll, 1,888 people—or just about half—were exclusively engaged in financial assistance activities. In the field, over 56 per cent of the employees were working full time interviewing loan applicants, contacting local banks, making loans, and so on.

These figures tell only part of the story of the relative importance of financial assistance programs within the SBA. Much of the rest of the personnel—lawyers, economists, auditors, bookkeepers—are engaged in providing staff support to the Financial Assistance Division.

To gain a little more insight, let us consider the number of people working on line, or program, functions in the agency. In 1965, 2,418 employees of the SBA were directly concerned with program activities; of these, 78 per cent worked for the Financial Assistance Division. In the field, over 83 per cent of the line personnel were employed by the Financial Assistance Division.

PRINCIPAL LENDING ACTIVITIES OF THE SBA

The SBA has provided more than $3.1 billion in financial assistance to small firms through its various lending activities during the period from 1953 through the end of 1966. More than 70,000 concerns have received financial aid through the regular business-loan program. And over 50,000 loans have been made to help victims of natural disasters.

In 1965, for example, the SBA approved:

1. 13,506 business loans for which the SBA share amounted to $408.9 million;

2. 26,310 disaster and displaced business assistance loans totaling $206.9 million (this was the year of Hurricane Betsy, of which more later);

3. 289 local development company loans amounting to $45.7 million;

4. 863 Economic Opportunity ("poverty") Loans totaling $10.5 million.

Business Loans. Traditionally, business loans have been the single most important function of the SBA. They are carried out pursuant to Section 7(a) of the Small Business Act. Under this program, the SBA makes loans to eligible small concerns to finance plant construction and expansion, to purchase equipment and inventory, and for working capital. The loans can be made directly by the SBA or in participation with commercial banks; also, the SBA can guarantee loans made by commercial banks. The current interest rate is 5½ per cent, except in areas of major persistent unemployment, where the rate is 4 per cent. The maximum amount that can be loaned to any one business is $350,000. With a couple of exceptions, loans are made for a period not exceeding ten years.

Over the years, the average size of SBA loans has been $50,000. But averages can be deceiving. Although the average size of a loan is $50,000, in 1965, for example, 86.2 per cent were in amounts of less than $50,000. Some 60 per cent of the loans were in the $5,000 to $25,000 range.

Disaster and Displaced Business Loans. Frequently, the SBA pops into the news when the President announces that he is asking the SBA administrator to proclaim a particular area, hard-hit by some sort of natural catastrophe, as a disaster area. Take 1965, for example. In that year, the SBA helped victims of sixty-three disasters in twenty-nine states rebuild or replace their lost or damaged homes, businesses, and other property.

Louisiana and some of its neighbors were lashed by Hurricane Betsy. After the storm subsided, SBA disaster assistance experts and other experienced personnel from Washington and the field were rushed to New Orleans to assist the New Orleans regional office. Volunteers were sought and helped the area organize to restore the damaged sections. The mayor of New Orleans and the governor of Louisiana, among others, joined forces with SBA officials. Widespread publicity was given to the disaster program on television and radio, in the local press, and in other media. Special offices were set up to interview loan applicants. Long lines formed. Many people had suffered severe losses to their property, to their businesses, and to their houses. Loan processing is a slow tedious process. Applications have to be made, loan applicants interviewed, assessment of damage determined, credit worthiness checked, and so on.

Before Hurricane Betsy struck, there were fourteen people in the New Orleans SBA office—seven professionals and seven clerical and administrative employees. Of the professionals, five were loan specialists, one an attorney, and one a management specialist.

At the height of the SBA activity following the storm, over 500 employees were at work in the area, interviewing applicants, and processing loans. By the end of 1965, there were still 247 people assigned to the New Orleans office, but emphasis had shifted away from financial assistance to administrative tidiness. Lawyers, auditors, and typists were now predominant. The SBA had moved swiftly to relieve the suffering. Inevitably some mistakes had been made, applications incorrectly filled out or partially completed. Now was the time to double-check and get all the books and records in order.

In all, the agency approved $91.5 million in loans in Louisiana alone. Probably 5,000 private citizens, including businessmen, were assisted in rebuilding homes and businesses that had been battered by the great hurricane.

These disaster loans are provided for in Section 7(b)(1) of the Small Business Act. They are not limited to small business alone, but are available to all concerns, regardless of size. The loans are made for a period not to exceed twenty years. The interest rate charged by the SBA is 3 per cent.

Physical damage loans have been by far the most important of the SBA's disaster loans. However, three other types of disasters are covered by the Small Business Act; and the SBA makes loans for these purposes, as well. Section 7(b)(2) provides for economic injury disaster loans. Under this authority, the SBA has made loans to small business concerns that have been injured economically as a result of drought or excessive rainfall. These disaster areas are determined by the President or the Secretary of Agriculture. This authority was recently broadened by the Congress. Now this kind of financial assistance may be provided in any area determined by the President or the Secretary of Agriculture to have suffered any major economic disaster. All these loans are limited to small businesses that have experienced substantial economic injury as a result of the proclaimed disaster.

Product damage disaster loans are covered in Section 7(b)(4) of the act. These loans are made to business concerns that have encountered substantial economic injury as a result of damage to a product arising from natural or undetermined causes. This section of the law was added in 1964. It came in the wake of the botulism problem in smoked fish which had been caught in the Great Lakes. Primarily, product damage disaster loans are made for working capital purposes to re-establish the affected business.

When the Housing Act of 1961 was passed by the Eighty-seventh Congress, it tacked on an amendment to Section 7 of the Small Business Act, giving the SBA authority to make loans to small firms that are forced to relocate because of federally sponsored urban renewal, highway, or construction programs. A business owner who is displaced by federal programs may acquire property in a new location if he so desires. And, although the SBA previously had not made loans to displaced businessmen who formerly rented but now wanted to own their own premises, the Congress made it clear in 1964 that they had intended for these businessmen to be able to do so.

To date, not much use has been made of the economic injury, product damage, or displaced business loans. From mid-1962 through the end of 1966, the SBA had made, in all, 913 displaced business loans totaling $59.1 million. As of mid-1965, the SBA had approved 943 economic injury loans, representing $17.5 million.

Interest rates and maximum term of the loans are similar to those under the physical damage disaster loans. The only exception is that the interest rate for the displaced business loans is higher than the 3 per cent charged for other disaster loans. The interest rate in early 1965 was 3¾ per cent. Under a complicated formula, the rate is based primarily on the current average annual interest rate of all interest-bearing obligations of the United States then forming part of the public debt.

ECONOMIC OPPORTUNITY LOANS (EOL's)

In 1964, an interesting, and potentially significant, program was added to the SBA's financial and management assistance programs with the passage of the widely heralded Economic Opportunity Act. This was, of course, the Johnson Administration's celebrated War on Poverty in America.

The act creates such undertakings as the Community Action Programs, the Neighborhood Youth Corps, the Job Corps, VISTA, and other poverty programs that have been so greatly publicized over the past few years. (The SBA's role in the passage of this legislation is chronicled in Chapter IX.) Title IV of the act provides: "It is the purpose of this title to assist in the establishment, preservation, and strengthening of small business concerns and improve the managerial skills employed in such enterprises; and to mobilize for these objectives private as well as public managerial skills and resources."

What do these murky, rather opaque words mean? They mean that the economically underprivileged—that is, those who are "living in poverty"—who wish to start a business or to expand an existing one can apply to the SBA for a Title IV loan, or EOL. To be eligible, the applicant must either be "in poverty" himself or, as a result of the loan, be able to take others out of poverty—primarily by providing them with jobs. Also, an applicant must have been turned down by at least two commercial banks and deemed ineligible for the regular SBA lending programs.

Terms are extremely liberal by normal banking standards. Little or even no collateral is required. Major emphasis is placed on the character of the applicant, his competence, and his general capacity to make a go of his business, financial considerations apart. The maximum amount of the SBA's share of a single loan is $25,000; the maximum term is fifteen years. Interest rates are the same as those for regular SBA business loans. Also, the SBA may, at its discretion, give a borrower a grace period for the repayment of principal and use other methods for repayment of the loans that will assist the borrower in making his business successful. For example, it might be prudent to make the borrower repay $1,000 a year for the first five years of a loan and $2,000 a year for the last five years. The borrower will thus have more working capital during the first five years than would be the case if he had received a typical bank loan. If all goes well, it should be easier for him to repay $2,000 a year, later on, than to repay $1,500 a year initially.

Until recently, the EOL program has been principally aimed at minority groups (mainly Negroes) in a score of metropolitan areas of the country. It is not clear at the present time how this program will turn out. It is an experimental undertaking operating in an area of great national concern and need, but it is fraught with many difficulties. Besides, it must be realized that this is a radical program by old SBA financial assistance standards. Credit men are justifiably proud of low loss ratios, which reflect sound credit judgment. It is unsettling to ingrained habits, thought processes, and standards of performance to place such a very different program in the midst of the Financial Assistance Division.

This program has received a lot of attention during the past few years. For example, in the President's annual budget message of January 1967, two brief paragraphs were accorded the SBA in the over-all scheme of things. One of the two paragraphs dealt exclusively with the EOL program. However, if one "looks at the record," the publicity does not appear to be justified. In 1965, only 863 "poverty loans" were made, totaling a mere $10.5 million. In dollars, this was roughly 2½ per cent of the regular business loans, 5 per cent of the amount lent to victims of natural disasters, and only one-quarter of the money lent to local development companies. The program has a handful of specialists in the Washington office who oversee it, but the loans are made by financial assistance men in the

field, many of whom, to put it judiciously, are not enamored
of the program and are skeptical of its soundness.

DEVELOPMENT COMPANY LOANS

The SBA makes loans to state and local development companies under Title V of the Small Business Investment Act of
1958. Section 501 of the act provides for SBA loans to state
development companies for the general purpose of providing
long-term loans and equity financing to small firms by the
development companies. To date, very little use has been made
of this program by state development authorities. As of the
end of 1965, only $3.6 million in loans and investments were
still outstanding. The main reason has been that state development companies have been able to borrow from the private
banking system at reasonable rates. Indeed, the interest rates
charged by the banks have generally been the prime rate,
which up to that time was usually less than the 5 per cent
charged by the SBA.

Section 502 provides for loans to local development companies for use in helping specific small businesses to expand
or modernize their facilities, or in helping new small firms to get
started. These loans may be made for a maximum of $350,000
for each identifiable small business concern. The maximum
term for a loan made under this program has been set at
twenty-five years.

These local development companies are playing an important role in economic development today. They are privately
owned and operate under state charter. The SBA works with
them to help restore vitality to areas that are lagging behind
the nation in economic growth and in general economic well-
being.

Primarily, the program is directed toward rural and small-
town America. It is a paradox that in the richest country of
the world, even at the prosperity peaks of the past seven years

or so, that almost everywhere there is concern about local economic situations. In some of the older areas of the United States, one often finds antiquated, inefficient plants, migration of industries to other regions, and a general state of depression relative to other areas. In regions where agriculture has been predominant, profound structural changes have taken place. The size of individual holdings has increased significantly; farms have become increasingly mechanized; and larger and larger amounts of capital are required to farm successfully.

While these trends are beneficial to the economy as a whole, they have caused serious dislocations to many people and communities. The farm population continues to shrink. People, especially the young, move from the town and the farm to the city. Local business, especially retail trade, dries up more and more. A striking manifestation of the magnitude and force of these local changes is revealed by comparing some figures from the 1950 and 1960 Censuses. During this decade, the population rose by more than 28 million people, a climb of over 18 per cent. However, during this so-called baby boom, approximately half the counties of the country lost population.

The areas that have been losing ground usually fall into one of these categories: (1) the small rural community that has little or no industry; (2) the community that actually depends upon one industry or derives its living from a seasonal industry or product; and (3) the community that has a fair amount of industry but a lagging growth rate. The lagging growth rate is usually due to two factors: over-all demand for the product or industry may be falling; and the local industry or product may have become increasingly noncompetitive. Sometimes a community or area has both problems.

The SBA gives first priority in its Development Company Program to America's smaller communities. In the period of July 1–December 31, 1966, for example, more than 67 per cent of SBA funds went to communities having populations of 5,000 or less; 11.1 per cent in the 5,000–10,000 range; 3.7 per cent in the 10,000–15,000 range; and 9.8 per cent in the 15,000–25,000 range. Only 8 per cent of SBA's local development money during this period went to areas with a population of 50,000 or more.

GOVERNMENT PROCUREMENT ASSISTANCE

The U.S. Government is the largest single purchaser of goods and services in America. In Fiscal Year 1965, it bought more than $38.5 billion of goods from American business. As with so many other things, the Department of Defense is by far the largest agency in terms of procurement. In Fiscal Year 1965, its purchases amounted to $27.9 billion, or just about three-quarters of the total.

Other important agencies, from the standpoint of government purchasing, are the National Aeronautics and Space Administration (NASA), which accounted for $5.1 billion during the same time span, and the Atomic Energy Commission (AEC), which made purchases costing $2.4 billion. Civilian executive agencies spent only $2.8 billion. Of these, the General Services Administration (GSA) is by far the most important. In Fiscal Year 1963, GSA purchases amounted to $812.1 million. This represented one-third of total procurement by the civilian executive agencies in that year.

The SBA is charged with responsibility for seeing to it that small business receives its "fair share" of government procurement and surplus property contracts. There are several ways in which the SBA has attempted to increase the small business share of government purchases and surplus sales.

Small Business "Set-Asides." The most important device has been the small business "set-aside." Under this system, procurement agencies set aside specific contracts, which may then be bid upon only by small business concerns. In Fiscal Year 1965, the Department of Defense awarded contracts worth $5.3 billion to small firms. Of this total, $2.4 billion, or about

PRINCIPAL FUNCTIONS OF THE SBA 67

45 per cent, were reserved for bidding exclusively by small business.

Until the middle of 1965, "set-asides" were made on a joint basis. That is to say, the procurement agency and the SBA jointly determined whether a particular contract should be reserved for exclusive small business bidding. In 1965, the SBA had forty-six representatives in the field engaged in seeing to it that small business received its "fair share" of government business. They covered thirty-four procurement centers on a full-time basis and thirty-six others on a scheduled part-time basis. They also visited 410 additional centers occasionally, to "spot-check" the trends in procurements.

In 1965, SBA administrator Eugene P. Foley decided to abandon the joint "set-aside" approach. Before the Senate Small Business Committee, he stated the findings of a survey indicated that what SBA procurement "representatives accomplish is more apparent than real." Foley also indicated that the SBA field men often only "rubber-stamped" decisions that had already been made by the procurement agency.

From now on, Foley said in effect, "set-asides" would be unilateral. In other words, these decisions would be made by the procurement agencies alone. The SBA would have no active role to play in this process. Instead, it would work with each of the agencies and help them set up over-all "goals" for awards to small business. Foley was a policy man; he did not think much of the joint "set-aside" program because the action there was "way down the line." "But," he said, "what does bring results is establishing goals and priorities right at the top."

The Senate Small Business Committee, including Chairman John Sparkman, did not appear overly impressed or convinced by Foley's proposal. Nevertheless, the program went into effect in July, 1965. The committee remained skeptical of the wisdom of this decision. Furthermore, in its Sixteenth Annual Report (June, 1966), the committee noted that the decision was of "questionable legal authority." It thought the new policy violated Section 15 of the Small Business Act, which provided for a joint-determination program. The committee also noted that "the SBA joint set-aside program [had] been operated successfully over the years, and SBA procurement center representatives [had] done yeoman's service in helping to channel Federal procurements to small business."

In testimony before the same committee in March, 1967, Bernard L. Boutin, Foley's successor as SBA administrator, indicated that he was not happy with the unilateral "set-aside" approach. Boutin said, in part:

> We have tentatively determined that we should combine several previous techniques. In the future, we think the best approach will be to station SBA representatives at major procuring centers (both military and civilian). These representatives would be responsible for a number of actions in connection with the procurement programs at these installations.
>
> We would, for instance, check procurements which have not been set aside to see whether in SBA's judgment they should be set aside.
>
> We would institute an appeal procedure to cover procurements that SBA recommends be set aside but the procuring agency does not agree [*sic*].

Certificates of Competency. The SBA's Certificates of Competency (COC) program is another instrument that has helped small businesses get government contracts. Sometimes a procurement agency will reject the low bid of a small business concern on the grounds of inadequate productive capacity or credit. The small firm has the right of appeal to the SBA. The agency will then undertake an independent study of its capabilities. If it concludes that the company is capable of carrying out the contract, a certification is issued which is binding on the contracting agency.

This SBA service has enabled many small firms to obtain

government contracts, which otherwise would have gone to higher bidders. It is helpful to both the small business community and the American taxpayer. Through 1965, the SBA had received 4,231 applications for certificates and has issued 1,859. The total amount of the contracts involved was $334 million. According to the SBA, approximately $27 million has been saved through eventual government acceptance of these low bids.

The Facilities Inventory. The SBA maintains a facilities inventory to help government buying offices and prime contractors locate small business suppliers. At the end of 1965, the inventory contained information about 63,406 firms supplying approximately 11,000 items, product lines, or manufacturing processes; 187 kinds of service businesses; about 500 specific types of research and development capabilities.

Each SBA regional office collects data on local small businesses for inclusion in this inventory. The registers are maintained at eighteen selected SBA offices, each responsible for information within a given geographical area. Information about the firms is kept on magnetic tape at the SBA's headquarters in Washington. Print-outs are sent twice a year to SBA regional offices, contracting offices, and business service centers of federal agencies.

Sales of Surplus Property. The SBA can help small firms buy surplus property, timber, and strategic materials sold by the federal government. The agency keeps a list of items small concerns have said they need. Whenever these items are to be offered for sale, small businesses are notified. Sometimes the government sales are set aside for small business.

MANAGEMENT ASSISTANCE

One of the most familiar clichés in the SBA lexicon is that poor management, not lack of credit at reasonable terms, not lack of long-term and equity capital, nor lack of government contracts, is at the root of small business failure. A survey by Dun & Bradstreet of all business failures in 1962 is often trotted out. The credit-rating firm concluded that the underlying cause of more than 90 per cent of all failures in that year was bad management. Since "management" is such a broad concept, the figure might as well have been 100 per cent, but it is likely that 90 per cent sounds more scientific and meaningful.

Be that as it may, there can be no question that poor management skills are the root cause of the failure, or unprofitability, of many ill-starred business ventures. But what can be done about it? Should the federal government really care? What *is* done about it?

The principal means offered by the SBA to upgrade the management skills of small businessmen are publications of varying kinds, conferences and seminars, and management counseling. All can be useful techniques. Publications have the advantage of being cheaper per small businessman reached than the other two activities, but they can miss their target. Often, the small businessman simply does not read them.

Seminars and conferences are useful. But it is essential that they be well organized, have a good roster of speakers, and be well publicized. They are considerably more expensive than publications. Furthermore, there is a clear limit to how far these activities can be expanded without suffering a rather grievous dilution of quality.

Many small business buffs believe that the SBA should expand its management counseling activities. It is felt that man-to-man counseling is the most effective way to improve the skills of small businessmen. An experienced counselor by actually going over the operations of a business with the owner can tell him what he is doing wrong and suggest ways in which his business can be improved. This is undoubtedly true. But several questions arise. One of the most important is cost. Extensive counseling would be quite expensive. Who is to pay for it—the taxpayer or the businessman? Suppose the advice is even worse than the opinions of the existing management? Would the government then be responsible?

Who is to be helped? Should the counseling be made available to all small businessmen? Or, say, should it be limited to those who are borrowers from the SBA? Should some of the businessmen pay for counseling? If not, would not government be invading the preserve of private management consultants?

Having raised these issues, let us look at the major SBA activities in the management assistance field.

SBA Management Publications. The SBA publishes and distributes many pamphlets. To illustrate the scope of these activities, let us look at what was accomplished during 1965. In that year, more than 4.1 million free leaflets were distributed. The various series have such titles as "Small Marketers Aids," "Small Business Bibliographies," "Technical Aids," and "Management Research Summaries."

More detailed booklets on management subjects are sold by the U.S. Superintendent of Documents. The price is nominal, usually less than 40 cents a copy.

A useful publication series is "Starting and Managing." It was originally sponsored by the Department of Commerce and the Veterans Administration, primarily to help servicemen returning from World War II. Many were interested in starting their own businesses, and the pamphlets outlined the essentials of running a particular kind of business enterprise. The advantages and disadvantages of starting and managing a business are weighed in the booklets. After the SBA was established, in 1953, it took over the responsibility for the series. A typical title would be "Starting and Managing a Small Retail Hardware Store."

One of the more popular SBA publications is "A Handbook of Small Business Finance." Over 160,000 copies were sold during the first eleven years after publication. In all, the Superintendent of Documents sold over 200,000 copies of SBA pamphlets in 1965. This is a rather modest figure when one considers that the potential market is nearly 5,000,000 customers.

Courses and Seminars. The SBA has developed training courses in such subjects as taxes, accounting, marketing, advertising, business law, and inventory management and control. These are given free or for a nominal fee to thousands of businessmen. They are offered by colleges and universities, high schools, trade associations, and local civic organizations, which act as cosponsors. As former administrator Bernard Boutin described the activity: "SBA acts as the liaison, the catalyst, between the educational institution and the business audience, providing training materials, publicity, and technical information."

One of the more interesting SBA educational activities is the one-day workshop seminar. In 1965, 197 workshops were conducted throughout the country and were attended by 7,734 new or prospective businessmen. The seminar is restricted to those who have been in business for a year or less and those who are contemplating going into business. The workshops are concerned with the fundamentals of good management and the problems of starting a business on a sound basis.

Among other things these seminars are useful because the pitfalls as well as the advantages of being a proprietor are illuminated. Often, people start a business with only a haphazard notion of what is involved. Many probable future business "failures" were dissuaded from going into business after attending such a seminar. Others redoubled their planning efforts before launching their enterprise. Originally, these one-day workshops were conducted exclusively by SBA management assistance personnel. But as demand increased, qualified volunteers, primarily local businessmen, have pitched in to help.

Management Counseling. The SBA provides personal counseling through its Washington and sixty-six regional offices scattered throughout the country. A small businessman with a business problem simply has to contact the nearest SBA office to seek advice. In 1963, its Washington and field offices assisted 18,000 people with their individual problems. The counseling can range from the simple matter of handing the businessman a pertinent pamphlet to a detailed, in-depth analysis of his problem.

The SBA counseling services have been considerably strengthened during the past three years with the introduction of the SCORE program. In announcing the program by press release in September, 1964, Administrator Eugene Foley said SCORE was

a nationwide pioneer program to concentrate the brainpower of retired business executives on management problems that beset thousands of small businesses. SBA has issued a call for volunteers from the ranks of retired businessmen who would be willing to help small businessmen, and is enrolling them in the Service Corps of Retired Executives (SCORE). By and large SCORE volunteers will work with problem loan cases, economic opportunity loans under the "poverty program," and community development surveys. The typical counseling case will involve a small business with less than 25 employees.

The SCORE system of counseling will identify the basic need for professional management consulting to small businesses. The program will not conflict with professional consulting because it does not provide the consulting-in-depth available from professionals.

By the end of 1965, SCORE had grown to include 3,000 retired business executives. Some 135 chapters had been formed throughout the United States, and during 1965, volunteers counseled 10,625 small business owners.

The Senate Small Business Committee, in 1964, commented on SCORE, as follows: "This appears to the committee to be a farsighted and unique approach to assisting small businesses with their managerial problems. It is felt that this program may have much merit. The manner in which it is received and utilized by the small business community will determine its efficacy."

Apparently, the SCORE program is efficacious. There is a large and growing demand for the services of these "senior citizens." And, as Administrator Bernard Boutin put it: "These volunteers are providing service worth many millions of dollars each year without charge."

SMALL BUSINESS INVESTMENT PROGRAM

The Small Business Investment program is unquestionably the most difficult of the SBA programs to grasp. Rather complex subjects are involved—the law, corporate finance, and capital markets. But the basic idea of the Small Business Investment program is quite simple. The Small Business Investment Act had its origins in the findings of Congress that there are many firms that are handicapped competitively by their inability to get long-term loans or equity capital from the public capital markets or from conventional financial institutions.

This conclusion was reached after several years of study and discussion, much of it within Congress itself. Indeed, at the time of the creation of the SBA, Senator John Sparkman had stressed the importance of providing long-term loan money and equity capital to small businesses. He proposed the organization of national investment companies to encourage the flow of private equity capital. The companies would have been supervised by the Federal Reserve Board. The Federal Reserve Banks would have been authorized to invest in the stock of the companies but would have been required to sell this stock as other purchasers could be found.

The capital of the investment companies would have been put up originally by the Federal Reserve Banks. The investment companies would then have been authorized to provide capital and credit by making loans to, or acquiring stocks or bonds of, small businesses. The maximum loan to any single company would have been $1 million.

The senator's proposal grew out of and closely paralleled earlier studies and recommendations made by Dr. A. D. H. Kaplan, of the Brookings Institution, and by the Committee for Economic Development (CED), in the late 1940's. Senators Paul H. Douglas, of Illinois, former professor of economics at the University of Chicago, and Ralph Flanders, of Vermont, former industrialist and trustee of the CED, supported Senator Sparkman's proposal. But it fell largely on deaf ears.

The idea of creating investment companies to extend long-term loans and equity capital to small business lay dormant for some time. Then in a series of studies, the widely respected Federal Reserve Board concluded that there was an equity and long-term credit gap for small business. This conclusion gave a powerful impetus to those who wanted to see the government set up investment companies for small concerns. The Federal Reserve's studies may well have been the crucial factor in passage of the Small Business Investment Act in 1958.

As provided in the act, the small business investment company (SBIC) is a privately owned and operated corporation. It is in business in order to earn profits for its shareholders. The principal reason for the establishment of the SBIC as an institution was to avoid the necessity for more direct government participation in meeting the equity gap. It was hoped, therefore, that with the help of the SBA, "private enterprise could do the job."

Under the law, the SBA is empowered to license SBIC's. Each company must have a paid-in capital and surplus equal to at least $300,000. The SBIC can obtain from the SBA additional capital equal to its paid-in capital and surplus by the sale of subordinated debentures to the agency. The amount of subordinated debentures of any single firm that may be held by the SBA cannot exceed $700,000.

Additionally, an SBIC can borrow money from the SBA. These borrowings cannot exceed 50 per cent of its paid-in capital and surplus. The maximum amount of such loans that can be made to a single SBIC is $4 million.

Over the life of the program, the SBA has issued 794 licenses; but as of the end of March, 1967, there were 624 licensed SBIC's. As of March, 1966, total *private* capital invested in the SBIC's was about $475 million. The SBA had advanced loans and had taken subordinated debentures aggregating $259.8 million. So at that time there was slightly less than $2 of private money in the program for $1 of government money.

Since 1958, the SBIC industry has made over 20,000 financings, involving about $1 billion, to all kinds of small concerns. As of March 31, 1966, some $552 million of small business equities and obligations were outstanding in the SBIC industry's portfolios. Of this amount, $279 million was in long-term loans, $180 million in debt securities, and $93 million in capital stock of small concerns. That last figure was most disappointing to those who had framed the program. Only $93 million, or less than 17 per cent of the total, was being used to close the "equity gap."

SBA rules fix the maximum cost of money to small concerns that can be charged by SBIC's at 15 per cent. In some cases, the maximum cost to be charged is less, because certain states have laws setting maximum legal rates below that figure. Usually, the state laws provide for a ceiling on rates well below 15 per cent.

However, the median rate charged has been far below the maximum permitted. Through March, 1966, the median rate in debt securities was in the range of 7 to 7.9 per cent. On straight loans it was 8 to 8.9 per cent.

The average size of financings for the SBIC fiscal year ending March 31, 1966, was $39,000 for loans, $70,000 for debt securities, and $45,000 for capital stock.

Since its inception the SBIC program has been beset by problems. Some of the difficulties are certainly traceable to the fact that the SBIC operation is a new, experimental program that is aimed at solving an extremely complex problem. Congress has understood these dilemmas and has attempted to shore up the program on four occasions. In 1960, it authorized SBIC's to acquire a wide range of equity securities from small business concerns financed by them and doubled the amounts that banks might invest in the stock of the SBIC's. In 1961, the amount of funds that the SBA might contribute to the capital of an SBIC was raised from $150,000 to $400,000. In 1964, the maximum was upped again to $700,000, and the Congress eliminated a previous restriction on the maximum amount an SBIC might invest in any one small business concern. At the same time, Congress directed the SBA to adopt effective regulations to deal with the conflicts of interest problem. And, late in 1966, Congress gave the SBA broad new enforcement and supervisory powers including the power to revoke licenses of SBIC's and to remove or suspend directors and officers of the investment companies.

IV

Organization and Administration

Organization and administration lie at the heart of modern governance. The formal structure of agencies like the SBA provides the arena in which the contest is waged for the prizes of government—money, jobs, glory.

Let us pause for a moment to consider our subject. Webster defines "adminstration" as "the total activity of a state in the exercise of its political powers including the action of the legislative, judicial and executive departments." Or, again, "the management of public affairs as distinguished from the executive or political functions of policy making."

Obviously, these are two quite different notions. Early students of public administration in the United States followed Webster's second definition, as represented by the theory of Frederick W. Taylor in *The Principles of Scientific Management* (1911). They believed that "politics," or "policy" could be separated from "administration." In describing administration, therefore, they stressed such antiseptically scientific factors as the line of authority, the need for staff offices, the span of control by supervisors over subordinates, the budget as an element of rational planning and coordination, personnel management, and administrative law.

In more recent years, many scholars have viewed administration less as an exact science than as what Charles E.

Lindblom has called "The Science of 'Muddling Through.'" This school of thought includes most of the leading lights in public administration today, including James G. March, Herbert A. Simon, Robert Presthus, and Victor Thompson. They see administration as an inseparable part of the larger society, particularly the political process. As Ernest S. Griffith has written in his book *The Impasse of Democracy:*

> One cannot live in Washington for long without being conscious that it has . . . whirlpools or centers of activity focusing on particular problems. The persons who are thus active—in agriculture, in power, in labor, in foreign trade, and the parts thereof— are variously composed. Some are civil servants, some are active members of the appropriate committees in the House and Senate, some are lobbyists, some are unofficial research authorities. . . . Perhaps special correspondents of newspapers are included. These people in their various permutations and combinations are continually meeting in each other's offices, at various clubs, lunching together, and participating in legislative hearings or serving on important but obscure committees set up within the departments. Among such human beings interested in a common problem, ideas are bound to emerge—ideas for programs, ideas for strategy. . . . There is nothing really mysterious about this sort of government. It is essentially "of men," and these men behave very naturally. "Who says what to whom, and what is the reaction?" This question, if we could obtain enough answers, would capture the spirit, the genius of our own or any government.[1]

One word of caution. To describe the SBA as a political institution may suggest the grimy image of politics often portrayed in editorial cartoons. What of the merit system, the notion of the public interest, dedication to public service? There is indeed a merit system, and upwards of 99 per cent of

[1] For more recent elaborations of the same viewpoint, see the article by Harvey C. Mansfield in the American Assembly volume and the book by J. Leiper Freeman listed in the bibliography.

SBA employees are covered by it. Both the civil servants and their political bosses probably believe more than most men do of themselves that they are doing what is right and thereby serving the public interest. Very many of them have chosen to work at the SBA in preference to more lucrative pursuits. But in making that choice, they have obliged themselves to work under the surveillance of the White House and Congress, which are supremely political institutions.

Thus, even in the age of the computer, the organization and administration of the SBA are based not only on a mechanical execution of its functions, described in Chapter III. They are also inescapably involved with the sort of politics chronicled in Chapter I and the needs of the small business community. The SBA is swept up in what Griffith calls a "whirlpool." It is always dealing with Congress, the public, and other agencies, as we shall see in subsequent chapters.

Since "administration" entails just about everything the SBA does, let us turn to the basic structure of the agency.

To put the SBA briefly in organizational perspective, it is a part of the executive branch of the U.S. Government. Outside the Presidential office, the executive consists of cabinet-level departments, independent agencies, and regulatory commissions. The SBA, an independent agency, is run by an administrator who is directly responsible to the President of the United States. The agency does not have the size and stature of a department. And unlike the regulatory commissions, it has a single head who oversees programs, which are primarily of an assistance, rather than a regulatory nature. The exception is the SBIC program, in which the SBA by law licenses SBIC's and monitors their activities.

Agencies are generally organized along three lines—clientele, functions, and geography; the SBA structure reflects all three. As the voice for small business in the executive branch, the agency was set up to serve that particular clientele. Internal SBA operations are in essence organized around its principal line functions—financial assistance, procurement and management assistance, and investment assistance—and the staff offices designed to serve them. The SBA employed about 4,000 people at the end of 1967, including a Washington headquarters of nearly 900 and more than 3,000 field workers, located in seventy-three communities across the nation.

SBA ORGANIZATION IN THE PAST

The SBA began as a modest amalgam of the small business lending functions of the Reconstruction Finance Corporation and the Small Defense Plants Administration. In January, 1954, five months after the agency was created, the SBA employed only 449 persons. Well over half worked in various field offices and fifty-five procurement centers where they met with small businessmen seeking government contracts.

In its earliest days, the SBA was headed by an administrator with three deputy administrators—one for Procurement and Technical Assistance, one for Financial Assistance, and one for Administration. In addition, official agency regulations, published in the *Federal Register,* authorized eight more major offices. These were the offices of General Counsel, Information and Managerial Assistance, Controller, Economic Adviser, Management, Financial Assistance, Procurement and Technical Assistance, and Compliance and Security. In addition, there was a Loan Policy Board, consisting of the secretaries of Commerce and the Treasury with the SBA administrator as chairman.

Gradually, over the years, the organizational pattern has changed. To a considerable degree, these shifts have resulted from functions added to the agency. For example, when the Small Business Investment Act was passed in 1958, it was necessary to create a position of deputy administrator for investment. Again, in 1963, the SBA administrator considered the civil rights movement of sufficient importance to justify a special assistant for minority groups at the agency. The emergence of data processing and the government's Planning-Programing-Budgeting System in the mid-1960's also brought new administrative units and techniques to the SBA.

Changes in organization patterns have also resulted from an increased volume of SBA activities. Take the major SBA program, financial assistance, for example. During the period from 1953 to January, 1967, the SBA approved about 70,000 business loans worth over $3 billion. More than 75 per cent of both the number and the dollar amount of these loans were made in the period beginning with 1960. Obviously, the stepped-up pace of loan processing demanded more personnel in the Financial Assistance Division. What is less apparent is the corresponding increase in the size of the agency's staff units. Thus, in January, 1954, the Office of General Counsel employed fourteen people, all of them located in Washington. In 1967, the office employed eighty people in Washington and 384 in the field.

Finally, the SBA has sometimes been reorganized because top officials preferred another way of doing business. To cite a recent example, SBA Administrator Robert C. Moot in April, 1968, issued National Directive Standard Change No. 15. This directive abolished the office of area program coordinator for the SBIC program in line with previous efforts to centralize control over the troubled SBIC program. The SBIC's had been investigated by two Congressional committees in 1966 (see Chapter VIII), and the agency in its attempt to make the SBIC's toe the line made the Washington Investment Division directly responsible for the supervision of all SBIC's. At the same time, the directive decentralized responsibility for the development company loan program from the eight area administrators to the more numerous regional directors, who serve a smaller constituency. It was felt that authority for this program should be administered at the agency level closest to the grass roots.

THE PRESENT ORGANIZATION OF THE SBA

The fundamental organization of the SBA is shown in the accompanying chart, which illustrates primarily the administrative set-up in SBA Washington headquarters. In the field, there are eight area administrators who oversee the activities of regional directors and, through them, branch managers. The field organization will be described later in this chapter. But it is the Washington operation which is the administrative nerve center of the SBA.

SBA Washington Headquarters. In essence, SBA headquarters consists of the administrator and deputy administrator and the units immediately responsible to them; the four principal staff officers—general counsel and three assistant administrators for Planning, Research and Analysis, Congressional and Public Affairs, and Administration—and the three associate administrators, who oversee the line program activities of Investment, Financial Assistance, and Procurement and Management Assistance.

The administrator is the commander-in-chief of all SBA operations. Reporting directly to him are the National Advisory Council, the special assistant for advisory councils, the special assistant to the administrator, and the hearing examiner. The administrator is given policy and program advice by the National Small Business Advisory Council, which he chooses from outstanding members of the public. The council works on a continuing basis with the special assistant for advisory councils. Probably more important is the special assistant to the administrator, his top multipurpose personal and confidential aide. This man serves as a troubleshooter for the administrator on various agency matters and also maintains a continuing contact with the White House staff. The hearing examiner presides over administrative tribunals at the SBA involving enforcement of the Small Business Investment Act,

ORGANIZATION OF THE SMALL BUSINESS ADMINISTRATION

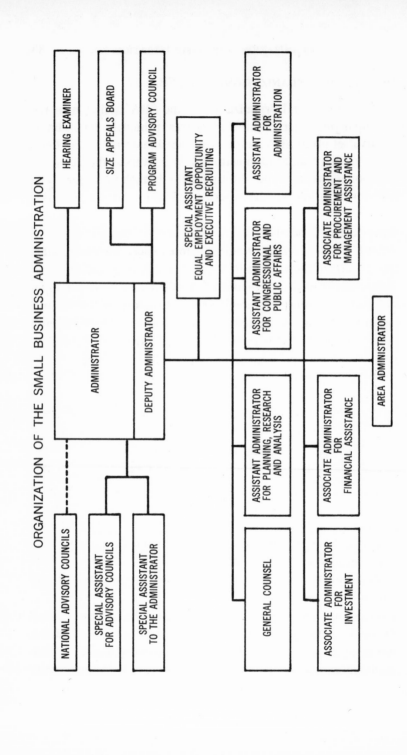

equal employment opportunity provisions of the Civil Rights Act, and disputes over SBA contracts.

The deputy administrator is the SBA's second in command. His post was created in 1963 by Administrator Eugene P. Foley, who wanted to concentrate on policy and delegate routine administrative decisions to his deputy (then called the executive administrator). Subsequent administrators have found the arrangement useful and maintained the position. The deputy administrator serves as chairman of the Size Appeals Board and the Program Advisory Council. The Size Appeals Board consists of the associate administrator for Procurement and Management Assistance, the associate administrator for Financial Assistance, and the assistant administrator for Planning, Research and Analysis, with the general counsel as legal adviser. The board reviews and makes recommendations to the administrator about specific size controversies. The Program Advisory Council includes all associate and assistant administrators and the director of the Office of Program Planning, who serves as its executive secretary. The council reviews and makes recommendations about the agency's Planning-Programing-Budgeting System.

The special assistant for Equal Employment Opportunity and Executive Recruitment performs two functions. As the fair employment officer for the agency, he reviews complaints of those who contend they have been discriminated against and makes recommendations to the administrator. As the executive recruitment officer, he heads the effort to interest college students—both minority and nonminority group members—in working for the SBA.

The general counsel, whose rank is equivalent to an assistant administrator, is the SBA's chief lawyer. As such, he is responsible for offering legal advice to the administrator on all the policies and programs of the agency. Under jurisdiction of the general counsel are the deputy general counsel, an administrative operations staff, and six offices concerned with the legal aspects of various agency programs—the Offices of Loans; Legal Investment (SBIC's); Liquidation and Litigation (dealing with "problem" loan cases); Legislation; Economic Development; and Procurement, Interagency, and Administrative Law. The SBA legal unit has over the years become one of the strongest administrative arms of the agency.

The assistant administrator for Planning, Research and Analysis is the SBA's chief economist. Just as the attorneys under the direction of the general counsel perform legal research upon which to base legal opinions about SBA operations, the agency economists carry on the staff work of an economic nature required by the SBA. This office has been organized and reorganized several times in recent years, and it is therefore somewhat difficult to describe its structure with any lasting accuracy. However, it is safe to say that it is grouped into units dealing primarily with the research and analysis of the economic functions of the agency—finance, investment, and procurement. From time to time, this office also contracts for economic research studies to be made by academic authorities.

The assistant administrator for Congressional and Public Affairs is the SBA's principal public relations man. He supervises about fifty employees in the offices of Congressional Relations, Public Information, and Public Inquiry and Analysis. (The two former offices are described in Chapters VIII and IX). The Office of Public Inquiry and Analysis handles priority correspondence requiring personal replies or clearance from the administrator.

The assistant administrator for Administration is in charge of keeping the agency humming. He and his staff of nearly 1,000 employees—slightly more than half of whom work in the field—are the SBA's record keepers, furniture movers, data processors, librarians, messengers, mailmen, accountants —virtually its jacks-of-all-trades. They handle the numerous administrative services required to keep a large organization functioning smoothly.

This assistant administrator has two deputies—one for management services and another for financial and data services. In addition to the Administrative Operations Staff common to all major SBA units, he has an Equal Opportunity Staff which reports directly to him. The latter group enforces within SBA Title VI of the 1964 Civil Rights Act, which calls for equal employment opportunity for minority groups within government agencies. Nine offices come under the wing of the assistant administrator for Administration: Audits and Investigations, Management and Organization, Personnel, Administrative Services, Budget and Finance, Program Planning (the central PPBS unit), Data Services, Reports, and Analytical Services.

The associate administrator for Financial Assistance commands the most important SBA operation—nearly 2,500 employees, less than 100 of whom are located in Washington. His administrative world consists of a deputy, a divisional Administrative Operations Staff, and five offices: Business Loans, Disaster Loans, Appraisals, Development Company Assistance, and Liquidation and Disposal. The associate administrator and his staff formulate and recommend SBA policy regarding financial assistance of all kinds.

The associate administrator for Investment supervises what has been the SBA's most troubled division, the unit responsible for planning and administering the Small Business Investment Company program. Assisted by a staff of around 100, the associate administrator for Investment carries on a highly centralized surveillance of SBIC operations. In addition to his deputy, the Investment Division includes a staff director who is in charge of the offices of Program Development, the Chief Accountant, and Administrative Operations. In the line end of things—operating assistance and service—are the two offices of, respectively, Eastern and Western SBIC operations. Everyone in the Investment Division works in Washington.

The associate administrator for Procurement and Management Assistance holds sway over two broad programs which were separate divisions before they were merged in 1965. Three staff units—the Administrative Operations Staff, the Size Standards Staff, and a Special Projects Staff—report to him. He and his deputy supervise two offices, Procurement Assistance and Management Assistance. The former includes a government liaison staff, which works with such contracting agencies as the Defense Department, and three divisions: Technology Utilization, Education, and Counseling. Some 550 people work on the procurement and management programs; about 450 of them work in the field.

SBA FIELD OPERATIONS

Most SBA employees work at the grass roots—or off the asphalt sidewalks—of communities across the United States. Appendix III lists all of the offices in the SBA's far-flung field operation. There are three levels of SBA field offices: The eight area offices, encompassing the largest amounts of territory and supervised by area administrators; the numerous regional offices, headed by regional directors; and the branch offices, headed by branch managers. The field operation of the SBA is of crucial importance. Financial assistance is the SBA's biggest program, and all credit decisions on loan applications are made in the field.

The area administrators are the principal representatives of the SBA's leadership within the geographical jurisdictions assigned to them. They are in charge of all agency operations within their territory. This includes all SBA programs except for the SBIC's, the responsibility for which is lodged in Washington (except for liquidation and disposal activities). The area counsel, equal opportunity staff, administrative staff, and appraisal staff serve as the area administrator's personal assistants. The area line programs reporting directly to the area administrator include financial assistance, procurement and management assistance, liquidation and disposal, and development company assistance.

The regional director is the chief representative of the area administrator within the region over which he holds sway. Under the general direction of the area administrator, he is responsible for all SBA regional operations in procurement and management assistance, financial assistance, and development company assistance. State advisory councils, the regional counsel and his legal staff, the SCORE chapter of retired business counselors, and the regional appraisal staff offer advice and assistance to the regional director. In addition, four divisions, representing the three line programs plus an administrative division, report to him. The financial assistance division is subdivided into assistance teams of specialists in finance, procurement and management, appraisal, and law, who work together to offer a variety of aids to small businessmen who come to the SBA in search of a loan.

The branch manager is the SBA spokesman in the smallest field offices. Typically, he supervises a small staff of which he is the only professional member. He serves as SBA liaison with businessmen and the community in localities that for one reason or another lack a regional office.

What Does the Future Hold?

Gazing into a crystal ball is a dubious enterprise. The future structure of an agency like the SBA depends to a considerable extent on the objectives of future Presidents, members of Congress, and SBA administrators. But there has been one recurrent proposal of this nature that would have a significant bearing on the SBA's future. That is the belief of many observers that the SBA should be made a part of the

Department of Commerce or perhaps a super department of economic affairs.

Rumors that the SBA would be merged with the Commerce Department have been persistent from the time of the agency's founding down to the present day. The speculation took concrete form in January, 1967, when President Lyndon B. Johnson in his annual State of the Union message surprised the Washington community by calling for a fusion of the Commerce and Labor departments and various related agencies, including the SBA. Creation of a new Department of Transportation involved transfer of a large chunk of Commerce Department activities and personnel, a shift which virtually gutted the older department. The Labor Department was already the smallest of the cabinet-level agencies. And there was ample precedent for the proposed merger: Commerce and Labor had been founded as a single department in 1916 and separated only several years later, largely at the behest of organized labor. Commerce for many years had had an Office of Small Business, and continued to interpret its mandate as service to all business, regardless of size.

There was strong support at the Budget Bureau[2] and elsewhere for putting the pieces back together and adding various related functions. Supporters of the move believed that for reasons of administrative consistency and efficiency, closely connected activities should be housed under a single roof. Seeking solid accomplishments, which would not involve sizable new government spending, President Johnson accepted the idea for a department of economic affairs.

A few months later, however, the notion was abandoned. Union leaders and their friends in Congress objected to loss of a department they could call their own. In addition, friends of small business on Capitol Hill were opposed to the demise of an independent small business agency. The department meas-

[2] For more on the central importance of the Budget Bureau, see Chapter X.

ure languished and expired in Congressional committee without ever being brought to a formal vote.

Still, the idea remains as a possibility for the days to come. The Budget Bureau continues to be skeptical of the administrative need for a separate agency to serve small businessmen and to believe in the desirability of the Labor-Commerce merger. Commerce continues to covet the SBA, albeit mildly. And many at the SBA fear that they may yet be merged—and submerged.

V

Financial Assistance Programs

As with most government lending, SBA financial assistance programs have been, and are, controversial. They are frequently attacked by "liberals" as too conservative and too "banker oriented." They are regarded as being totally inadequate in terms of financial resources and unimaginative in terms of their objectives.

Many "conservatives," on the other hand, think the SBA has no business lending the taxpayers' money to "marginal," inefficient business concerns. These views have sometimes found expression in the pages of the influential *Wall Street Journal*. An editorial comment, published in that newspaper on July 8, 1963, under the title, "Flexible Federal Ethics," concluded: "It could be noted that the SBA is a dubious enterprise from many points of view with its subsidized competition for private banks and its program of reserving Government business for small business merely because they are small."

In considering charges of "subsidized competition for private banks," and as a matter of fact in viewing SBA financial assistance activities as a whole, it should be born in mind how truly insignificant SBA loans are, quantitatively, in relation to the money provided to American business by private financial institutions. At the end of 1965, commercial banks and mutual savings banks held over $435 billion in assets. Of these, about $72 billion were in the form of industrial and commercial loans.

On the other hand, the SBA's total business and economic opportunity loans outstanding at that time amounted to $724.5 million or about 1 per cent of those of private institutions. Furthermore, SBA loans were, on the average, for a much longer term of repayment. Thus, the private lenders' funds could be turned over more times than the SBA funds.

One cannot escape the conclusion that while SBA loans might be "subsidized" in character, they certainly were not providing much money to promote "competition" for our private banking system.

Is There a Credit Gap for Small Business?

Underlying the SBA's financial assistance programs has been the widespread belief that the small businessman is discriminated against in the money markets. He is expected to pay higher interest rates; repayment terms are more stringent; conditions attached to the loan are more restrictive; and collateral required is higher. When money is tight, it is the little fellow, invariably, who doesn't get the loan.

These views are held by many small businessmen, many congressmen, and many ordinary citizens. How much validity is there to them? And if these views are essentially correct, should we be concerned about the credit situation of small business or simply look at it as one of the facts of life?

Studies of the Federal Reserve System

In 1957, the research staffs of the Board of Governors and Federal Reserve Banks undertook a major study of the financing problems of small business. According to Federal Reserve Chairman William McChesney Martin, Jr., the study was conducted "for the information of the Federal Reserve System, the interested committees of the Congress, as well as the public generally."

The studies (*Financing Small Business,* 1958) were submitted to the House and Senate Banking and Currency committees and the Select Committees on Small Business. There were three parts to the studies.

Part I, *Background Studies,* contained sixteen studies of various aspects of small business. They were prepared as independent papers by individual scholars at leading universities as well as by individual members of the Federal Reserve research staff.

Part II, *Surveys of Credit and Capital Sources,* presented the results of survey data obtained from commercial banks, commercial finance companies, and others supplying equity capital. These surveys were carried out by the Federal Reserve research staff.

Part III was a longer-range, experimental study designed to obtain information on the financial structure, practices, and problems of small concerns. The study was based on interviews with, and questionnaires sent to, the businessmen themselves. The Bureau of the Census helped the Federal Reserve research staff in carrying out the study.

The 1957 and 1958 studies of the Federal Reserve research staff remain the most comprehensive inquiry into the financing problems of small business ever undertaken. The questions about small business raised at that time are essentially the same questions that are raised today. What were the major findings of these reports?

For one thing, the analysts concluded that the core of the small business financing problem was in manufacturing, which in 1957–58, accounted for less than 8 per cent of the number of small business concerns. In all lines of endeavor, the short-term credit needs of small business firms were considered to be adequately met by the private banking system.

According to the Federal Reserve research staff, the small business financing problem is primarily an unfulfilled need for long-term loans, equity or equity-type capital. In other words, it is the firm with the ambition to grow, and to grow rapidly, that is most affected. Although certain mining and construction firms and some service, wholesaling, and retailing concerns are in this category, it was the growing manufacturing company that was most often faced with the need for long-term credit. Such companies often need working capital, and, even more important, investment funds to finance plant and major equipment installations.

Their problem was viewed essentially as one of faulty, or inadequate, capitalization. A balance sheet for such a firm all too often showed too much debt, especially short- and medium-term debt, in relation to equity capital. The small, growing manufacturer was chided by the Federal Reserve writers for his reluctance to share control of his business with outside shareholders. He was described as seeking venture capital, but on a long-term loan basis. Many small businessmen thought they could obtain equity capital only at too great a cost. The Federal Reserve authors concluded: "Perhaps the range of needs includes a hybrid financing instrument, partly [long-term] loan and partly equity, such as the convertible debentures, developed to a high degree in recent years by many large, publicly financed companies."

While recognizing the long-term capital problems of the growing small business, the Federal Reserve's analysis was fundamentally a defense of the *status quo*. The concluding two paragraphs of the essay by George Garvy of the Federal Reserve Bank of New York set forth the "banker's view" of the small business financing problem:

In examining the existing financial situation of small business, as well as in appraising financing needs, it is essential to keep in mind a basic fact that underlies the allocation of resources in a free economy: real capital, as all other real resources, is scarce. The allocation of financial resources that give command over real resources involves some element of rationing, and that must always be so. To maximize potential output in a freely functioning economy, such allocation must be guided by the prospective profitability of alternative uses of available resources. In a dynamic and growing economy, the number of entrepreneurs who expect to be able to use additional funds successfully is likely to exceed, most of the time, the actual capabilities of the economy as a whole to provide the corresponding real resources.

A properly functioning financial system should allocate financial resources according to the potential profitability of their use, without regard to the size of the receiving unit. The process of allocation must, nonetheless, involve the peeling off of successive layers of less efficient seekers of funds. It is in this way that the economy can best limit the volume of funds channeled into new investment to the amount of real resources available. Even when this process of selection meets all conditions laid down to assure equality of treatment, as long as demand (and ambitions) exceed the resources available, there will be a variable fringe of unsatisfied demands. It should be the responsibility of public policy to keep the process of allocation from being disturbed or distorted by the exercise of monopoly powers or by imperfections in the financial mechanism. But public policy can neither aim nor hope to find ways of fulfilling all unsatisfied demands.

Other studies of this question have come essentially to the same conclusion. G. L. Bach and C. J. Huizenga, of the Carnegie Institute of Technology, conducted research sponsored by the Ford Foundation. Their findings were set forth in an article entitled, "The Differential Effects of Tight Money," which appeared in the March, 1961, issue of *The American Economic Review*. They studied the lending-investing pattern of commercial banks during 1955–57. Bach and Huizenga concluded that discrimination among borrowers was largely based on traditional banking standards of credit worthiness. They attributed shifts in loans among various borrower groups to differences in demands for loans. Their conclusion was that "widespread criticisms of tight money as [being] unfairly discriminating against small borrowers, both in availability of loans and interest costs, are not supported by the data."

The December, 1964, *Journal of Finance* contained an article which took the same tack. The study, "Commercial Bank Price Discrimination Against Small Loans," by George J. Benston, was supported by the Federal Reserve Bank of Chicago and the Ford Foundation. Benston focused on the 1959–61 period. The first of those three years was a tight money year; 1960 and 1961 were years of relative monetary ease. The author came to the rather unstartling conclusion that the higher interest rates charged by commercial banks on small business loans were explained by the greater costs of lending and the greater element of risk. This study reiterates the Bach-Huizenga findings in the following terms: "the data are inconsistent with the hypothesis that banks discriminate against small borrowers in times of tight money."

In considering the question of whether a credit gap exists for small business, one inevitably must consider interest rate differentials and concepts of availability of credit. Small business firms pay more for short- and long-term credit than large firms do. Table XI illustrates this point. The interest rate on short-term loans made by commercial banks is higher for smaller loans than for larger loans. The differential rate between the smallest ($1,000–$10,000) and the largest ($200,000 and over) loan size classes varied from 0.9 per cent to 1.6 per cent in the thirteen-year period shown in the table. Of the nineteen large cities covered, the highest rates charged were in the Southern and Western cities, for all loan sizes, followed by the Northern and Eastern cities. The rates in New York City were the lowest.

Most economists would certainly agree with the bankers that a small business loan should generally bear a higher interest rate than a big business loan. Interest rate differentials should exist because there are differences in lending costs and differences in risk.

TABLE XI

Bank Rates on Short-Term Business Loans[a]
(Per Cent Per Annum)

Area and Period	All Loans	Size of Loan (In Thousands of Dollars)			
		1–10	10–100	100–200	200 and Over
Year					
19 Large Cities					
1953	3.7	5.0	4.4	3.9	3.5
1954	3.6	5.0	4.3	3.9	3.4
1955	3.7	5.0	4.4	4.0	3.5
1956	4.2	5.2	4.8	4.4	4.0
1957	4.6	5.5	5.1	4.8	4.5
1958	4.3	5.5	5.0	4.6	4.1
1959	5.0	5.8	5.5	5.2	4.9
1960	5.2	6.0	5.7	5.4	5.0
1961	5.0	5.9	5.5	5.2	4.8
1962	5.0	5.9	5.5	5.2	4.8
1963	5.0	5.9	5.5	5.2	4.8
1964	5.0	5.9	5.6	5.3	4.8
1965	5.1	5.9	5.6	5.4	4.9
Quarter[b]					
19 Large Cities					
1965 September	5.00	5.90	5.60	5.32	4.80
December	5.27	5.96	5.74	5.51	5.11
1966 March	5.55	6.13	5.96	5.76	5.41
June	5.82	6.39	6.25	6.03	5.68
September	6.30	6.73	6.65	6.51	6.18
New York City					
1965 September	4.76	5.65	5.37	5.13	4.64
December	5.08	5.74	5.59	5.13	4.99
1966 March	5.41	5.92	5.78	5.66	5.34
June	5.65	6.14	6.11	5.87	5.57
September	6.13	6.60	6.57	6.39	6.05
7 Other Northern & Eastern Cities					
1965 September	5.03	5.88	5.62	5.31	4.87
December	5.32	5.95	5.80	5.56	5.19
1966 March	5.58	6.10	6.05	5.82	5.46
June	5.86	6.32	6.35	6.08	5.74
September	6.40	6.62	6.75	6.60	6.31

[a] Loans maturing in less than one year.
[b] Based on new loans and renewals for first fifteen days of the month.

TABLE XI—CONTINUED

11 Southern & Western Cities					
1965	September	5.31	6.02	5.73	5.45	5.03
	December	5.46	6.07	5.80	5.59	5.23
1966	March	5.70	6.23	6.01	5.77	5.50
	June	6.00	6.52	6.28	6.08	5.82
	September	6.42	6.84	6.65	6.51	6.26

The cost (per dollar amount loaned) of lending to a small business generally is proportionately greater than the cost of a large loan. This is one of the inherent disadvantages of running a small business. Every financing transaction involves certain fixed costs which are not related to the size of the loan; these costs are, therefore, relatively more expensive for the small borrower. Since lenders must cover their costs, commensurate rate differentials may be perfectly justifiable.

One of the authors of the Federal Reserve study puts it this way:

> If a small firm should be able to borrow at the same interest rate as a large firm, it should be able to purchase materials at the same price, irrespective of the fact that materials may be sold more economically in large quantities; less-than-carload freight rates, and so on. Adoption of such a principle would inevitably involve a reduction in real output. Furthermore, it seems to be a well-established principle, embodied in the Robinson-Patman Act, for example, that price differentials which reflect cost differentials are not contrary to the public interest.

Small business loans are generally riskier for lenders than large business loans. As a group, small firms have relatively the weakest position as reflected in various financial ratios, such as current assets to current liabilities, net working capital to total assets, and net worth to total debt. On the whole, they also have the lowest credit ratings and the highest loss ratios. Table XII illustrates the fact that the smaller loans

TABLE XII

Default Rates and Realized Loss Rates on RFC Direct Business Loans,
by Size of Firm
(Ratios, in Per Cent)

Assets of Borrowing Firms (In Thousands of Dollars)[a]	Number of Outstanding Loans, December 31, 1951[b]	Ratio of Loans in Default to All Outstanding Loans, December 31, 1951		Ratio of Realized Net Loss to Amount Disbursed, 1934–51	
		Number	Amount	On All Loans[c]	On Extinguished Loans[c]
Less than 5	200	11.1	3.6	6.2	7.7
5 to 24	872	12.0	8.7	4.6	6.5
25 to 49	1,032	17.4	22.0	1.7	3.5
50 to 99	1,009	11.1	14.0	1.1	2.1
100 to 249	986	12.3	11.0	2.9	5.7
250 to 499	484	20.7	19.1	1.2	2.4
500 to 999	222	11.6	19.2	0.9	1.4
1,000 to 4,999	165	18.7	11.6		
5,000 to 49,999	23	4.5	2.8	0.7	1.2
50,000 and over	6	0	0		
All loans	5,700[d]	13.2[d]	9.6[d]	1.3[e]	2.1[e]

Source: Federal Reserve System, *Financing Small Business*, Part I (1958). Unfortunately, there are no data available after 1951. There is no reason to believe, however, that the general situation has changed.

[a] At time of loan application.
[b] Total number of active loans, December 31, 1951.
[c] Based upon expanded amounts and numbers of loans from a sample of 2,851 out of 17,000 net RFC authorizations, 1934–51, covering all loans of $500,000 or more, roughly 50 per cent of loans between $100,000 and $500,000, and 10 per cent of loans of $100,000 or less.
[d] Includes 701 loans on which information on assets of borrowing firm at time of loan application was not available, on which the default rates were 8.1 per cent (by number) and 8.4 per cent (by amount).
[e] Includes loans on which information on assets of borrowing firm at time of loan application was not available, on which the loss rates were 1.9 per cent (on all loans) and 2.3 per cent (on extinguished loans).

involve higher risk. Generally speaking, the lower the assets of the borrower, the higher the loss rate.

There is unanimity among observers that small business pays more proportionately for its loans than do large borrowers. The economist generally views this matter with equanimity because it is an inevitable result of the presumed efficient allocation of capital carried out by the market.

What is of concern to the economist, the political scientist, and the small businessman, is whether the differential that the small businessman is forced to pay truly reflects the additional element of risk and the higher fixed cost relative to the size of the loan which is incurred by those who lend to him. This is the crux of the matter, and here we find no unanimity. Some would say the small business pays too much, and others say the rates fairly accurately reflect the situation.

SBA BUSINESS LOANS

"Regular business loans," as Chapter III points out, have been the single most important activity of the SBA.

Section 7(a) of the Small Business Act provides the statutory basis for making small business loans. There are two types of SBA business loans: *direct loans,* where the funds are advanced directly by the SBA; and *participations,* involving agreements by the SBA to participate in loans made by private lenders. There are two principal types of participations: *immediate participation,* a loan in which SBA agrees to advance a definite proportion immediately; and *deferred participation,* a loan in which the financial institution makes and administers the entire loan, with the SBA agreeing to purchase, on demand, an agreed portion of the outstanding balance.

Somewhat similar to a deferred participation loan is a loan guaranty. In 1963, a Loan Guaranty Plan supplemented the Deferred Bank Participation Plan at the SBA. Under the Loan Guaranty Plan, the bank and the SBA enter into a written guaranty agreement whereby the loan is disbursed and serviced by the bank, with SBA guaranteeing repayment of not more than 90 per cent of the unpaid principal and interest.

Table XIII shows the amount of business loan applications received, the number of loans approved, and the percentage

Table XIII

Statistical Summary of Loans Approved,
Fiscal Year 1954 Through December 31, 1967
(In Millions of Dollars)

Fiscal Year	(7a) Business		Economic Opportunity		Displaced Business		Economic Development		Investment		Total All Loans (Excluding Disaster)	
	No.	Amount	No.	Amount	No.	Amount	No.	Amount	No.	Amount	No.	Amount
1954	473	27.7	—	—	—	—	—	—	—	—	473	27.7
1955	1,172	56.0	—	—	—	—	—	—	—	—	1,172	56.0
1956	1,915	82.0	—	—	—	—	—	—	—	—	1,915	82.0
1957	3,536	159.1	—	—	—	—	—	—	—	—	3,536	159.1
1958	4,014	195.0	—	—	—	—	—	—	—	—	4,014	195.0
1959	5,582	267.0	—	—	—	—	15	2.0	9	1.3	5,606	270.3
1960	3,670	168.4	—	—	—	—	37	5.1	74	11.7	3,781	185.2
1961	4,989	250.4	—	—	—	—	73	10.9	209	35.6	5,271	296.9
1962	6,203	360.8	—	—	90	5.0	80	14.8	322	50.6	6,695	431.2
1963	6,073	313.9	—	—	93	5.6	116	17.9	409	83.4	6,691	420.8
1964	6,288	312.2	—	—	95	6.9	154	23.0	334	58.8	6,871	400.9
1965	13,420	418.1	159	1.8	199	12.5	256	40.2	221	47.0	14,255	519.6
1966	10,404	354.8	1,689	17.6	276	18.3	317	54.1	178	50.0	12,864	494.8
1967	8,070	385.3	3,034	31.9	385	32.7	341	54.6	72	15.4	11,902	519.9
1968 to Date	4,973	252.3	1,415	14.6	170	15.9	189	27.7	26	4.5	6,774	315.0
Total	80,782	3,603.0	6,297	65.9	1,308	96.9	1,579	250.3	1,854	358.3	91,820	4,374.4

By Type of Loan										Total (Excluding Investment)	
Direct	32,791	892.8	5,849	59.9	1,179	81.7	780	131.6		40,599	1,166.0
Participation	47,991	2,710.2	448	6.0	129	15.2	799	118.7		49,367	2,850.1
Immediate	33,102	1,963.4	155	2.5	125	14.9	769	116.3		34,151	2,097.1
Guaranteed	9,170	480.1	293	3.5	4	0.3	30	2.4		9,497	486.3
Deferred	5,719	267.7	—	—	—	—	—	—		5,719	266.7
Per Cent of Total											
Direct	40.6	24.8	92.9	90.9	90.1	84.4	49.4	52.6		45.1	29.0
Participation	59.4	75.2	7.1	9.1	9.9	15.6	50.6	43.4		54.9	71.0
Immediate	41.0	54.5	2.5	0.8	9.6	15.3	48.7	46.4		38.0	52.2
Guaranteed	11.3	13.3	4.6	5.3	0.3	0.3	1.9	1.0		10.5	12.1
Deferred	7.1	7.4	—	—	—	—	—	—		6.4	6.7

Source: Small Business Administration.

and amounts of loans made on a direct and participation or guaranteed basis.

AVOIDANCE OF COMPETITION WITH PRIVATE LENDERS

One of the principal concerns of the SBA has been to avoid, as far as is practicable, competition with private lenders. Much store is laid on friendly relations with the American Bankers Association and lending institutions generally.

Of the 71,264 business loans made by the SBA through the end of 1966, over 58 per cent were made on a participation basis, and over 41 per cent were immediate participation loans. To lessen the risk of competition with private lenders, the SBA has interpreted quite strictly the phrase of the Small Business Act to the effect that "the financial assistance applied for is not otherwise available on reasonable terms." To satisfy this requirement, the SBA has insisted that an applicant must submit evidence that he has been turned down by at least two private banks.

In processing a loan, the SBA explores with the applicant the possibility of obtaining the loan from another source. If none is available on reasonable terms, the SBA loan officer must consider the form of the loan in the following order: guaranty, deferred participation, immediate participation, and direct. Thus, the SBA makes a direct loan only if guaranties or participations cannot be obtained.

EMPHASIS ON SECURED LOANS

The SBA has always placed emphasis on secured loans. This differs somewhat from the commercial banks, where unsecured term loans are far from uncommon. There is nothing in the Small Business Act which prescribes that collateral must be put up by the borrower. It is an administrative interpretation of the statute which requires that "all loans shall be of such sound value or so secured as reasonably to assure repayment." Since by definition many of the borrowers are substandard by private bank credit standards, it is perfectly understandable why loan officers at the SBA have been so insistent upon collateral. If many loans are not deemed to be of particularly "sound value," then they must be "so secured as reasonably to assure repayment."

In recent years the rather stringent interpretations of the SBA have been relaxed for certain programs. This has been particularly true of the Economic Opportunity Loan program, launched in late 1964. To avoid misunderstanding of the intent of the law, the Economic Opportunity Act of that year and the agency regulations for the new program were worded to make it clear that little or no collateral would be required for so-called "poverty loans."

LARGE PROPORTION OF LOANS TURNED DOWN

During the years 1961–66 some 83,292 applications for regular business loans were received by the agency. Of this total, only 48,981 loans were approved. Thus, about 41 per cent of all loan applicants were either turned down or withdrew their applications voluntarily. The major reasons for this high rate of turndowns have been cited as inability of the applicant to demonstrate sustained earning power, insufficiency of collateral, and undercapitalization of the business venture. These are all, of course, characteristics of relatively poor credit risks. The government loan officers, if they must err, choose to err on the side of caution.

UNIFORM AND RELATIVELY INFLEXIBLE INTEREST RATES

Another feature of SBA loans is the fact that the interest rates are uniform and quite inflexible relative to those in the private sector. When the SBA was established in 1953, the interest rate on direct loans or on the SBA portion of a loan was set at 6 per cent. In 1958, the statutory rate was changed to 5.5 per cent where it remains at present. By way of contrast, the average rate of interest on short-term loans made by private banks was 3.2 per cent in 1953 and 6 per cent in 1967.

CONCENTRATION OF LOANS AMONG MANUFACTURERS

Table XIV shows the number of business loans approved, by industry, from July 1, 1953, through December 31, 1967. A high proportion of the loans went to the manufacturing sector of the economy. During this period, manufacturers received 23.9 per cent of the loans and 37.6 per cent of the loan money made available by the SBA; but they comprised, in 1966, only 6.4 per cent of the business population. On the other hand, retail trade—which made up 41.6 per cent of the business population—received only 35.9 per cent of the loans and 21.6 per cent of the loan money.

The usual explanation for this concentration in lending is that the manufacturers have greater need of the financing provided by the SBA. SBA lending is generally for a longer term than funds provided by the private banking system. Manufacturers require a higher proportion of fixed assets in relation to total assets than are required for most other forms of business activity.

But it is also partly a reflection of the fact that SBA loan officers are for the most part conservative credit men. It will be recalled that, SBA lending policies are conservative because the law requires them to be "of such sound value or so secured as reasonably to assure repayment." Since manufacturers generally can offer better and more substantial collateral than wholesalers or retailers, there is an inherent bias toward lending to manufacturers.

TABLE XIV

Business Loans Approved, by Industry, Fiscal Year 1954 Through December 31, 1967
(In Thousands of Dollars)

Fiscal Year	Total No.	Total Amount	Manufacturing No.	Manufacturing Amount	Construction No.	Construction Amount	Wholesale No.	Wholesale Amount	Retail No.	Retail Amount	Services No.	Services Amount	Other No.	Other Amount
1954	473	$ 27,739	269	$ 16,531	26	$ 1,496	17	$ 1,092	66	$ 2,270	—	—	95	$ 6,350
1955	1,172	55,975	579	31,117	76	3,682	63	3,620	247	7,518	121	$ 3,831	90	6,207
1956	1,915	81,977	722	43,465	112	3,910	146	6,592	577	13,692	195	5,501	163	8,817
1957	3,536	159,095	1,182	76,598	202	8,931	303	14,230	1,196	29,584	393	15,747	260	14,005
1958	4,014	194,997	1,250	87,728	279	14,348	312	14,205	1,185	29,681	498	20,388	490	28,647
1959	5,582	267,042	1,517	111,244	308	15,571	465	22,371	1,872	46,396	911	38,284	509	33,176
1960	3,670	168,366	884	60,824	202	10,923	293	13,748	1,269	32,641	709	30,574	313	19,656
1961	4,989	250,432	1,226	93,843	315	15,937	430	20,750	1,670	45,354	945	46,111	403	28,437
1962	6,203	360,762	1,696	146,022	330	20,963	560	33,961	1,943	60,050	1,201	65,869	473	33,897
1963	6,073	313,904	1,496	119,506	341	16,529	577	29,745	2,108	65,732	1,155	58,588	396	23,804
1964	6,288	312,212	1,405	112,973	337	15,329	552	31,044	2,311	67,784	1,242	57,421	441	27,661
1965	13,420	418,057	2,362	136,484	771	23,956	1,051	34,580	5,534	115,250	2,924	77,043	778	30,744
1966	10,404	354,841	1,965	113,559	669	18,219	789	31,261	4,189	98,084	2,198	65,601	594	28,117
1967	8,070	385,300	1,719	126,975	412	15,734	708	40,429	2,985	98,703	1,733	69,391	513	34,068
1968—12/31/67	4,973	252,309	1,059	78,528	269	11,799	440	29,160	1,853	67,246	1,018	42,699	334	22,877
Total	80,782	$3,603,008	19,331	$1,355,397	4,645	$197,327	6,706	$326,788	29,005	$779,985	15,243	$597,048	5,852	$346,463
Percentage	100.0	100.0	23.9	37.6	5.8	5.5	8.3	9.1	35.9	21.6	18.9	16.6	7.2	9.6

Source: Small Business Administration.

Subsidy Aspects of SBA Financial Assistance

It has been mentioned that SBA interest rates are uniform and inflexible. They are also quite low by any standard. As market rates of interest have increased almost steadily over the life of the agency, the subsidy aspects of SBA financial programs have become greater and greater.

The SBA Annual Report for 1966 noted that

> the maximum interest rate on disaster loans (other than "displaced business" loans) is fixed by statute at 3 per cent, and the maximum interest rate on business loans is set at 5½ per cent. At the same time, in Fiscal 1967, SBA is paying the Treasury Department interest on disbursements from the funds at the rates of 4⅝, 4⅜, and 4⅞ depending on the particular program involved. In Fiscal 1966, interest paid to the Treasury was at a rate of 4⅛ per cent for all programs.

The result of this policy has been that the SBA's financial assistance programs consistently operate at a loss. In 1966, the net loss was $54.4 million; in 1965, $39.6 million, and in 1964, $29.7 million.

To illustrate the bind the SBA is in, the interest earned on business loans during 1966 was $28 million, but the interest paid to the Treasury was $25.4 million. Administrative expenses were $27 million. All in all, SBA operating income on the business loan portion of its financial assistance programs was $30.4 million. Its operating expenses were $55.6 million. Thus, the SBA business loan program ran at a loss of $25.2 million.

Should the taxpayer pay for this subsidy? Adherents would say that it is peanuts compared to the depletion allowances granted to the oil and mineral industries, the various subsidies paid to the nation's farmers, or the subsidies paid to the shipping interests.

But is this a good answer? It is certainly not a good answer from the standpoint of economics. SBA loans are made to those who must demonstrate that they cannot borrow from private lenders on reasonable terms. By definition, the borrowers from the SBA are less attractive credit risks than business firms borrowing from private financial institutions. Since the risks are higher, economic logic would say that the interest rates should be higher, not lower, than the private rates of interest.

That subsidies to small businessmen are minute in comparison to those paid to others is also probably an inadequate justification from a practical standpoint. If SBA rates are below market rates, some borrowers will be attracted by this fact. As the spread between the two rates becomes wider, the more attractive an SBA loan becomes. It does not require too much imagination to realize that turndowns from local banks can be advantageous if a prospective borrower is shopping for the lowest possible interest rate. This has happened, but to what extent is not known.

Surely the intent of the Small Business Act was not to provide the small business borrower with a subsidy in the form of below-the-market interest rates. It was to assure that a small businessman could get his loan if it was not obtainable from private lenders at reasonable terms.

SBA Administrator Eugene P. Foley was concerned about this problem. Testifying before the Senate Small Business Committee in May, 1965, he stated that a study in Connecticut covering the period from 1955 to 1959 indicated that "about one-third of all our loans are made to people who privately concede that they could have obtained the loans in the marketplace. In other words, our loans aren't reaching the risky type of business that really needs it so badly." Foley added, "We want to put our money with the firm which can't get it in the marketplace. When the figure is as high as one-third who can otherwise get it, then our SBA program is not doing the job it ought to do."

Instead of asking for a hike in the statutory interest rate and for some flexibility so that the SBA rate would move with the market, however, Foley had another idea. He recommended utilization of a complicated "escalation clause" which would have been inserted in all SBA business loan agreements. The agency would have been authorized to dispose of any business loan to a bank at the interest rate prevailing in the area where the small business concern was located. Foley contended that "this new feature, permitting banks the returns to which they are accustomed, should facilitate loan sales." He added: "It will have the desirable side effect of discouraging those who apply to us solely as a means of evading the market rate."

This seems an unnecessarily complicated approach to the problem. Also, it is an inequitable approach. It hardly seemed fair to the senators to leave the interest rate a small businessman might have to pay to an *ex post facto* decision of an SBA loan officer and a local bank officer.

The escalation clause idea was never endorsed by the Senate. It is unfortunate that the interest rate question was raised in this backhanded and complicated fashion. It is to be hoped that some future SBA administrator and some future Congress will address themselves to the question more directly and frankly. After all, the SBA—like all government agencies—receives a finite amount of money, not a blank check. The more the SBA interest rate goes below the market rate, the higher the subsidy element in the loans made and the fewer the effective funds made available to the small business community. And it increases the likelihood that loans may be made more and more on a political basis rather than on their merits.

DISASTER LOANS

As has been mentioned in Chapter III, the Small Business Act authorizes the SBA to make loans to victims of disasters of various kinds. Disaster loans may be summarized as follows:

1. During Fiscal Year 1967, 2,017 loans for $24.2 million were approved to alleviate suffering from physical disasters—flooding, high winds, hurricanes, tornadoes, and so on. Over the life of this program through Fiscal Year 1967, almost 59,000 loans for $536 million had been approved. These loans were made primarily to homeowners, not necessarily small businessmen.

2. Small businessmen who suffered economic injury as a result of such events as drought,. hurricanes, and floods, obtained 1,158 loans for $22.3 million through June 30, 1967.

3. Small businesses that had been displaced by federally assisted or financed construction projects, principally urban renewal and highways, obtained 385 loans for $32.7 million in Fiscal Year 1967. On a cumulative basis, some 1,138 loans for $81 million had been approved since 1961.

4. Thirty-six loans for $2.6 million had been made to small businessmen as a result of their inability to market a product for human consumption due to circumstances beyond their control.

5. During 1967, loans were made to homeowners and businessmen who suffered losses as a result of riots. Loans totaling $3.4 million were made in Detroit, Michigan, and Newark, New Jersey, after the riots there. The National Advisory Commission on Civil Disorders report—the so-called Kerner report —in 1968 called for a broadening of this type of assistance.

LEASE GUARANTEE PROGRAM

Small businessmen have been hurt increasingly by their inability to compete with large firms for favorable business locations. Retail sales keep climbing in the new shopping centers of constantly growing suburbs, while retail sales in the central cities do not keep pace. Many a small druggist, for example, faced with declining sales and increasing crime with its attendant costs, feels trapped. He can either continue in his deteriorating neighborhood or sell his business at what often amounts to a distressed price. He finds that he cannot relocate his drugstore in a shopping center in a thriving suburban area. That territory has been pre-empted by the big drug chains. Mortgagors much prefer to have such a tenant rather than a small businessman.

To attempt to cope with this problem the SBA launched a pilot program in 1967 under which the agency stands ready to guarantee or insure lease rental payments. Provisions for such a program were included in the Housing and Urban Development Act of 1965, and a $5 million pilot project program was authorized.

The lease guarantee program got under way on an experimental basis in May, 1967. It was confined at that time to small business firms that had been displaced by federally financed or assisted construction and to those firms that were operated by persons who were economically disadvantaged.

Approval of the first project under this program came in August, 1967. It involved the development of a shopping center to provide space for twelve small businessmen in Mobile, Alabama, who had been displaced by an urban renewal program.

The lease guarantee program was broadened by Congress early in 1968 to extend to small businessmen generally. A uniform fee schedule has been established in order to assure that the program will operate on a self-sustaining basis. A maximum rate of 2.5 per cent of the annual rental has been set.

Guarantees may be made by the SBA directly when they cannot be made by private sureties; as with all SBA financial assistance programs, however, maximum participation by the private sector is sought. To this end, the SBA held a series of regional conferences at which officials explained the program to state insurance commissioners and the major insurance companies.

This is an interesting new program which promises to be of great assistance to small businesses—especially retailers—in overcoming one of their most difficult problems.

SBA AND THE WAR ON POVERTY—
    ECONOMIC OPPORTUNITY LOANS

Unquestionably, the major new financial assistance program unveiled by the SBA in recent years has been its Economic Opportunity Loan (EOL) program. Statutory authority for this effort came in the Economic Opportunity Act of 1964, which launched President Johnson's widely heralded War on Poverty.

Title IV of this act is devoted to employment and investment incentives. R. Sargent Shriver, director of the Office of Economic Opportunity, the principal antipoverty agency, in early 1965 exercised his authority under the law to delegate this program to the SBA administrator. This delegation was by no means unexpected, for SBA Administrator Eugene P. Foley had pushed actively for enactment of Title IV. (The background leading to passage of this legislation is described further in Chapter IX.)

The program has been run in a rather erratic fashion since its inception, for two principal reasons. First, the personalities involved have been constantly shifting. Second, budgetary and administrative objectives and requirements have been constantly shifting, as well.

Originally, the EOL program was to be directed to new entrepreneurs or small businessmen who were either "in poverty" themselves or who, as a result of the loan, would hire one or more of the long-term unemployed. Maximum loans were $25,000 for fifteen years. Little or no collateral was to be required; and emphasis was to be placed on the loan applicant's character, integrity, and presumed ability to operate a business successfully.

As a component part of Title II of the Economic Opportunity Act, which provided for the establishment of Community Action Programs, the SBA insisted upon creation of Small Business Development Centers (SBDC's). The SBDC's were to be set up locally to screen applicants for referral to the local SBA field offices. The centers were also to organize management training and counseling activities. Only loan applicants from communities that had organized an SBDC were to be eligible to apply for an EOL. Also, the EOL was to be the last loan window for applicants. Applicants were not only required to have been turned down by at least two private banks, as is customary with all SBA loans; they also had to be not sufficiently credit worthy for other forms of SBA financial assistance.

In 1965, acting SBA Administrator Ross D. Davis limited EOL's to applicants who were themselves poor. At the same time, he cut back the maximum amount that could be borrowed to $15,000. His action was taken for two principal reasons: the SBA was suffering from an acute case of the "shorts" (see the discussion later in this chapter of the SBA revolving funds) and OEO, then being criticized for not doing enough for the poor, insisted that the SBA directly help more poor people.

With the appointment of Bernard L. Boutin as SBA administrator in May, 1966, several changes were made. For its part, Congress insisted on these changes. Although the SBDC's were not scrapped, they were de-emphasized. No longer were loans to be made only to those whose businesses were located in communities having an SBDC. The program was opened to the nation.

The program was also revamped. Loans were classified as being either EOL I—loans of up to $15,000 to the poor, particularly proprietors of existing businesses; or EOL II—loans of up to $25,000 to persons of proven managerial capability, who were not themselves poor but lacked the capital necessary to expand their firms. Finally, full responsibility for the program was transferred from the OEO to the SBA, and the provisions of Title IV were incorporated in the Small Business Act.

The EOL program was set up to help eliminate what Michael Harrington has called "the other America." As SBA Administrator Eugene P. Foley told Chairman Adam C. Powell's House Education and Labor Committee in April, 1964, "I want to add right here that this program will not be limited to Negroes, but I would be less than frank or candid if I did not suggest that the greatest opportunity and the greatest need exists in the Negro community."

In a nutshell, the aim of the EOL program is to give poor people, especially Negroes and other ethnic minorities, a chance to succeed in business—a chance which, for a variety of reasons, has all too often been denied them. In the economic and social sphere there is still much truth in Calvin Coolidge's dictum that "the business of America is business." It was felt that unless and until a much higher number of disadvantaged people have a stake of their own in America through business ownership, they will remain second-class citizens.

Thus, EOL's are given on what are for the SBA or any financial institution very liberal conditions. Also, because very few of the poor have managed their own businesses or even studied some of the principles and techniques of business administration, much emphasis has been placed on management training and counseling.

What has happened since the program got under way in December, 1964? Through December 31, 1967, some 6,297 EOL's had been made in a total amount of $65.9 million. In

Fiscal Year 1967 and the first half of Fiscal Year 1968, loans were running at an annual rate of about 3,000 in the amount of about $30 million.

Statistics, usually dry, point up dramatically the contrast between regular SBA business loans and the EOL's. From Fiscal Year 1954 through the end of 1967, some 24.8 per cent of the total SBA assistance lending was on a direct basis. In other words, over three-fourths of these regular business loans in dollar terms were made in participation with private banks. In stark contrast, 90.9 per cent of the EOL's were made by the SBA directly; that is, the private banking community participated in less than 10 per cent of the loans. These numbers speak volumes. They indicate that the banking community thinks that EOL's are too risky. But, conversely, the figures may well indicate that the SBA is filling an important economic gap in our society, which bankers—and other businessmen for that matter—may be ignoring at their peril.

How well is the EOL program doing? It is very hard to tell. First of all, it must be kept in mind that $30 million in loans a year is Lilliputian. The EOL program accounted for only about 6 per cent of SBA loans during Fiscal Year 1967. The staff that oversees the program from SBA headquarters in Washington consists of only three or four professionals. Also, it should be remembered that to date about 60 per cent of the money has gone to whites and the remainder to Negroes and others.

It is clear that loss ratios in the EOL program will boggle the eyes of some congressmen, the rather conservative SBA loan officers, and businessmen generally. The default rate on SBA regular business loans over the years has been slightly under 3 per cent. Although it is too early to be anywhere near precise or authoritative about prospective EOL defaults, a guess would put the range from 30 to 60 per cent.

Is it worth it? The answer to that question depends to a great extent on the importance which society—both black and white—attaches to the idea of assisting disadvantaged groups to own and operate their own businesses. It is undeniable that very few minority group citizens today have the kind of stake in society represented by ownership and management of a business. It is also clear that their lack of such a stake is socially undesirable.

But is such a program practical? This depends, in part, on how effective SBA personnel are in carrying out the idea. It also depends on how well our new American entrepreneurs perform. There is no reason to believe that Negroes or other minorities, given the opportunity, lack the native ability to succeed in business. What is needed is skill, experience, and capital.

Just because the loss ratio may be high during the first few years of the program does not mean that the propensity to succeed will not increase. But the effort will take a good deal of time. As experience is gained by both the SBA and the new entrepreneurs, real progress should be made and loss ratios move downward.

When it is learned that such loans are bankable, the private financial community should take over. The gradual involvement of bankers is entirely proper. After all, the SBA does not have to show a profit, but private lending institutions do. The SBA should continue to take the lead in breaking this important new ground, with the private financial community taking on the job from there.

WHERE THE MONEY COMES FROM: THE REVOLVING FUNDS

The money required for carrying on the SBA's various financial activities comes from its revolving funds. The Business Loan and Investment Fund is drawn upon for the following programs: business loans (including EOL's), state and local development company loans, and SBIC loans. In 1966, a separate Disaster Loan Fund was established by act of Congress. As of December 31, 1966, the net assets of the Business Loan and Investment Fund were over $1.3 billion and the net assets of the Disaster Loan Fund were $349 million.

The noted economist Arthur Smithies, of Harvard University, in his authoritative study, *The Budgetary Process in the United States* (1955), pointed out that there are three major ways in which government enterprises have been organized: the traditional agency, such as the Post Office, whose expenditures are appropriated by Congress and whose receipts are paid into the Treasury; the corporation, such as the Tennessee Valley Authority, which relies on its own earning or lending powers to cover expenses and not on Congressional appropriations; and the revolving fund.

The revolving fund is a hybrid device—a cross between the traditional agency and the government corporation. The initial fund is provided by appropriation. The appropriation, however, is intended to be used for an indefinite period, certainly much longer than a year. Like the corporation, receipts arising from the operation of the revolving fund are not paid into the Treasury; they are used to replenish the fund for further operations.

SBA Revolving Funds. The SBA has had continuing difficulty in keeping its revolving funds nourished. As acting Administrator Ross D. Davis stated before the Senate Small Business Committee late in 1965, "Our revolving fund has never revolved."

As Tables XV and XVI show, the SBA has gone to the well time and again. This history of regular and supplemental appropriations required to replenish the revolving fund during Fiscal Years 1954–66 indicates that $1,805 million was appropriated for the revolving funds during that period—$1,215 million in regular appropriations and $590 million in supplemental appropriations. One could say that the SBA was a *de jure* revolving fund agency but a *de facto* traditional agency.

TABLE XV

Regular Appropriations to SBA Revolving Funds, 1954–66
(In Millions of Dollars)

Fiscal Year for Which Requested	Public Law No.	Date	Amount
1954	83–207	August 7, 1953	$55
1955	83–428	June 24, 1954	25
1956	84–219	August 4, 1955	25
1957	84–604	June 20, 1956	50
1958	85–170	August 28, 1957	100
1959	85–766	August 27, 1958	200
1960	86–88	July 13, 1959	150
1961	86–451	May 13, 1960	50
1962	87–125	August 3, 1961	20
1963	87–843	October 18, 1962	300
1964	88–245	December 30, 1963	90
1966	89–164	September 2, 1965	150
Total			$1,215

Source: Senate Small Business Committee, *Small Business Administration Lending Programs* (1966).

TABLE XVI

Supplemental Appropriations to SBA Revolving Funds, 1954–66
(In Millions of Dollars)

Fiscal Year for Which Requested	Public Law No.	Date	Amount
1956	84–533	May 19, 1956	$20
1957	85–19	April 20, 1957	45
1958	85–457	June 13, 1958	20
1962	87–332	September 20, 1961	160
1962	87–545	July 25, 1962	40
1965	88–635	October 7, 1964	45
1965	89–16	April 30, 1965	100
1966	89–309	October 31, 1965	160
Total			$590

Source: Senate Small Business Committee, *Small Business Administration Lending Programs* (1966).

These shortages in the revolving fund have caused the agency throughout its history to operate in fits and starts. Table XVII shows the chronology of suspension and curtail-

TABLE XVII

History of Business Loan Approvals' Being Suspended or Curtailed Because of Shortage of Funds

Period	Basis
April 10 to May 21, 1956	Suspended to reserve funds for disaster loans
February 1 to April 22, 1957	Suspended to reserve funds for disaster loans
June 6–13, 1958	Suspended to reserve funds for disaster loans
December 1, 1961, to October 12, 1962	Applications were restricted to a maximum of $200,000 SBA share for other than defense-oriented firms
March 2 to August 31, 1962	Funds available only for urgent cases and released on a case-by-case basis. From continuing resolution amount in both July and August, some funds were released for approval of oldest cases in backlog.
November 10, 1964, to October 12, 1965	Effective November 10, 1964, applications limited to $15,000 direct loans and $50,000 SBA share of immediate participations. Effective December 18, 1964, priority order by program for loans approved in field offices was established and modified on December 23. Use of advice of favorable consideration instituted.
May 19, 1965, to May 1966	Application ceiling was raised to $100,000 for direct loans and SBA share of immediate participations with less than 25 per cent bank participation. Discontinued use of advice of favorable consideration technique.
October 12, 1965, to May 26, 1966	Discontinued acceptance of business loan applications except under loan guarantee program.

Source: Senate Small Business Committee, *Small Business Administration Lending Programs* (1966).

ment of loan activities because of depletions in the revolving fund. Certainly the leanest period came from November, 1964, through May, 1966. On November 10, 1964, loan applications were limited to $15,000 on direct loans and $50,000 for the SBA share of immediate participations. The statutory limit for each, of course, is $350,000. With these ceilings still in effect, a priority order for loan applications was established. The priorities became: (1) EOL loans, (2) physical disaster loans, (3) guaranteed business loans, (4) all other disaster loans, (5) local development company loans, and (6) all other business loans.

In May, 1965, fortified momentarily by a supplemental appropriation of $100 million in April, the application ceiling was raised from $15,000 to $100,000 on direct loans and the SBA share of immediate participations from $50,000 to $100,000.

This prosperity proved short-lived. Despite a regular appropriation of $150 million in September and a supplemental of $160 million in October, business loan applications were not accepted after October, with the exception of those under the loan guarantee program. The latter, of course, did not involve any outlay of SBA money.

It was not until May, 1966, when Bernard L. Boutin was appointed SBA administrator, that the moratorium on business loans was lifted. At that time, the agency began accepting applications for direct loans up to $50,000 and the SBA share of immediate participation loans up to $100,000, and guaranteed loans up to $350,000.

This is a sorry record. What are the reasons for the "non-revolving" character of the SBA revolving funds? What can be done?

In trying to explain why there was a moratorium on business loans in December, 1965, acting Administrator Davis laid much stress on the drain upon the funds caused by the aftermath of Hurricane Betsy. Although disaster relief explains a large part of the problem in 1965, it fails to explains all of it, by any means. It also does not explain what happened in all the other years when additional appropriations were required.

In calendar 1965, SBA loans for disaster assistance totaled $206.9 million. Appropriations for the calendar year, as we have already noted, were $410 million. What happened to the rest of the money?

The answer is relatively simple. The demands for SBA financial assistance have consistently exceeded the amount of money in the revolving fund. There are only two ways out of this dilemma. The agency either has to increase the supply in the form of ever-increasing amounts of money in the revolving fund or has to reduce the demand by curtailing or suspending lending programs. The practice has been this: as funds run low, activities are slowed down or suspended. Then, when funds run out, appropriations are sought.

Why does the SBA, and other agencies, run credit programs in this fashion? The SBA administrator will not ask for the money that is required because it is presumed that the Bureau of the Budget will not go along. The Budget Bureau seeks to cut "the fat" out of the budget and raises an arched eyebrow at new spending plans of low-priority outfits like the SBA. So the SBA and the Bureau of the Budget consistently ask for less from Congress than is politically realistic.

An alternative approach would be for the administration to request of Congress that the lending programs pay their way, or at least pay substantially more of their way. Since this might mean interest rates of, say, 9 to 11 per cent, rather than the statutory rate of 5½ per cent, it is considered realistic not to ask for something so revolutionary—one might even say elementary—from the Congress. And so it goes. That is the way the game is played.

Participation Certificates. With these apparently being the ground rules, alternative approaches have been sought to ameliorate the situation. The most prominent of these has been the introduction of participation certificates with passage of the Independent Offices Appropriation Act of 1967.

Under this act, the Federal National Mortgage Association (FNMA)—often inelegantly referred to as Fanny Mae—sells participation certificates to the public.[1] The sale is underwritten by such large investment banking companies as the First Boston Corporation and Merrill Lynch, Pierce, Fenner & Smith.

The certificates are hardly for the common man. They are issued in denominations of $5,000, $10,000, $25,000, $100,000, $500,000, and $1,000,000. They bear interest, and principal will be paid on maturity by Fanny Mae. In fact, the issues are quite attractive to investors. In April, 1968, participation certificates were issued bearing interest of 6.45 per cent. This was described in *Business Week*'s April 6 issue of that year as "the most paid on any government-guaranteed obligation since the Civil War." Upon reading that comment, an SBA wag added: "Yeah—and that was for Confederate bonds."

Under the participation certificates scheme, pools of government loans are assembled. The certificates are shares in these pools which are sold to the public. During Fiscal Year 1968, sales of these certificates are expected to total $5.3 billion.

The principal agencies involved in this scheme are the Farmers Home Administration (Department of Agriculture), the Office of Education (Department of Health, Education, and Welfare), the Department of Housing and Urban Development (HUD), the Veterans Administration, and the SBA. The Farmers Home Administration, HUD, and the SBA are by

[1] FNMA was incorporated on February 10, 1938. It is a government-owned corporation and its operating funds are borrowed almost entirely from the Treasury. Its principal business is the purchase and sale of mortgages insured by the Federal Housing Administration. Since 1948, FNMA has also purchased and sold mortgages guaranteed by the Veterans Administration. The purpose of Fanny Mae is to provide a secondary market for such mortgages.

far the most important contributors to the principal assembled.

Stripped of all its technicalities, what is actually happening here is that the government is borrowing money from the public and putting up its loans as collateral. As far as the loans are concerned, the whole thing is essentially a paper transaction. Private investors do not take over the loans. The government agencies continue to hold and service them.

Participation certificates are eagerly sought by private investors. Issues are quickly snapped up. Yields are highly attractive. In addition, according to an opinion of the Attorney General of September 30, 1966: "FNMA's guaranty of a participation certificate brings into being a general obligation of the United States backed by its full faith and credit." The Attorney General went on to assure potential investors: "The holders of participations guaranteed by FNMA hold valid general obligations of the United States and are in a position to reach beyond the assets of FNMA to the United States Treasury for payment, if necessary."

The arrangement is also advantageous to the federal government. To the extent that the device is used, agencies like the SBA can replenish their revolving funds without having to suffer through the often painful appropriations process. But the major gain, politically, has been that this operation serves to reduce the almost perennial deficit of the federal budget proposed to Congress every year. This is because of some rather archaic accounting concepts. Until now, when the participation certificates have been sold, the transactions have been treated in the budget as a sale of assets by the government and, thus, reduced the size of its deficit. The whole thing has been more illusory than real.

Actually, the device merely buys time. Agencies have to turn over to FNMA money to meet interest payments to private investors who hold participation certificates. Eventually, payments of principal will have to be made.

There is a price to be paid for this type of financing, and

it is a stiff one. In Fiscal Year 1967, the SBA paid 4⅝, 4¾, and 4⅞ per cent for the money it obtained from the Treasury for its various programs; in Fiscal Year 1968, it has paid 4⅞ and 5 per cent. But in calendar year 1967, the SBA paid rates ranging from 4.75 up to 6.40 per cent as interest on participation certificates. And in April, 1968, as we have mentioned, participation certificates carried an interest rate of 6.45 per cent.

Perhaps this does not sound like a stiff price. But let us spell the matter out more clearly. Say the average amount paid to the Treasury as interest is at 5 per cent, and 6.5 per cent is paid to the private investor on the participation certificates. A difference of 1½ per cent may not sound like much. But as any student of finance or mathematics knows, there is a great difference. It is a difference of only 1½ percentage points; but with the 6.5 per cent rate the government is paying 30 per cent more for interest than it pays at 5 per cent.

The worm will begin to turn for the SBA in Fiscal Year 1969. In 1967, sales of SBA participation certificates were $520 million and retirements were $70 million. In 1968, it is estimated, sales will be $315 million and retirements $70 million. But in 1969 it is estimated that sales will be only $200 million with retirements rising to $213 million.

In the 1969 federal budget, following the recommendations of the President's Commission on Budget Concepts, a fundamental change took place in the accounting for participation certificates. The practice of handling the transactions as being disposals of assets was scrapped. They are now treated as borrowing.

This change is eminently sound. But it should take much of the steam out of the drive for participation certificates. Participation certificates, instead of reducing the budget deficit as formerly, will now be accounted for in precisely the same way as drawing upon the Treasury.

One problem that was of particular concern to the President's Commission on Budget Concepts has also been of central concern in much of this chapter. It is the fact that many federal loans, including all SBA loans, are made on such favorable terms in an economic sense that they carry an implicit subsidy. The commission did not call for an end to the subsidy element, but it urged that the government find out what the subsidy amounts to.

The Budget Concepts Commission recommended first:

> that the full amount of the interest subsidy on loans compared to Treasury borrowing costs be reflected and specifically disclosed in the expenditure account of the budget and, furthermore, that it be measured on a capitalized basis at the time the loans are made.

In addition, the commission urged that subsidies be disclosed:

> Effective measures [should] be developed to reflect (in the expenditure rather than in the loan account of the budget) the further subsidy involved in the fact that Federal loans have a larger element of risk than Treasury borrowing. This should be done by creation of allowances for losses and making appropriate credits to those allowances and charges to expense as new loans are extended.

VI

Procurement and Management Assistance

Helping small business get government contracts and subcontracts and upgrading the managerial skills of entrepreneurs have traditionally been two of the major functions of the SBA. Why is this aid needed? What are the problems encountered in operating SBA programs? How effective are its activities? These are some of the questions that need to be raised now.

PROCUREMENT ASSISTANCE

Statutory authority for the procurement assistance program comes from Section 2 of the Small Business Act. It states, in part:

> It is the declared policy of the Congress that the Government should aid, counsel, assist, and protect, insofar as is possible, the interests of small-business concerns in order to preserve free competitive enterprise, to insure that a fair proportion of the total purchases and contracts or subcontracts for property and services for the Government (including but not limited to contracts or subcontracts for maintenance, repair, and construction) be placed with small-business enterprises, to insure that a fair proportion of the total sales of Government property be made

127

to such enterprises, and to maintain and strengthen the overall economy of the Nation.

Underlying this legalistic phraseology is the belief that small firms had not received a fair share of federal procurement. It was also believed that continuance of this situation would lead to a lessening of free competition, a further concentration of economic power, and a weakening of the private enterprise system.

The policy of assisting small firms to obtain a fair share of federal government procurement is not new. It was put into effect during World War II. However, the tendency of federal procurement to lead to a pattern of concentration is still manifest. In Fiscal Year 1964, for example, the 100 companies that received the largest dollar volume of military prime contracts received almost three-fourths of the money. The top five companies alone obtained approximately one-quarter of the total.

The government market is huge and seems ever-growing. In 1967, government purchases of goods and services amounted to $176.3 billion, slightly over 22 per cent of the gross national product. These purchases were pretty evenly balanced between the federal government, on the one hand, and the state and local governments, on the other. The preponderance of federal purchases was for national defense; about four out of every five of these dollars were spent for defense purposes.

To illustrate the tremendous growth in federal purchases of goods and services, let us look at the magnitudes in a few representative years. In 1929, they amounted to $1.3 billion, or slightly more than one per cent of the gross national product. In 1937, a typical Roosevelt peacetime year—if there was such an animal—they were $4.7 billion, about 5 per cent of the gross national product. In 1947, in the early days of Harry Truman's Fair Deal, federal purchases were $12.5 billion, again only about 5 per cent of the total.

Starting with the build-up in the Korean War in 1951, federal purchases have absorbed a much higher proportion of the gross national product than in any of the years before or immediately following World War II. In 1952, for example, federal purchases were $51.8 billion, about 18 per cent of the gross national product.

The years 1952 and 1953, as a matter of fact, were the years in which federal purchases were at their peak in relation to total product (World War II excluded). Although purchases had risen to $89 billion by 1967, they constituted only about 11 per cent of the total—much higher than in the prewar or postwar total but considerably lower than in 1952 and 1953.

FEDERAL PROCUREMENT PRIME CONTRACT AWARDS

The statistics that are watched most closely by SBA procurement officers are the prime contract awards of the most important federal agencies. Table XVIII sets forth the totals for the years 1953 through 1967.

Transcending all other agencies in importance is, of course, the Department of Defense. Total prime contract awards of the federal government in 1967 were $49.8 billion. The Pentagon awarded $40.6 billion, over 81 per cent of the total. Aside from the Defense Department, the most important procurement agencies are the National Aeronautics and Space Administration (NASA), the Atomic Energy Commission (AEC), and the General Services Administration (GSA). But as huge as their dollar expenditures on prime contracts may seem, they are quite small when compared to military contracts.

SMALL BUSINESS SHARE OF PRIME CONTRACT AWARDS

Table XVIII also shows the share of total federal prime contracts that were awarded to small business. In Fiscal Years 1960–67, they ranged from a low of 17.3 per cent of total prime contracts to a high of 21.3 per cent.

TABLE XVIII

Federal Procurement—Prime Contract Awards

Fiscal Year	Total All Agencies			Department of Defense			Civilian Agencies		
	Total Contract Awards (In Millions)	Awards to Small Business		Total Contract Awards[a]	Awards to Small Business		Total Contract Awards[b] (In Millions)	Awards to Small Business	
		Amount (In Millions)	Per Cent of Total		Amount (In Millions)	Per Cent of Total		Amount (In Millions)	Per Cent of Total
1967	$49,807	$10,232	20.5	$40,609	$8,361	20.6	$9,198	$1,871	20.3
1966	44,249	9,409	21.3	34,878	7,612	21.8	9,371	1,797	19.2
1965	34,765	6,976	20.1	26,113	5,305	20.3	8,652	1,671	19.3
1964	34,985	6,453	18.4	26,920	4,842	18.0	8,065	1,611	20.0
1963	34,426	5,959	17.3	27,793	4,597	16.5	6,633	1,362	20.5
1962	31,549	6,093	19.3	26,147	4,622	17.7	5,402	1,471	27.2
1961	27,664	4,876	17.7	22,992	3,657	15.9	4,672	1,219	26.1
1960	25,916	4,735	18.3	21,302	3,440	16.1	4,614c	1,295	28.1
1959	24,376	4,623	19.0	22,744	3,783	16.6	1,632	840	51.5
1958	23,425	4,497	19.2	21,827	3,729	17.1	1,598	768	48.1
1957	20,512	4,514	22.0	19,133	3,783	19.8	1,379	731	53.0
1956	18,909	4,043	21.4	17,750	3,475	19.6	1,159	568	49.0
1955	15,969	3,768	23.6	14,930	3,214	21.5	1,039	554	53.4
1954	12,510	3,393	27.1	11,448	2,902	25.3	1,062	491	46.2
1953	29,334	5,414	18.5	27,822	4,608	16.6	1,512	806	53.3

Source: Small Business Administration.

a Military functions (includes civil functions) beginning Fiscal Year 1963.
b Excludes purchases of less than $10 for 1953; less than $25 from January 1954 to June 1961; $100 or less beginning Fiscal Year 1962. Includes AEC and NASA beginning Fiscal Year 1960.
c NASA for 1960 excludes Procurements placed under GSA contracts.

Subcontracts are also made by prime contractors with small business concerns. Of the $49.8 billion in prime contracts in Fiscal Year 1967, for example, $7.3 billion of the work was subcontracted to small business firms.

INSTALLATIONS ACTIVELY COVERED BY THE SBA

In Fiscal Year 1967, about $17.3 billion in prime contracts were made at Defense Department installations covered by SBA personnel. Of this total, $3 billion, or about 17.5 per cent, was awarded to small business concerns. By far the most important installation from the standpoint of the SBA was the Defense Supply Agency's installation in Philadelphia.

The Defense Supply Agency (DSA) is an interesting innovation. It was created to procure for and distribute common-use commercial-type supplies and services to the military departments. It buys such things as blankets, sheets, beds, socks, shoes, tableware, soap, maps—all the items that are common to all branches of the service.

Previously, each branch of the service did its own purchasing. Certain congressmen, usually but not always of the opposition party, made an avocation of ferreting out examples of poor purchasing practices. It might be found, for example, that the Navy had a seventy-eight-year supply of mosquito nets or that the Army had a ninety-two-year supply of atabrine tablets. Such a situation was always juicier if the Air Force then proceeded to buy atabrine tablets or mosquito nets or both.

Such revelations made news, and properly so. The Defense Supply Agency was set up to eliminate these wasteful practices. It also enables the Defense Department to place larger orders, presumably at lower prices, than was the case when the services bought separately. Apparently, DSA has been quite successful in improving DOD's procurement efficiency on common-use commercial items.

TECHNIQUES FOR INCREASING THE SMALL BUSINESS SHARE

Over the years a rather comprehensive set of policies and programs has been developed by the SBA to carry out the intent of Congress with respect to procurement assistance for small business. The programs include the small business "set-aside," the certificates of competency, technical assistance, the facilities inventory, procurement counseling and procurement conferences (most of these programs were already discussed in Chapter III).

WHAT IS A "FAIR SHARE" FOR SMALL BUSINESS?

It can be stated unequivocally that no one knows what a "fair share" for small business would be. The procuring agency is concerned, of course, with price, quality, good delivery dates, assurance of completion of the contract, good maintenance, spare parts, and so on. The SBA, for its part, is concerned that the small business share of total procurement increases year by year.

The Defense Department keeps elaborate records on its prime contract awards to small business. Table XIX is a typical display. It is taken from the testimony of Secretary of Defense Robert S. McNamara before the Senate Small Business Committee in 1967. The data consists of twenty-seven "claimant programs" of the Defense Department with percentages of small business shares and small business "goals," claimant program by claimant program.

Unfortunately, as impressive and precise and scientific as these figures might appear to be, they are of very little use to SBA analysts. The statistical information which the SBA possesses about small business is based on the Standard Industrial Classification (SIC) code, which is used by the Bureau of the Census and most other government agencies that use statistics. This system is much more detailed than the data

TABLE XIX

DOD Small Business Claimant Program—Goals and Actual Awards and
Percentage, Fiscal Year 1966
(Dollar Amounts in Billions)

| Claimant Program | Actual | | | Goals, Small Business Per Cent |
	Total Awards	Small Business Awards	Small Business Per Cent	
Total	$34.9	$7.6	21.8	18.3
Airframes and spares	4.4	.08	1.8	1.2
Aircraft engines and spares	2.1	.03	1.5	1.5
Other aircraft equipment	1.0	.16	15.9	14.8
Missile and space systems	4.1	.09	2.2	1.4
Ships	1.3	.2	16.1	10.0
Combat vehicles	.6	.08	14.6	12.5
Noncombat vehicles	1.0	.13	12.8	9.6
Weapons	.5	.13	26.2	28.5
Ammunition	2.8	.5	16.8	7.8
Electronics and communications equipment	3.6	.5	12.7	12.6
Petroleum	.9	.2	24.1	20.5
Other fuels and lubricants	.023	.008	35.6	29.4
Containers and handling equipment	.007	.001	15.6	32.6
Textiles, clothing, and equipage	1.2	.7	58.7	55.0
Building supplies	.4	.14	38.8	22.5
Subsistence	1.0	.5	52.2	46.6
Transportation equipment	.008	.001	9.6	—
Production equipment	.2	.05	26.0	33.1
Construction	1.0	.7	63.2	58.0
Construction equipment	.2	.03	15.9	27.2
Medical and dental supplies and equipment	.2	.05	25.1	20.9
Photographic equipment and supplies	.16	.02	14.8	12.4
Materials handling equipment	.1	.04	36.1	38.7
All other supplies and equipment	1.3	.6	46.8	38.4
Services	2.3	.5	23.0	20.5
All actions of less than $10,000	3.5	1.8	51.1	50.6
Civil functions	.9	.3	40.2	45.0

Source: Senate Small Business Committee, *Status and Future of Small
Business*

supplied by the Pentagon. The Defense Department's system,
the Federal Supply Classification Code (FSC), is product-
oriented, while the SIC is industry-oriented.

The SBA knows, for example, how important a factor small

business is, industry by industry, in the American economy. Unfortunately, there is no link between the Defense Department's statistical system and the SBA's. Until such a link is forged, the SBA cannot participate knowledgeably in the setting of small business procurement goals for the Department of Defense.

For several years, the most common measuring rod used in evaluating the program has been the percentage of prime contract procurement awards going to small business. The SBA, and the small business community, are supposed to be encouraged when the small business share of total awards rises from 18 per cent to 20.3 per cent, as it did from Fiscal Year 1964 to Fiscal Year 1965.

A cruder or more misleading statistic could hardly be devised. Changes in the program mix are the more important factor in determining whether the over-all small business share goes up or down and not the vigor and efficiency of SBA procurement specialists or their counterparts in the Defense Department.

There are certain claimant programs, such as airframes and spares or missile and space systems, where the small business share is understandably low—less than 2 per cent. There are other claimant programs, such as construction, textiles, clothing, and equipage, where the small business share is high; in these instances, it is usually about two-thirds of total procurement. Other things being equal, a rise in awards for construction, textiles, clothing, and equipage and a decline in awards for airframes and spares and missiles and space systems should obviously lead to an unaided and undirected rise in the small business share. This is hardly a remarkable achievement.

Situations like this are difficult to resolve in the government. The SBA is obviously overmatched with a giant like the Defense Department. For practical reasons, the Pentagon's private views on small business' fair share of military procurement do not always coincide with those of the SBA. The Defense Department has many other concerns, many of which it deems to be far more important than—and sometimes antithetical to—the small business interest. As long as the meaningless statistic of the small business share of defense procurement goes up or remains relatively stable, it is likely that nothing will be done to change the present way of doing things. The Defense Department will be happy and so will the SBA and Congress.

THE PROBLEM OF MEASURING THE CAPABILITY OF SMALL BUSINESS

Apart from these important informational problems of a statistical character, another great cloud hanging over this whole operation is the stark fact that often very little is known about the capability of small business to carry out important kinds of work for the federal government. The certificates of competency are, of course, an attempt to surmount this problem, at least in part. But essentially the certificates of competency approach, however worthy, can only scratch the surface. This is because the certificates of competency are issued on a case-by-case basis. In 1966, there were only 357 contract awards resulting from this program, amounting to $11.9 million. Approximately, $1.1 million was estimated to have been saved by these 357 contract awards.

There is an indeterminate amount of contracts that are awarded because of the program which did not require issuance of a formal certificate. Sometimes cases are referred to the SBA and, after information has been gathered, a contract is awarded with no formal certificate required.

Let us assume that the certificates of competency may have resulted in $20–30 million in awards in that year which would not have otherwise gone to small business. This is about one twenty-fifth of 1 per cent of total federal prime contract awards.

In other words, for each $1,000 of federal procurement awards about 40 cents may have gone to small business through the certificates of competency program that would otherwise have gone to large business.

Of the $10.2 billion in prime contracts awarded in Fiscal Year 1967, the certificates of competency program made a contribution of about one-fifth of 1 per cent.

There are only a handful of people who work on the certificates of competency program. They are highly skilled. Most of the professional personnel have degrees in engineering, as well as extensive experience in industrial production and in government procurement. To expand this program greatly would not only be increasingly and rather prohibitively expensive—the law of diminishing returns would quickly set in—but it would also be difficult to recruit the personnel required.

A more promising over-all approach would be to study much more intensively than heretofore specific "products" or "industries" of major importance to the federal government. For example, in 1966 some 12.7 per cent of total Defense Department awards for electronics and communications equipment were to small business. Should this figure have been 15 per cent or 25 per cent or 50 per cent? No one knows because no one knows that much about the capabilities and efficiency of small business in making these products. Well-designed and well-executed research studies could strip this subject of much of its mystery. Then the SBA and the Defense Department could set much more realistic goals for the small business share.

THE GROWTH OF RESEARCH AND DEVELOPMENT
IN THE AMERICAN ECONOMY

Research and development (R&D) expenditures are of ever-increasing importance to the American economy and to the small business sector. As Daniel Hamberg wrote in 1966:

The magnitude of the current research effort and its rate of advance have inspired awe and generated a torrent of enraptured expletives describing the promise it holds forth in the form of lifesaving and life-serving new products and processes. How important technological change has been to our present living standards has recently been statistically verified in a number of independent studies. By various means a succession of economists has estimated that between 50 and 90 percent of the advances in productivity (output per man hour) in our economy have originated in technological progress.[1]

For many years the interest of executives in understanding research was dampened undoubtedly by the fact that both the costs and the results of research were extremely uncertain. Uncertainty about results, however, cannot be regarded as a primary cause for the tardiness in American industry's willingness to spend large amounts of money on research and development. Businessmen are used to taking chances, often when the odds are long. As an example, oil companies, which were perfectly willing to gamble extravagantly to discover oil and to bring in producing wells, were slow in spending money on the much less risky ventures of research on refining processes and the development of petrochemicals.

What was needed was proof that research pays off. Dramatic results were shown in a few industries—notably the electrical equipment, communications, chemicals, electronics, and airplane industries. Technical knowledge is so essential in these lines of endeavor that improvement of products and processes could not be relegated to a task to be performed by operating men and engineering staffs as a sideline activity.

In addition, tremendous expansion in research and development activity in the United States has also been generated by government research contracts arising out of the needs of World War II and the ensuing cold war.

---

[1] Daniel Hamberg, *R & D: Essays on the Economics of Research and Development* (New York: Random House, 1966), p. 3.

Staggering as the amounts of money spent on R&D may appear today, technological research is probably still in an early stage. There is still a considerable concentration of R&D expenditures in a few industries. This, of course, is partly the result of the defense and space needs of the federal government.

In 1962, for example, two industries accounted for 58 per cent of the $11.6 billion spent on R&D in the industrial sector. The aircraft and missiles industry spent $4.1 billion and the electrical equipment and communications industry spent $2.5 billion. These two industries plus chemicals accounted for 69 per cent of the total R&D outlays. If one adds the motor vehicle and transportation industry to the list, the four industries accounted for three-fourths of all industry spending on R&D.

There is obviously considerable room for expansion of technological research, especially into areas where little has been done. The huge iron and steel industry, for instance, still spends a negligible amount on R&D. It spends about one-fifth of what the much smaller professional and scientific instruments industry spends.

Research has become a major method of competition, and it will play a far bigger role in the economy of the future than it does today. One result of the age of intensified research is that the rates of innovation and of obsolescence are far higher than we have known in the past. Industry will have to change its ideas about the useful life of equipment and be prepared to finance a considerably faster rate of replacement.

THE ROLE OF THE FEDERAL GOVERNMENT IN R&D

World War II and the years that have followed have had the effect of pushing the federal government into technological research on a giant scale. Although most research is done privately, primarily by industry, most of it is paid for by the government. In 1962, for example, the government laid out

$9.6 billion, or 65 per cent, of the $14.7 billion spent in the United States on R&D. In constant prices, the $15 billion government outlay for R&D in 1965 was $2 billion more than all government purchases of goods and services in 1940.

Small business gets a very small share of the federal R&D dollar. In Fiscal Year 1964, for example, small business received only 3.7 per cent of the Defense Department awards in experimental, developmental, test, and research work.

It is not known to what extent government R&D contracts are subcontracted to small business. How much of the federal R&D dollar finds its way to small business in this fashion is highly conjectural, but it is likely that it is not much. It should be noted that the concentration indexes for the important industry recipients of federal R&D funds are quite high relative to most other industries.

It will be recalled that four industries account for three-fourths of the total industrial R&D spending in the United States—aircraft and missiles, electrical equipment and communications, chemicals, and motor vehicles and transportation equipment. Concentration is rather extreme in these industries. For instance, in electrical equipment and communications, 75 per cent of total R&D expenditures in 1961 were made by the eight largest companies. These companies also received 79 per cent of the federal money received by industry.

THE ECONOMICS OF R&D

During the past two decades, a growing body of economists has focused upon the process of technological change and its relationship to economic growth.

One of the reasons for this heightened increase in interest in the economics of technological change has been the Cold War. We have become increasingly aware that our national security may well depend on the success of the military R&D effort in the United States. It behooves us, therefore, to understand this complicated business as well as we can.

Another source of this increased interest is the changing way that some economists are looking at the competitive process. Increasingly, the focus is on competition through new products rather than on direct price competition.

There has been no definitive work on the question of the relationship between size and efficiency in R&D. Some economists—Richard R. Nelson, John Kenneth Galbraith, and the late Sumner Slichter, to name a few—have thought that size is a great advantage. They have argued that economies of scale seem to result from the abilities of large laboratories to make profitable use of a wide range of expertise (division of labor) and their ability to carry a large number of projects (reduction of risk).

Others would argue to the contrary. Several economists have concluded in their studies of particular industries—radio, aircraft engines and fuels, electric lamps—that the birth of new firms was an important part of the development of these products and industries. The British economist John Jewkes studied sixty-one important inventions and innovations and found that over half came from independent inventors or small firms. Two recent examples of this phenomenon in the United States are the Polaroid camera and the ubiquitous Xerox machine. These products were developed by small concerns, which then rose quickly to giant size.

The recent report of the Commerce Department's Panel on Invention and Innovation accorded small business an important role in technological progress. It stated:

It goes without saying that the United States could not depend solely on the innovative contributions of small firms. The large firms are indispensable to technological and economic progress. From a number of different points of view, however, we are persuaded that a unique cost-benefit opportunity exists in the provision of incentives aimed at encouraging independent inventors, inventor-entrepreneurs, and small technologically-based businesses. The cost of special incentives to them is likely to be low. The benefits are likely to be high.

And yet very little federal research money goes to small business. In 1961, the House Committee on Science and Astronautics conducted a study of the impact of federal R&D programs. In a rather classic statement of the reasons why small business did not receive a larger portion of the contracts in weapons, space, management and operational system awards, the Committee's staff study said:

1. Small business is unable to compete with the large prime contractors from a financial, facilities, and technical talent standpoint. . . .

2. Small business is not represented when a large prime contractor determines his "make or buy" policy. . . . If the prime contractor is "hungry" and needs work to keep his own people and facilities busy, his decision will be "make" rather than "buy," even though this means entering a new field and purchasing additional equipment.

3. The reluctance of small business to become a subcontractor under a prime for fear of being absorbed by the prime either through "osmosis" or outright purchase or forced merger after the small business firm becomes entirely dependent on the prime. . . .

4. The large prime contractor is able to provide a management base and administrative service encompassing a complete program, therefore, relieving the responsible Government agency of having to establish an "in-house" overall technical management and administrative capacity. . . .

5. The built-in organizational flexibility of the large prime contractors assures rapid execution of a program.

Some economists have argued, however, that the great uncertainties inherent in R&D should mean that several efforts should be run in parallel. A good strategy for a group of inventors initially might well be to diversify their efforts and undertake parallel work on several alternative approaches. This, of course, is a strong argument to advance on behalf of increased small business involvement in the nation's R&D efforts.

How Can the Small Business Share of Federal R&D Be Increased?

We find ourselves on the horns of a dilemma. The national need for federal expenditures on R&D has resulted in a heavy concentration of expenditures in a few industries and a few firms. On the other hand, there is ample proof that small firms are capable of producing inventions of great commercial and social value.

Federal expenditures are extremely concentrated even though the government is traditionally committed to the preservation and expansion of free competition. Small business fears that the giant concerns will become even more dominant thanks to the R&D policies of the Defense Department and NASA. New processes are developed and proprietary rights are obtained through the patent system. A monopoly pattern is aided and abetted with the taxpayers' money.

The SBA has been keenly aware of this problem. In March, 1964, a comprehensive 110-page report, "Federal Research and Development Expenditures: Problems and Prospects for Small Business," was submitted by the SBA to the House Select Committee on Government Research. Recent SBA administrators have underscored the importance of small business involvement in R&D. Loan applicants who wish to develop new products or processes are accorded top priority status. The SBA procurement officers push for R&D awards to small business, but accomplishments seem slight in view of the magnitude and complexity of the problem. The small business share is still very small, while big business is deeply entrenched. To get meaningful results in this key area will require herculean efforts.

SBA MANAGEMENT ASSISTANCE PROGRAMS

Good management is the key to successful business. The businessman finds his world subject to constant change. New techniques and ideas must be constantly absorbed and put into practice if the businessman is to compete successfully. In the world of the corporate giants, a man can carve out a highly successful and remunerative niche for himself by knowing only one phase of business management well—sales, production, purchasing, or whatever.

Not so in small business. The small businessman is the generalist supreme. To be a crack small businessman, he must know all phases of his enterprise well. This is why more big companies are looking to heads of smaller firms in filling the post of chief executive officer than was formerly the case. Often, the head of a small business is better qualified. He is used to command and has a better conception of the total needs of the business and a better feel for the workings of the various parts of the organization. He is not afflicted with the narrow-mindedness of many specialists, nor does he usually attach too much importance to a single phase of a business as specialists are inclined to do.

This is true of the successful small businessman; but many small businessmen are poor managers. A majority of them certainly could improve their skills significantly. Over 350,000 businesses die each year. A much higher number of small businesses just hang on. Many of them do not provide a good income for their owners.

The small businessman has a variety of avenues to improved managerial knowledge and skills open to him. For the reading of papers and periodicals, he can select from many excellent general business publications, such as *The Wall Street Journal, The Journal of Commerce, Business Week, Fortune,* and the *Harvard Business Review.* The financial page of his daily newspaper is often a good source of general information. His trade association is often a useful source, as well. Its publications are geared to his industry and contain valuable information on developments in the industry and new techniques that have been developed. Sometimes the association provides comprehensive material on various aspects of managing an enterprise successfully. They also conduct meetings and seminars that are informative.

A small businessman often belongs to one or several business or quasi-business groups, such as the local chamber of commerce, the Kiwanis, the Lions, and the like. These can be helpful and contribute in various ways to his improvement as a businessman. Many also belong to more general national groups like the Chamber of Commerce of the United States. The Chamber provides many services designed to improve the knowledge and skills of managers of small businesses. Also, it provides him an opportunity to learn more about vital economic issues, such as taxation, government spending, foreign economic policy, and so on.

In his own home town, the small businessman can frequent the public library to great advantage. In addition, many of America's larger cities have excellent business libraries. Many colleges, junior colleges, and high schools offer evening courses especially designed for the small businessman or the aspiring entrepreneur. Predominantly, these courses focus on such basic tools as accounting, business law, marketing, and general principles of management. In addition, there are excellent management education groups—notably, the American Management Association—which offer a wide variety of conferences, courses, and seminars on a large number of business and management subjects.

Fundamentally, the small businessman has a problem of

selection in his attempt to improve his management capability. Information and organized activity are all about him. Which to select? Which to reject? Which to give a lick and a promise? Which to devote real time and energy to? These are problems that face all those who are determined to advance professionally, but they are particularly acute for a small businessman. There is so much he should know, and what is known or believed is constantly changing.

SBA MANAGEMENT PROGRAMS

The small businessman is confronted with two fundamental problems common to most humans—time and money. But his problem, particularly with respect to time, is probably more acute than it is with many other people. So much of his waking hours is completely bound up with his business; he simply has to be there for long hours each and every day. Or as is often the case, he feels compelled to be there.

The SBA's management programs are designed to supplement the activities available to small businessmen, but they can often be a substitute for some of them, for the SBA activities are framed for the small businessman and his special problems and needs. Some of the SBA's management assistance programs were described in general outline in Chapter III. Here, we shall take a closer look—and, in some instances, a more detailed look—at the more important of them.

COURSES, CONFERENCES, AND SEMINARS

In Fiscal Year 1967, the SBA held courses, conferences, seminars, clinics, and business workshops in over 400 communities. Typical subjects were business law, the use and abuse of credit, money management, bookkeeping, and inventory management and control. Over 89,000 small businessmen attended these functions. In Fiscal Year 1968, it is expected that 2,700 training sessions of various kinds will be held. More than 100,000 small businessmen will probably attend.

PUBLICATIONS AND FILMS

The SBA had available in 1968 over 900 different publications on business management. They range from one-page leaflets to thoroughly documented studies on various aspects of business. The publications may be obtained through any SBA field office or directly from the Government Printing Office in Washington. Some are free; others are for sale at a nominal price.

A very popular publication is "Starting and Managing a Small Business." Another, in these days of apparently rising crime, is "Preventing Retail Theft." Other typical subjects are inventory control, effective advertising, maintaining accurate records, tax planning and management, quality control for the small firm, and effective hiring and personnel policies. The publications are usually written by authorities on the various subjects. They are frequently prepared as a public service. Sometimes a modest fee is paid to an author. During Fiscal Year 1968, it is estimated, 3 million copies of such SBA publications will be distributed.

In addition to publications, the SBA produces short training films. A recent production, for example, consists of a series of four film strips on advertising for the small firm. Films are written, produced, and directed by outside experts under contract with the SBA.

MANAGEMENT COUNSELING

The SBA devotes more resources to management counseling of various kinds. According to the SBA, over 60,000 small businessmen were given information and guidance during Fiscal Year 1967. In 1968, it was anticipated that over 80,000 small businessmen would receive management counseling.

Counseling can range from a telephone call or brief visit to one of the SBA's seventy-three offices throughout the country to an intensive analysis of a company's problems. SBA advisory services are being stepped up. The need has increased since inception of the EOL program, since many recipients of these loans have no experience in running a business. In addition, many have little or no educational background in business or management. Under these circumstances, management counseling is often the best way to improve the management skills of a loan recipient. The SBA considers management counseling, and management education generally, so important that it sometimes makes these a precondition for an EOL.

In recent years, the SBA has also accelerated its management counseling activities related to loan servicing. Since poor management is invariably the underlying cause of business failure, it is reasoned, improvement of management skills will not only help the small businessman but will also help assure that the government gets its money back.

The SBA field offices have adopted what is called a "team approach." According to former Administrator Bernard L. Boutin:

> Each team processes, closes, and services loans for which it is responsible, including business loans, economic opportunity loans, disaster loans, rehabilitation loans for the Department of Housing and Urban Development, and lease guarantees. The teams are self-contained units. Each member has the capability of performing any necessary processing, servicing, or closing activity. . . . Great importance is given to management counseling. Teams offer management assistance both to borrowers and to those whose applications are denied.

SERVICE CORPS OF RETIRED EXECUTIVES (SCORE)

One of the more important—and newsworthy—SBA efforts is the SCORE program. It was launched in 1964 by Administrator Eugene P. Foley. SCORE is composed of over 3,500 retired business executives, many of them formerly successful small businessmen, who assist the SBA and the small business community on a volunteer basis.

The program is simple. Retired businessmen, voluntarily and without compensation, counsel the small businessman at his shop, office, or plant. According to a 1966 *Business Week* article, SCORE has had two important factors working for it: "It offered an outlet for the pent-up energies of the nation's fastest growing bank of talent: retired executives. And it offered small businessmen, without charge, the commodity that they may well be shortest of: objectivity."

SCORE is organized into chapters throughout the country. At present, there are over 150 of them. A typical chapter elects officers from among its active members and maintains a duty roster for the membership. Often the SCORE chapter is located in an SBA field office. Sometimes the SCORE office will be housed in space donated by the local chamber of commerce or by a local business. The SBA provides administrative and clerical help. Many of SCORE's clients have heard of the program through the local newspaper or over the radio. SCORE also gets a lot of clients by referral from SBA loan officers and management assistance personnel.

The retired executives receive no fees for their services. They can collect travel expenses, but few of them even ask for reimbursement of these personal outlays. Because the SBA does not wish to invade the territory of management consult-ing firms, SCORE assistance is usually made available only to firms with twenty-five or fewer employees. Businesses of that size are nearly always unable to afford the services of a professional management consultant.

How Effective Is SBA Management Assistance?

It is difficult to assess the management assistance programs of the SBA. For one thing, benefits from educational efforts generally are extremely difficult to measure in quantitative terms. The SBA Financial Assistance Division can say how many loans it has made, what its loss ratio has been, and how many jobs it has "created." It can even estimate the total costs and benefits of its operations. The procurement assistance group can crow about how many government contracts were set aside for small business. But all the management assistance people can do is say how many pamphlets were distributed, how many conferences were held, how many people attended the conferences, how many people received "counseling"— often only a brief telephone conversation—and so on. There is no real measure of how effective all this activity has been and is.

The other point to note is that very few people are engaged in the management assistance programs of the SBA. In Fiscal Year 1967 there were only ninety-six management counselors in the field offices, and there are over 5 million small businesses in the United States. To be sure, SCORE—with its 3,500 members—boosts the attempt to strengthen the SBA's management assistance capability. But it should be pointed out that the SCORE workers are part-time volunteers. Many, in fact, are inactive. While SCORE members can be of great help, they cannot carry the SBA management program—nor should anyone expect it of them.

VII

Small Business Investment Companies: Providing Venture Capital for Small Business

The Small Business Investment Company (SBIC) program is the SBA's newest major activity—and its most controversial, as well. The Small Business Investment Act was approved on August 21, 1958. With passage of this legislation, a "fourth banking system" was believed to have been created.[1] A new financial institution, the SBIC, was to be added to the three traditional financial institutions in the United States—the commercial banks, savings institutions, and investment banks.

The act also marked the entry of the SBA into the long-term financing field. The Investment Division was set up in accordance with the law. It administers the government aspects of the program and regulates and polices the SBIC's.

Almost a decade later, as of early 1968, there were over 500 licensed SBIC's in operation. On March 31, 1967, the assets of the SBIC's stood at slightly over $670 million. During the history of the program through March 31, 1967, SBIC's

[1] Dr. Neil C. Jacoby, Dean of the Graduate School of Business, University of California at Los Angeles and a member of the President's Council of Economic Advisers during the Eisenhower Administration, is believed to have coined this phrase.

had made over 26,000 separate small business financing transactions and had disbursed over $1.2 billion.

The SBIC's were the device by which the so-called equity gap that exists for small business would be closed. It will be recalled that the exhaustive study of small business financing problems made by the research staff of the Federal Reserve Board had confirmed the widespread belief that an equity gap existed for small firms. Sometimes this is referred to as the capital gap.

The investment program has undoubtedly been the SBA's most widely debated activity. Let us examine the major operating details of the program.

THE CAPITAL GAP

The studies carried out for the Federal Reserve Board provided the rationale for the SBIC program. The program's legislative history underscores this point. The report of the House Banking and Currency Committee on the enacting legislation, relying on the reports of the prestigious Federal Reserve Board, succinctly underlined the need for the program:

> The Board's study found that the financial needs of small business vary among different categories of small concerns and that such needs are most complex. Information and data compiled clearly indicated that most of the unsatisfied demand of small business is for long-term loans, equity, or equity-type credit. The commercial banking system is not prepared or designed to satisfy needs for equity or long-term credit. . . .
>
> As indicated by the Federal Reserve Board's study, the unavailability of long-term loan and equity capital is clearly one of the most important problems of small business today. Such investment capital must necessarily come from the personal savings of the people and most of these savings are going into existing financial intermediaries, such as our large insurance companies, savings banks, and others which in turn reinvest these funds. . . .

Institutional investors generally are limited by law in the choice of their investments. When these institutions can exert judgment in the matter of making investments it is found they prefer investing their funds in those securities which have active national markets. . . .

Most of the testimony received by the committee, and in particular the study of this problem by the Federal Reserve Board, points to the fact that there is a real need at this time to stimulate the availability of capital funds to small business; and there is a gap in the economy's present financial mechanism which prevents the small businesses of the country from obtaining needed long-term and equity-type financing.

The prospects for government involvement in helping to close the long-term capital gap were warmly received in the Congress. However, as is usually the case, some conservatives, principally Republicans, opposed the idea. An extract from the dissent of Republican Senators Homer E. Capehart, of Indiana, John W. Bricker, of Ohio, and Wallace F. Bennett, of Utah, gives the flavor of their views:

There is no justification for using the taxpayers' money to finance this venture by the Federal Government into private business. . . .

This bill should be defeated. In sum, it would place the Federal Government in the position of undertaking an impossible assignment with impossible tools. It would be a disservice to the small-business concerns of our country to present this program as an effective means to meet their long-term financing problems. It would be more realistic and practical for the Congress to strengthen the existing programs of the Small Business Administration rather than to perpetrate this new intrusion by the Federal Government into private business.

There were two approaches to the subject by those who supported small business investment legislation. In the Senate, both ideas were introduced as bills by the majority leader, that master of consensus politics, Senator Lyndon B. Johnson, of Texas. One bill (S. 3651), with modifications, was finally adopted. (It will be described in the next section.) The second grew out of a series of hearings held by Congressman Wright Patman, of Texas. This bill looked to the creation of a Small Business Capital Bank System, organized with a branch bank in each Federal Reserve district. Under these branch banks, small business investment associations would have been formed to serve the equity capital and long-term loan requirements of small business in their areas.

The Patman-inspired bill had two distinguishing features. First of all, appropriations would not be required; the initial capital was to have come from funds of the Federal Reserve System. Secondly, it provided that the Small Business Capital Bank System would be patterned after the Federal Home Loan Bank System. The system would have been privately owned through a provision which would have required borrowers to take shares of stock in the banks and associations.

The bill also provided for a separate Small Business Investment Administration, which would have been an independent government agency, managed by an administrator appointed by the President with the consent of the Senate. The idea of a separate agency was strongly supported by many of the senators, particularly many of the Democratic sponsors of the bill. Senator John Sparkman, of Alabama, who was one of the prime movers in the course of this legislation, pointed out why he wanted an independent agency. Originally, the senator had wanted the function put in the Federal Reserve System; but the Federal Reserve did not want the job. Sparkman then advocated the separate agency. He gave his reasons on the floor of the Senate:

> As I pointed out, the SBA was created to handle a different kind of lending program. The SBA was established for the purpose of handling relatively small loans for operational purposes and

handling disaster loans in distress cases. This program has a very different purpose. It calls for what are supposed to be long-term capital loans.

I feel very strongly . . . that there should be provided a separate agency. This program should not be part of the Small Business Administration. I say that without any desire to reflect upon the Small Business Administration. As a matter of fact, I think the Small Business Administration, by and large, has done a good job in the handling of the types of loans it is supposed to handle.

I have felt this program should be handled by a separate agency because it involves a separate type of financing.

However, the Eisenhower Administration was opposed to the creation of a new agency; in fact, it was tepid, at best, about any proposal for closing the small business capital gap. As Senator Paul Douglas, of Illinois, said, "the Administration said that it supports the bill, then it is against it when it comes to the floor." Senator Sparkman observed that "it was difficult to determine at any particular time just where the Administration stood."

One by one, the main features of the two pending bills were changed, and the legislation began to resemble the administration bill, put forward by Republican Senator Edward Thye, of Minnesota, chairman of the Senate Small Business Committee.

The idea of a separate agency was dropped and gave way to the idea of having a deputy administrator for Investment in the SBA who would be appointed by the President and approved by the Senate. However, this was opposed by the Eisenhower Administration; and the deputy administrator (the title was later changed to associate administrator), eventually came to be appointed by the SBA administrator. He merely took his place alongside the other three deputy administrators, one for Financial Assistance, one for Management Assistance, and one for Procurement Assistance.

The capital bank idea was opposed by the Board of Governors

of the Federal Reserve System, the Treasury, and others; and it was scrapped. Fiscal conservatives, such as Senator A. Willis Robertson, of Virginia, were up in arms about another scheme for "backdoor financing" and, as is customary in such circumstances, trotted out Article I, Section 9 of the Constitution, which provides: "No money shall be drawn from the Treasury, but in Consequence of Appropriations made by law. . . ." Their views prevailed, and anything which smacked of "backdoor financing" was stricken from the legislation.

Stripped of most of the basic provisions of both bills introduced by Lyndon Johnson, and much more in accordance with Senator Thye's bill, the legislation sailed through Congress. It was debated and passed by voice vote by the Senate on June 9, 1958. It went to the House Banking and Currency Committee on June 10 and was reported favorably on June 30. On July 23, it was debated and amended and passed by the House by a vote of 131 to 5. The Senate disagreed with certain House amendments and a conference was agreed to on July 30. The conferees agreed to two major changes in the House-approved legislation: (1) regular appropriations made by Congress were substituted for "backdoor financing" through Treasury borrowing; and (2) federal charters for SBIC's for up to three years were authorized in addition to the state charters provided for by the House.

The conference report was approved by the Senate on August 7 and passed by the House later the same day. The bill was signed by President Eisenhower, and the Small Business Investment Act became law on August 21, 1958.

MAJOR PROVISIONS OF THE ACT

The principal innovations of the Small Business Investment Act of 1958 may be summarized as follows:

Establishment of a Small Business Investment Division of the SBA. As already noted, the new SBA division set up under the act was to be headed by a deputy administrator named by the SBA administrator. Through its Investment Division, the SBA licenses, regulates, and helps finance privately organized and privately operated SBIC's. These, in turn, provide equity capital and long-term loans to small business firms.[2]

Small Business Investment Companies. The act provided for the formation of SBIC's. Under the law, as adopted and amended, an SBIC must be incorporated and have a minimum of three stockholders. The SBA may issue a license to a company that has met the statutory and regulatory requirements.

As the bill was originally enacted, SBIC's were authorized to make long-term loans to small business and to buy convertible debentures from them. The SBA's money comes from a revolving fund. Section 304 of the act states that a primary function of an SBIC was to provide equity capital for small firms through the purchase of convertible debentures from them. At the option of the SBIC, the debentures could be converted into stock of the small business. The value of the stock—so-called sound book value—was to be determined when the debentures were issued.

The SBIC's received a large infusion of capital from the federal government. The act stipulated that an SBIC had to have a paid-in capital and surplus of at least $300,000 before it would be eligible for a license from the SBA. However, the SBA could supply up to half this amount by purchasing subordinated debentures of the nascent SBIC. These subordinated debentures, purchased by the government, were considered part of the "statutory capital" of the SBIC.

Nor was this all the capital injected by the government. Additional loans from the SBA could amount to as much as 50 per cent of the "statutory capital" of the SBIC. Thus, an SBIC could open up for business with as much as two-thirds of its capital provided by the SBA. In the example given, it

[2] A discussion of what is considered "small" for the purposes of carrying out the Small Business Investment Act is found in Chapter II.

could start with $450,000, of which only $150,000 came from private funds. The SBA would have matched the initial $150,000 by buying $150,000 worth of the SBIC's subordinated debentures, and then by making a loan to the SBIC of 50 per cent of the $300,000 of "statutory capital," or another $150,000. Thus, an SBIC could get started with two government dollars for each dollar of its own.

The act sought to broaden the ownership of the SBIC's and eventually to reduce their reliance on government funds. In line with this policy, it provided that a small business receiving capital from an SBIC had to buy stock in the SBIC equal to at least 2 per cent but not over 5 per cent of the amount of capital supplied. The act also allowed SBIC's to make long-term loans to incorporated and unincorporated small businesses. Furthermore, it permitted SBIC's to furnish consulting services for a fee.

The Small Business Investment Act also gave tax advantages to encourage the formation and profitability of the SBIC's. Taxpayers investing in the stock of SBIC's were allowed an ordinary loss deduction rather than a capital loss deduction on losses incurred in the sale or total depreciation of such stock. Similarly, SBIC's were to treat losses on convertible debentures, including losses on stock received when their conversion privilege was exercised, as ordinary losses instead of capital losses. Additionally, SBIC's were allowed to deduct 100 per cent of dividends received from taxable domestic corporations, rather than the 85 per cent deduction allowed corporate taxpayers generally.

THE 1960 AMENDMENTS

The Small Business Investment Act has been amended on several occasions. The original provision stipulating that equity capital could only be provided in the form of convertible debentures proved too restrictive. Both the SBIC's and small business firms stated that it was essential to tailor the instruments of financing to the needs and the situation of the firm. Another objection concerned the requirement that the small businesses receiving SBIC financing purchase stock of the SBIC. This was looked upon by many small businesses as essentially an additional charge for the money received from the SBIC's.

In June, 1960, the act was amended to take care of these and other objections. The law was changed to provide that SBIC's could supply equity capital to small firms, "in such manner and under such terms as the small business investment company may fix in accordance with the Regulations of the Small Business Administration." The 1960 amendments also deleted the requirement that the provision of equity capital be a primary function of the SBIC. The requirement that small firms receiving capital from an SBIC had to buy stock in the SBIC was modified. Henceforth, the firm would not be required to purchase SBIC stock but could do so only if it so desired.

THE 1961 AMENDMENTS

During 1961, the act was amended again. The maximum of $150,000 that SBA could supply to SBIC's to form part of the "statutory capital" was raised to $400,000, provided matching funds were invested in the SBIC from private sources.

The original act had permitted the SBA to make operating loans to SBIC's up to 50 per cent of their "statutory capital." This provision was open ended. The 1961 amendments tightened this provision by limiting the amount of such loans to $4 million or 50 per cent, whichever was less.

Commercial banks had been permitted by the original act to invest in an SBIC an amount not to exceed 1 per cent of the bank's capital and surplus. To encourage bank support of the program further, the amount was upped to 2 per cent of capital and surplus.

The SBA was also given authority to conduct administrative proceedings which could lead to show-cause orders, cease-and-desist orders, and the suspension of SBIC licenses. Revocation of licenses continued to require a federal court proceeding, but the SBA was given additional investigatory authority.

Finally, the provisions relating to the maximum amount that an SBIC might lend to one firm were tightened. In the original act, a limit of 20 per cent of the SBIC's capital could be invested in or lent to a single small business firm. The 1961 amendments went one step further and provided, in addition, for a maximum of $500,000 to be made available to a single small business unless prior SBA approval was obtained.

THE 1963 AMENDMENTS

The 1963 amendments, which actually passed in February, 1964, called for a further increase in the matching funds from $400,000 to $700,000. At the same time, a five-year limit was placed on the availability of this amount. The amendments also removed the $500,000 lending limit to one small business, which had been inserted in the act only two years previously. The amendments also required the SBA to adopt regulations to deal with conflicts of interest.

THE 1966 AMENDMENTS

The 1966 amendments had an entirely different focus and tone. As detailed later in this chapter and in Chapter VIII, they were addressed to well-documented and rather widespread instances of wrongdoing in the SBIC industry and to well-documented evidence of lax administration on the part of the SBA.

In 1966, Congress gave the SBA administrator additional

powers to supervise the SBIC program more effectively. These additional powers included authority to remove or suspend officers and directors and power to revoke SBIC licenses as well as to suspend them. The 1966 amendments also provided for a civil penalty for late filing of reports by SBIC's to the SBA and a criminal penalty for the use of SBIC stock as collateral for loans to purchase stock in an SBIC. The amendments also provided for appropriate administrative proceedings and judicial review by federal courts to assure that the new powers granted to the SBA administrator would not be used in an arbitrary and capricious manner.

THE 1967 AMENDMENTS

The 1967 amendments have been described by SBA Administrator Robert C. Moot as "the most significant alteration of the SBIC program since its inception." Among other changes, the legislation provided for new standards for the licensing of SBIC's, a further increase in the amount of money an SBIC might draw from the SBA, an additional increase (to 5 per cent) in the percentage of the capital and surplus a commercial bank might place in an SBIC, and the establishment of the SBIC Advisory Board. The SBA can now match private funds on a two-for-one basis up to $7.5 million.

THE RECORD TO DATE

Generous allowance must be made for the growing pains of an infant industry. Time has also been needed to shake the kinks out of the SBIC legislation and to build the experience required for effective administration. Nonetheless, even given these factors, the record of the SBIC industry after a decade is far from impressive. Indeed, one could well question whether the whole exercise is worth the effort.

From the inception of the program through March 31, 1967, SBIC's had made 26,751 separate financings, totaling

$1.2 billion. As of that date, the assets of the SBIC's were $672 million, but these were below the total assets of each of the previous two years. It should also be remembered that a large portion of these assets were provided by Uncle Sam. During this period, the SBA took over $184 million of subordinated debentures and lent the SBIC's over $173 million to add to their capital.

Profits have been meager by any yardstick. It was not until the year ending March 31, 1967, that the SBIC industry ever showed an over-all profit. It was extremely modest—$10.7 million was earned after taxes for the 600-odd companies then active in the program. This represented a 2.4 per cent return on invested capital, hardly an attractive return for the investors (yields on many government issues exceed 6 per cent).

Another disappointing aspect of the SBIC performance to date has been the low proportion of equity financing (or a reasonable facsimile thereof) provided by the companies. As of March 31, 1966, for instance, the SBIC's had investments and loans outstanding of $552 million. Of this, $279 million was in long-term loans, $180 million in debt securities, and $93 million in capital stock. Thus, over half the money was used for long-term loans and only 17 per cent was being used for purchases of capital stock.

PROBLEMS OF THE SBIC PROGRAM

The year 1966 was one that saw an intensive investigation into the SBIC program. On July 15, 19, and 29, the Senate Banking and Currency Subcommittee on Small Business, under the chairmanship of Senator William Proxmire, of Wisconsin, held hearings to review the operations of the program. The House Small Business Committee, chaired by Representative Joe L. Evins, of Tennessee, held similar hearings on July 21–22. The really significant hearings were those held on

August 2–4 by the Permanent Subcommittee on Investigations of the Senate Government Operations Committee. Senator Fred R. Harris, of Oklahoma, served as acting chairman of the panel at the request of the chairman, Arkansas' Senator John L. McClellan. These investigations led to the Small Business Investment Act amendments of 1966 and 1967.[3]

Senator Harris and his staff had done their homework. The Investigations Subcommittee went into every aspect of the program with thoroughness and precision. The hearings were held during exceptionally troubled times for the SBIC program. Many of the SBIC's were in serious financial difficulty. Former SBA Deputy Administrator for Investment[4] Richard E. Kelley, who had just resigned after a little more than two years service, had created something of a sensation in the financial press when he stated publicly that 232 of the 700 SBIC's were on the SBA's "problem list" as of April 30, 1966. He referred to certain "dubious practices" in the industry, and he estimated that, because of "the wrong people" who operate SBIC's, the government was likely to lose about $18 million of the $275 million it had invested in the program.

The Congressional hearings were a shocker. Conditions were even worse in actuality than those described by Kelley in his swan song. The hearings were to reveal the failure of the SBA to screen properly the individuals who received government funds, the inadequacy of existing examination and investigation procedures and practices, and widespread instances of conflicts of interest, self-dealing, and outright fraud.

A "crash program" was initiated in July, 1966, by Administrator Bernard L. Boutin. Boutin had been in office for only two months at the time, but much of that period he had spent studying the SBIC morass. The "crash program" was completed by the end of November. It revealed conclusively that

[3] For more on the Congressional investigations of the SBIC industry, see Chapter VIII.

[4] The position is now called associate administrator for Investment.

former Deputy Administrator Kelley's appraisal of the problem was a serious underestimate.

There were 686 licensed SBIC's at the time Boutin launched his investigation. Some 107 had been investigated during the first six months of the year. Another 145 SBIC's were already under investigation or in litigation. As a consequence, these companies were not re-examined.

The SBA examined the remaining 434 SBIC's. No violations were found in only thirty-eight companies. Another ten were dormant; that is, they had been formed but had not been operative. The remaining 386 companies were found to be in violation of the regulations. Some twenty-eight of these had violations that were considered serious enough to require additional review to determine whether a full-scale investigation should be opened. Over 1,300 violations of varying degrees of seriousness were found in the 386 SBIC's.

The potential loss to the government was also carefully assessed. A loss of $50.5 million was estimated, rather than the $18 million figure mentioned by Kelley. Accordingly, the reserve for losses was increased to $54 million in March, 1967. However, the ultimate loss to the government will probably exceed this figure, as many of the loans are for a long term and may yet go sour. In its report of January 31, 1968, the Senate Permanent Subcommittee on Investigations concluded "that a substantial, although undetermined, part of this loss was due to the failure of the SBA to establish and enforce proper procedures to protect U.S. funds."

In its report, the subcommittee made the following recommendations regarding the SBIC program:

1. The subcommittee recommends that the Small Business Administration and the Justice Department make all necessary efforts, including litigation, to recover Government funds in cases where a loss is now anticipated.

2. It is recommended that the SBA's examination and investigation program for the SBICs be maintained at its present

level of activity. Prompt and vigorous action should be taken to intervene when an SBIC is found to be in serious financial trouble in order to prevent any further dissipation of assets.

3. The Administrator of SBA is requested to advise the subcommittee about his views on the effectiveness of the new statute enacted by the 90th Congress, and to indicate whether the "completely new approach" advocated by Bernard Boutin, former Administrator of the SBA, is still considered by the agency to be required to make the SBIC program workable and to avoid further deterioration from an already shaky position.

OUTLOOK FOR THE SBIC PROGRAM

In his testimony of April 12, 1967, before the Senate Permanent Subcommittee on Investigations, Administrator Boutin made the following statement about the future prospects of the SBIC program:

> From my experience of the past 11 months, I am convinced that a new approach is necessary if the SBIC program is to meet its potential in supplying needed equity and long-term financing to the small businessmen of this country. I have, therefore, developed a program to help accomplish this which we are currently discussing with the Bureau of the Budget and interested agencies. Briefly, this program proposes in part:
>
> (a) Raising the minimum capital requirements for SBICs; both for those remaining in the program and new licensees;
>
> (b) Combining section 302 and section 303 to provide a single investment vehicle with more adequate dollar limitation and a stable maturity;
>
> (c) Raising the percentage which banks may invest in SBICs to stimulate their participation in the program, since our experience reveals that bank-affiliated SBICs are among our more successful companies;[5] and
>
> (d) Increasing the leverage for those companies which concentrate in equity financings.

[5] For a thorough study of this subject, see the book by S. J. Flink listed in the bibliography.

It is my honest conviction that the SBICs represent a necessary and valuable tool to assist small business. However, I also believe that the experience of the past 9 years has proven that the industry cannot survive as presently constituted. Without the minimum reforms which we plan to propose to the Congress, the industry, in my opinion, will deteriorate further from its present shaky position. The support of Congress is needed to make the SBIC program a strong, properly constituted vehicle for filling the small business equity and long-term financing needs.

The proposals that Administrator Boutin developed were adopted in the main by Congress in the 1967 amendments. Like most proposals in the past for strengthening the SBIC industry, they amounted in effect to a further subsidization of it, either in the form of tax concessions—usually called "tax incentives" by publicists—or in the form of larger infusions of government money.

It is likely that the SBIC's will become larger and larger. The SBA has advocated that the minimum capital of an SBIC be $1 million. According to a special study, it was found that the majority of SBIC's with less capitalization were unlikely to be profitable operations. SBIC's were broken down in the study into four size categories—those with statutory capital and surplus of not more than $325,000, those from $325,000 to $1 million, $1 million to $5 million, and $5 million and above. The rate of return on invested capital of companies in these size categories in 1966 was, respectively, a loss of 2.3 per cent, a profit of 0.3 per cent, a profit of 4.4 per cent, and a profit of 3.3 per cent. Analysis of the upper quartile of the companies in each category showed these rates of return: 8.3 per cent, 9 per cent, 14.4 per cent, and 9.2 per cent.

A study of the eighty-eight largest SBIC's was also made. Sixty-nine of these SBIC's had statutory capital of from $1 to $5 million; the remaining nineteen had capitalization of $5 million and above. Although they amounted to only 13 per cent of the companies by number, they had earned 64 per cent of the total net income from operations and had made 60 per cent of all the dollar financings made by the SBIC industry. The study further revealed that while these eighty-eight companies had about 72 per cent of the total private capital in the program, they had received only about 34 per cent of the government funds. This was a result for the most part of the legal upward limit on the two-for-one formula; the large SBIC's could not get two government dollars for each private dollar, as the small SBIC's could.

It is also likely that the average size of SBIC equity financing and loans to small business will also become larger and larger simply because larger financings are more profitable. And the larger loans are given to firms somewhat larger than "the little fellow," whose needs are more modest.

It is undeniable that SBIC's can be made profitable, given the proper mix of government subsidy and encouragement of larger and larger SBIC's and larger and larger outlays by SBIC's. We shall then have large SBIC's making long-term loans and providing equity financing for what are in effect medium-sized firms. The little fellow will be lost in the shuffle again simply because there is not much money to be made out of him.

VIII

Relations with Congress

The SBA has always been a creature of the Congress. Members of Congress have throughout the agency's history been its strongest supporters. The activities of the SBA—potentially on behalf of 4.8 million citizens—are of great interest to most legislators. Accordingly, they have exercised close surveillance over the agency's operations. And similarly, SBA officials have always had their ears closely attuned to any rumbles from Capitol Hill.

From its beginnings, the SBA has had an Office of Congressional Relations; however, the number, variety, and—occasionally—importance of Congressional inquiries has meant that a very large proportion of its professional employees, including the administrator, must be concerned almost daily with some aspect of Congressional relations.

Individual members of Congress deal directly with the SBA in efforts to assist their constituents. The SBA receives hundreds of letters each month from congressmen and senators calling attention to the cases of businessmen back home seeking a loan, an SBIC license, a job at the agency, or any number of other benefits.

Take the matter of size standards. A few days before the SBA Size Appeals Board hears a case, each of its members gets many telephone calls daily from Capitol Hill. Some call-ers seek to have an individual business declared small; others, to have a constituent's competitor declared not small. Anyone who has an opportunity to influence decisions within the SBA is subject to similar pressures.

There is nothing irregular about this practice. An elected representative, after all, is just what his title says—a spokesman for the people of his district. As the veteran Congressman Emanuel Celler put it in the title to his autobiography, "you never leave Brooklyn." Intervention by congressmen in matters like SBA size standards cases also often serves to provide useful factual information to officials who make the final decisions. Taken together, requests for help from congressmen are important in terms of time spent, administrative and investigative tools and skills required, real aid rendered or denied, and good or bad feelings established.

COMMITTEES: HOW CONGRESS DEALS WITH THE SBA

The committees and subcommittees that matter most to the SBA fall into four groupings: those subcommittees of the Banking and Currency committees in both the Senate and the House that are concerned with small business and to which the SBA is substantively responsible; the subcommittees of the Appropriations committees of both houses, to which the SBA is financially responsible; the Government Operations committees, to which it is administratively responsible; and the two Select Small Business committees, to which it is perhaps emotionally responsible.

Banking and Currency Committees. Although the Banking and Currency committees are concerned with a plethora of other and apparently more significant matters, they are active in the small business area. To the SBA, their importance lies in their power to write the laws upon which most small business programs are based.

In the Senate, the Banking and Currency Committee has a

Small Business Subcommittee. In the House, the subcommittees of Banking and Currency are numbered rather than having formal names.

Yet small business is by no means neglected in the House. Indeed, Congressman Wright Patman, chairman of the full House committee, has long been a strong proponent of antitrust measures and opponent of high interest rates by lending institutions. As such, he has been a friend of the small businessman. Patman was active in promoting the establishment of the Small Defense Plants Administration and the SBA. Under this strong, though controversial, chairman, the House committee has generally treated the SBA well.

On the Senate side, the committee has been more conventional and somewhat more conservative. However, most requests for new SBA authority have been approved there. Senator William Proxmire, of Wisconsin, served for some time as chairman of the Subcommittee on Small Business. Another Congressional maverick, Proxmire is author of *Can Small Business Survive?* (1964), a question which he answers in the affirmative. The interests of the SBA—or, at least, Proxmire's conception of the interests of the small businessman—received a boost in 1967 when Proxmire became chairman of the Congressional Joint Economic Committee. There was hope that Proxmire would remember small business in his leadership of Congressional deliberation on broad economic policy.

Appropriations Committees. At least equally important to the SBA are the two appropriations subcommittees to which it is responsible. Generally, House appropriations subcommittees review the expenditures of executive agencies more extensively than do their Senate counterparts. The SBA has had no exceptional treatment. The chairman of the SBA's subcommittee is the legendary Congressman John J. Rooney, of New York. A State Department official who also had to appear regularly before Rooney's subcommittee has been quoted as saying: "Let's face it. When Rooney whistles, we've just got to dance."

Every year Rooney and the members of his subcommittee painstakingly scrutinize lengthy SBA statements describing program operations and costs. The SBA administrator and his top staff are then questioned at some length by the subcommittee, with Rooney asking nearly all the questions. Although he has been consistently tough with the SBA—as with the other agencies under his jurisdiction—Rooney has been reasonable. If he considers the SBA justification of its undertakings a careful, thoughtful, and responsible statement, the budget proposal passes through his committee relatively unscathed. A phenomenally hardworking man, Rooney regards himself as a trustee of the taxpayer's money. He has been determined in reviewing agency appropriations requests to justify every penny spent.

Once a budget measure has been approved by the Rooney panel and the House, the rest is easier. The Senate Appropriations Committee is widely known as less tight-fisted than its House counterpart. According to folklore, the Senate appropriations panel always restores the budget cuts, at least in part, made by the House unit. To a considerable extent, that has been the SBA's experience. Still, with such noteworthy investigators as Senator John L. McClellan, of Arkansas, acting as chairman of its Senate appropriations subcommittee, the SBA can hardly expect to breeze through the upper chamber.

Government Operations Committees. McClellan has also simultaneously served as chairman of the Senate Government Operations Committee, which, along with the parallel House group has jurisdiction over the SBA. These two committees have a broad mandate to follow the administrative activities of all executive agencies. They have the power to consider legislation, much of which deals with organizational matters affecting the various agencies. In addition, the Government

Operations committees have the power to conduct investigations of specific programs and practices to determine whether an agency is conforming to Congressional intent in its programs and to common sense and conventional ethics, as well.

Although the Government Operations committees are not considered a prize assignment and are far less glamorous than policy-oriented committees, occasionally Government Operations probes catch the public eye. For example, Senator Joseph R. McCarthy, of Wisconsin, used the panel's Permanent Subcommittee on Investigations as a forum for his charges during the 1950's of Communist penetration into the federal establishment. Somewhat less sensationally, Senator McClellan has used the same subcommittee as a vehicle for investigating crime. It was in this series of hearings that Jimmy Hoffa, president of the Teamsters' Union, came to national attention. And it was also this subcommittee that was assigned to probe summer racial riots in 1967.

Nonetheless, investigations of the SBA's operations by the Government Operations committees have been relatively rare. In 1966, however, there was a notable exception. The Senate Government Operations Committee launched an inquiry into the workings of the SBA's controversial SBIC program. The investigation will be described more fully later in this chapter. Despite this hearing, which generated considerable publicity, it is accurate to say that the Government Operations committees have generally been less concerned with the SBA than the other major Congressional units that are responsible for the agency's activities.

The Small Business Committees. Both the House and the Senate select committees on small business have probably been the most involved with the SBA over the years. As select committees, they lack the power to consider bills and recommend them. Their mandate is to inquire into the problems of American small business and to bring their general conclusions to the attention of Congress, the executive, and the public.

These two committees consider themselves spokesmen for the small businessman on Capitol Hill. Their investigations on behalf of what they consider to be small business interests have considerable influence. It will be recalled that the Small Business committees in both chambers were very active in the movement to create the SBA and its predecessor agencies. Although the committees lack the power to affect SBA activities from a legal standpoint, they do have and exercise the power to discuss and criticize SBA operations.

The Senate committee, particularly, has followed the agency very closely. Its long-time chairman Senator John J. Sparkman is widely considered to be very knowledgeable about small business. When Sparkman left his position as chairman of the committee, in 1967, in order to become chairman of the Banking and Currency Committee, he was succeeded by Senator George A. Smathers, of Florida. Evidently anxious to live up to Sparkman's lofty stature, Smathers undertook a lengthy series of hearings involving numerous high government officials from various agencies, noted scholars, and businessmen, all discussing the role and problems of American small business.

The House Small Business Committee has in recent years been somewhat less active than its Senate counterpart; but it has performed much the same role. It has held extensive hearings on various government policy and program matters affecting small business. Frequently its members have attempted to intercede in government agencies and elsewhere on behalf of individual small businessmen whose dilemmas have been brought to their attention. The SBA has been the prime but not the sole focus of their efforts.

For example, the House committee, in 1966, was largely responsible for the issuance of a permit to ship goods in interstate commerce to the owner of a small Atlanta trucking firm. The Interstate Commerce Commission had at first refused to grant the permit to one Joe Jones, a Negro entrepreneur. In the meantime, Jones had received an Economic Opportunity

Loan—whose purpose was the expansion of his business into the interstate market—from the SBA. After several months of effort by the House committee, the Interstate Commerce Commission finally saw the issue their way and gave Jones his permit.

In the broadest sense, the two Small Business committees have served primarily as advocates of the small business sector, of specific small firms, and of government programs to assist small business. Accordingly, more frequently than not the committees have been allies of the SBA. Members of the committees have acted as friends of small business and—usually— of the SBA when they served on other committees. This kind of leverage has helped boost the SBA's strength.

Many examples may be cited. Congressman Patman and Senator Sparkman both left their respective Small Business chairmanships to move up to the top jobs on the Banking and Currency committees. Both Senators Leverett Saltonstall, of Massachusetts, and Jacob K. Javits, of New York, have served as ranking Republicans on the Small Business Committee while also as members of the Appropriations Committee. Still more usefully, Javits was a member of the SBA's Appropriations subcommittee and Senator McClellan's investigations unit. Senator Proxmire's chairmanship of the Joint Economic Committee has already been mentioned. In addition, he has served as chairman of the Banking and Currency small business subcommittee and a member of the Appropriations Committee. Congressman Joe L. Evins, of Tennessee, was a member of the House Appropriations Committee during his tenure as chairman of the House Small Business Committee.

Another notable champion of small business who served for a time on the Senate Small Business Committee was the former pharmacist, Hubert H. Humphrey. Even after becoming Vice-President, Humphrey's interest in the small businessman and the SBA continued. This was particularly true during 1963– 65 when one of Humphrey's protégés, Eugene P. Foley, served as SBA administrator. Strategic positions such as these have been very useful to the SBA when these legislators have supported the agency's actions.

Occasionally, however, dissatisfaction has arisen within the Small Business committees over the SBA's handling of a particular matter. Disagreements have stemmed from personal confrontations, the state of a program in a particular Congressional district, genuine policy differences, or even the agency's failure to consult a committee or key members in making some decision. In early 1964, for example, the SBA scuttled a research contract of nearly $150,000 after members of the Senate Small Business Committee raised questions about it. The senators had not been informed of the contract negotiations before it was awarded. Such disputes, however, have been relatively rare.

In the main, the Small Business committees have been a weathervane by which the SBA has tested the climate of "the small business community." The SBA has often acted as though these two committees are truly representative of their common clientele.

Other Committees. In addition to these principal committees in each house of Congress, the SBA also has dealings from time to time with other legislative panels.

In its program authorized under the 1964 Economic Opportunity Act, the SBA went to the House Education and Labor and Senate Labor and Public Welfare committees. These two panels dealt with all agencies involved in the poverty program. Again, hearings were held, in 1964, by the Senate Commerce Committee on the possible effects of cutbacks in defense spending. The SBA administrator testified before that committee about the impact such a move might have on small business defense contractors and subcontractors.

SBA officials also attend hearings of the Joint Economic Committee in order to monitor its activities. This enables the agency to get some perspective on the place of small business in the economy as a whole. And many hearings held by the subcommittees on Antitrust and Monopoly of the Judiciary committees have considerable relevance to small business problems.

Tax matters affecting small business come up in the House Ways and Means and Senate Finance committees. And many bills with important implications for procurement policies in which numerous small firms are interested are handled by the Armed Services committees.

So it goes. Although the SBA deals most closely with less than a handful of committees in each chamber, it must keep abreast of, and occasionally even involved in, the operations of other panels as well.

How the SBA Deals with Congress

The committees of Congress are set up on a functional basis so as to deal with various government policies and programs effectively. Similarly, government agencies like the SBA are divided into staff and line units responsible for specific programs and problems. As previously described, the divisions of the SBA appear to be neat and tidy, with clear-cut jurisdictions and duties. In fact, quite the opposite is the case. The structure of the SBA's relations with Capitol Hill illustrates this fact.

SBA Washington Headquarters. We have already seen that there is within the SBA an Office of Congressional Relations, which is under the general supervision of the assistant administrator for Congressional and public affairs. It would seem simple enough to channel all questions raised by members of Congress through this central office. Simple, perhaps, in theory; but impossible in practice.

For one thing, the sheer volume of Congressional inquiries would overwhelm any modestly staffed office; and the SBA office in charge of Congressional liaison has been modestly staffed, with only a handful of professionals and their secretaries.

Upon reflection, moreover, it is unreasonable to expect any one office to be technically capable of handling every sort of Congressional demand. There are requests for economic data, speeches to be written for the administrator's testimony, inquiries about various SBA programs, inquiries about particular loan applications or small business "set-asides," and so on. Some Congressional relations matters are of considerable political importance, requiring personal attention by the administrator; others are of a more routine or at least nonpartisan nature.

For these reasons, the SBA Office for Congressional Relations performs only a minute fragment of the Congressional liaison work. The principal job of the office is to keep tabs on what is happening on Capitol Hill. The Congressional liaison staff spends most of its time chatting with members of Congress and their staffs in order to learn what individual legislators and various committees are doing that is of interest to the SBA. They attempt to accommodate the Congressmen as much as possible while guarding the agency's interests. Their basic task is to assure good relations between the SBA and the legislature. As a result, they act primarily as brokers.

Since many dealings with Congress fall outside the jurisdiction of the Congressional relations office, most SBA administrators try to maintain a checkrein over the dealings of SBA employees with members of Congress and their staffs.

How can the administrator keep close watch over the relations of SBA employees with Congress? Various systems have been tried, and a general routine has been established. Nearly all official contacts with the legislature eventually come to the SBA in the form of a letter. To be sure, there may be unofficial face-to-face or telephone conversations over a given matter, but the very nature of administration eventually requires some sort of written record.

In recent years, all the official mail received by the SBA has been channeled through a central office now called the Office of Public Inquiry and Analysis. This unit sorts the correspondence and routes it to the appropriate SBA office for action. For Congressional letters, the Office of Congressional Relations is generally consulted, but does not usually provide the substantive reply. Mail for members of Congress is customarily referred to either one of the associate administrators or to a top staff official, such as the general counsel. The reply, including supporting material such as testimony for a Congressional hearing or comments on proposed legislation, is prepared by a member of his staff. He then approves the letter and either signs it himself or sends it to the administrator for his signature. The Office of Congressional Relations automatically receives a carbon copy of all material sent to Capitol Hill.

Thus, the Office of Congressional Relations is not responsible for all dealings with Congress—or, indeed, even most of them. Rather, there are many individual relationships which grow up between the Capitol and various SBA offices. The Congressional liaison staff primarily expedites the handling of Congressional requests, gathers information about Congressional interest in SBA activities, and tests Congressional support for pending measures.

Substantive material requested by Congress is prepared by various program officers and other experts and approved by the top staff officials, who are personally responsible to the administrator. For instance, the Office of General Counsel prepares most of the legislation submitted by the SBA and comments on bills originating elsewhere for which the SBA's opinion is sought. The Office of Public Affairs is responsible for drafting much of the testimony made by the administrator at Congressional hearings, although specific material about SBA programs is generally prepared by the agency's line offices. The Office of Budget draws together much of the data for the annual presentations to the Appropriations committees. Offices under the assistant administrator for Planning, Research, and Analysis are responsible for providing necessary economic data. The administrator's special assistant for Equal Employment Opportunity is custodian of information in that realm.

SBA Field Offices. Congressional relations is not solely the responsibility of SBA's Washington staff. The agency has regional and branch offices throughout the country. It is far from uncommon for a member of Congress who seeks something from the SBA—particularly those who seek something for an individual constituent, most often an SBA loan—to express his interest at the local level to SBA officials in his constituency.

Loan approval is the responsibility of local SBA offices; the Washington headquarters has sought for some years to remove itself from such operations and deal primarily with broader matters. Thus, if a congressman wants to put in a good word for a project being considered for his district, he is better advised to do so with a regional director rather than with a Washington official. For one thing, the regional director is much better known to the Congressman. Sometimes he is a close friend.

However, Congressional intervention on the local level is restricted primarily to the representative function of a senator or congressman as spokesman for his constituents. In his role as a policy-maker, he deals directly with the policy level of the Washington operation.

Red Tape and Snafus. Because of the complexity of the SBA's Congressional relations, the formal procedures—as in the words of Robert Burns—"gang aft a-gley." Occasionally, more than one SBA officer is charged with responsibility for a single project; and sometimes the coordination between various SBA men is less than perfect.

A notable example concerned the opening of a Small Business Development Center in Atlanta, Georgia, in 1965. An SBA assistant deputy administrator was assigned to handle a Congressional hearing in Atlanta where the project was to be unveiled. He arranged to have the congressman who represented the district question the SBA administrator, who would announce the project and thank the congressman for his help on it. Shortly before the hearing was to take place, however, the SBA administrator decided that the chief Congressional liaison man should be handling the hearing arrangements. A snarl ensued. Ultimately, the question about the project was first raised at the Atlanta hearing by a congressman from Rochester, New York. He made his query not of the SBA administrator but of an official of the Office of Economic Opportunity, which was funding the project. Both the SBA chief and the Atlanta congressman were red-faced from anger and embarrassment.

A more frequent sort of problem arises when a member of Congress makes a deliberate attempt to deal simultaneously with more than one office at the SBA on a single matter. It is generally to the advantage of congressmen and senators to open up as many points of access to an agency as possible. For instance, if a congressman cannot extract information he wants through official requests to the SBA, he may appeal to others at the agency who will supply the information. Sometimes they may not realize that the congressman is not supposed to know, and sometimes they may want to foil an administrator's attempt to keep the information confidential. Congressional dealings such as these tend to work a hardship on the SBA, sometimes by causing its personnel to duplicate their efforts and sometimes by making its leadership appear foolish.

Another factor that serves to blur the lines of the SBA organization is the frequency of informal contacts between officials and members of Congress and their staffs. It is only natural that such relationships develop. Indeed, there is some exchange of personnel between small business circles on Capitol Hill and in the executive branch.

In general, top officials at the SBA seek to keep dealings with Congress within official channels, where they can control them better. They do not want, for example, a disaffected employee to tell his troubles to his old friends at the Capitol. Such situations are highly embarrassing to top administrators, whatever the agency. As a result, internal memoranda are periodically circulated requesting that dealings with Congress be officially reported or cleared. Some more fastidious SBA personnel prefer to check with the Office of Congressional Relations before having official dealings with Congressional employees. Others consider such caution excessive.

CONGRESS MAKES A LAW

Within this general setting of relationships between the SBA and Congress, two important kinds of activities take place: legislation and Congressional supervision of administration. Legislation takes two general forms: bills affecting SBA programs and appropriations bills. The process for both is the same except that appropriations bills are always considered first in the House, whereas other legislation affecting the SBA may originate in either chamber. Money bills go to the Appropriations committees and other measures to different committees, generally Banking and Currency.

The bill establishing the SBA's EOL program, first proposed to the House Education and Labor Committee and the Senate Labor and Public Welfare Committee as part of the poverty program, illustrates how the SBA works with Congress.

In August, 1963, Eugene P. Foley became the new SBA administrator. One of his first acts was to ask his top staff members for ideas about how SBA programs might be improved. One suggestion, made by the economic adviser, was that a program be established to provide equity-type financing to small firms, particularly sole proprietorships. Many applicants, the adviser contended, had been refused SBA loans because they lacked capital and collateral and could not "reasonably assure repayment," as required by the Small Business Act.

Asked to comment on the economic adviser's proposal, the head of the SBA's Financial Assistance Division said that "few qualified applicants" had been turned away for such reasons. He added that he did not think the SBA should provide equity money to small businessmen. In his comments, the SBA's general counsel expressed some concern over whether the proposal was legal in view of the requirement of reasonable assurance of repayment. The administrator, however, liked the idea. It fit with his policy persuasion and with another idea proposed by sources outside the SBA.

After several years' planning, a project was about to be launched in Philadelphia aimed at assimilating minority groups into the middle class. An organization called the Philadelphia Small Business Opportunities Corporation was established to provide credit for business establishment or expansion, generally unavailable to Negroes and other minority group members, and also management instruction necessary for successful enterprise. The pilot project was sponsored jointly by local Philadelphia groups, the federal Area Redevelopment Administration, and the President's Commission on Equal Employment Opportunity.

The SBA administrator, a strong civil rights advocate, saw to it that SBA management and financial assistance were available at the center when it opened its doors in January, 1964. The loans came in a new SBA program called the 6 x 6, which offered up to $6,000 for a six-year period. The response was enormous; in following months centers were also set up in Harlem and Washington. Dozens of beauty parlor operators, dry cleaners, dressmakers, and other firms received 6 x 6 loans. The program got widespread publicity.

This liberalized loan program might have remained a matter of small short-term loans within the SBA's independent province; but at about this time, President Johnson was planning a broader program to aid those on the lower levels of the economy. Previously President Kennedy had told Walter Heller, chairman of his Council of Economic Advisers, to develop plans for a major attack on poverty. President Johnson adopted the idea, giving the War on Poverty highest priority in the program he presented to Congress in January, 1964. A task force of key government officials, headed by Peace Corps Director R. Sargent Shriver, was formally established February 1. On February 12, the President underscored the importance of the proposed program by asking Shriver to sit with the cabinet henceforth. Six days later Shriver was sworn in as a Presidential special assistant. Throughout the month, leading economists, sociologists, and other policy advisers from outside the government met with Shriver and his aides.

The SBA was directly involved in these activities. Its deputy general counsel was chosen by the administrator to meet with the legislative drafting team of the poverty task force. The poverty drafting team was headed by an assistant attorney general in charge of the Justice Department's office of Legal Counsel. Lawyers from a number of relevant agencies, plus a Budget Bureau official, were included in the group. The SBA deputy general counsel set to work with the general counsel of the Area Redevelopment Administration to draft what was designated as Title IV of the proposed legislation. Part A of the title would have established a program of twenty-five-year loans to private borrowers for purposes of stimulating employment; it was to be administered by the Area Redevelopment Administration. Part B called for a program of character loans to small businessmen who would create jobs by starting or expanding a firm; it was to be administered by the SBA.

Various SBA officials, at their own initiative or that of the administrator, were working on aspects of the poverty program. The administrator sent a memorandum to Sargent Shriver describing the SBA's success in the Philadelphia 6 x 6 program. The Labor Department expressed interest in some sort of SBA program to hire the long-term unemployed; the administrator arranged to have an SBA economist work with them to study the problem. The assistant administrator for Administration was requested to estimate the cost of SBA's loan-guarantee program. The general counsel was asked for an advisory opinion about whether the SBA had legal authority to make unsecured business loans; he replied that it did, so long as there was reasonable assurance of repayment. The special assistant for minority groups, who was already working on the Philadelphia project, was brought into the informal group advising the administrator on poverty legislation.

Several issues arose in drafting the bill. How was the program to be new? With the 6 x 6 innovation, why was additional legislation necessary?

The SBA deputy general counsel wanted something different —either a longer term for repayment or more money available. After considerable thought, the administrator decided to increase the maximum term of loans from ten to fifteen years. He firmly kept the loan limit down, however, setting the ceiling at $15,000. The SBA's statutory authority on loans went to $350,000; in this program, however, the administrator wanted to keep the loan amount small, like the 6 x 6. He referred to the latter program privately as "rinky-dink" loans for very small businesses.

Several specifications of the poverty measure were new. Financial assistance under Title IV was limited to cases in which no other aid was available from private or public sources, including other SBA loan programs. In addition to the extended term of the loan, it was liberalized in several other ways. The SBA was authorized to guarantee up to 100 per cent, as opposed to the existing 90 per cent, of both direct and bank participation loans. More importantly, no collateral

was required of the borrower. Certain other requirements, relating to over-all policy objectives, were stiffened. Thus, management training might be made a precondition of the loan
if the prospective applicant lacked managerial skills. Moreover, no loan would be approved unless its purpose was consistent with an over-all economic development program—
which in most cases would be the Community Action program
under Title II of the bill.

With these specifications, the Title IV draft legislation was
submitted to the Budget Bureau for clearance as a part of the
omnibus bill. The Bureau's Legislative Reference Division
reviewed the draft and referred it, with corrections, to the
relevant agencies for their clearance. No significant changes
were made. The measure was ready to go to Capitol Hill.

The President's message on poverty, calling for "total vic-
tory" in the poverty war, was sent to Congress March 16.
Hearings began in the House the following day. They were
held by the War on Poverty Program Subcommittee of the
House Education and Labor Committee and chaired by the
full committee chairman, Adam C. Powell, of New York.
Under consideration was the poverty bill introduced on March
17 by Representative Phil Landrum, of Georgia, at the President's request. An identical bill, had been introduced in the
Senate on the same day by Senator Patrick V. McNamara, of
Michigan.

Little attention was paid to the SBA-sponsored measure in
the House hearings. Various administration witnesses mentioned Title IV in passing, including it in a general endorse-
ment of the bill. The SBA administrator's testimony came
April 8. He told the subcommittee that most of the SBA's
Title IV activity would probably go to very small clients who
employed three or fewer persons and needed both financial
and managerial aid. He said that commercial banks and the
SBA as well had been traditionally conservative in their lending policies, and that the pending proposal would liberalize

that policy to some extent. Then, taking up the matter of race, about which there had been some discussion at the previous day's hearing, SBA Administrator Foley said, "I want to add right here that this program will not be limited to Negroes, but I would be less than frank or candid if I did not suggest that the greatest opportunity and the greatest need exists in the Negro community."

Foley then cited the Philadelphia experience, describing that pilot project as a prototype of the small business component of a Community Action Program. He explained that Title IV (B) had been incorporated in the bill in order to obtain a specific legislative mandate for lending up to $15,000 for up to fifteen years under the newly liberalized credit criteria. There was no significant discussion of his statement by the subcommittee.

There was, indeed, little further discussion of Title IV during the rest of the House hearings. The measure was supported in the course of general endorsements of the legislation by the AFL-CIO, the United Auto Workers, several governors and mayors, and spokesmen for various minor groups.

Curiously enough, the only major objection to Title IV voiced at the House hearings came from the business community. Carl H. Madden, speaking for the U.S. Chamber of Commerce, opposed the bill as a whole. He termed it federal intrusion into a rightfully local sphere and a duplication of existing federal programs. Of Title IV, Madden said:

A primary objective of Title IV is to provide a new mechanism for the continuation and expansion of the ARA [Area Redevelopment Administration] and APW [Accelerated Public Works] subsidy programs.

The failure of those programs to achieve their job-creating objectives; the boondoggling that has accompanied their administration; the refusal of Congress to approve an ARA extension bill; the stated desire of President Johnson to "phase out" the APW program; and the pledge in Title I of the tax bill to forego pump-priming programs as a means of stimulating the economy, are just five of many reasons why Title IV should not be enacted.

This kind of business community hostility to the poverty program generally was by no means unexpected.

Sargent Shriver and his aides gave their final testimony April 28, and a meeting to begin voting was scheduled for May 1. Republican committee members protested at what they called undue haste. Republican Representative Peter Frelinghuysen, of New Jersey, introduced a substitute for the administration bill which would have given general supervision of the program to the Secretary of Health, Education, and Welfare. Among other modifications, the Frelinghuysen Bill had no provisions resembling Title IV.

House committee Democrats held a series of private caucuses to iron out disagreements. This meant postponement of any full committee meetings on the bill. Protesting Republicans picketed outside the caucus room door and carried a sign that read, "Open the door, Adam." The House committee finally met as a whole and, on a straight party-line vote, approved an amended bill on May 26. The changes were substantial. A clean bill, which incorporated the committee amendments, was favorably reported on June 3.

By this time, a stormy climate of opposition threatened the Economic Opportunity Act. Republicans on the Education and Labor Committee had written a sharply critical minority report on the bill. The House Republican Policy Committee came out against the administration measure. Meanwhile, Southern Democrats were concerned that the poverty bill would serve as a kind of economic buttress to the civil rights bill passed by the House in February and still being debated by the Senate.

On June 17, the Senate began its hearings. No major issues were brought forth that had not been aired at the House sessions. The SBA administrator did not testify before the Senate panel, submitting instead a printed statement setting forth the agency position. Most references to Title IV during the Senate hearings were routine. The White House wanted to finish Senate deliberation quickly. It was presumed that the Senate would pass the bill, thus encouraging the House to do likewise. There was also a desire to accomplish as much as possible before Congress recessed for the Republican National Convention, scheduled to begin July 13 with platform committee meetings during the preceding week.

The bill was marked up by the Senate committee, and among the numerous changes were the striking of Part A of Title IV, which the House had also deleted, and the increase in Part B of the SBA loan ceiling from $15,000 to $25,000, in the belief that a larger loan would have more impact. On July 2, the bill was ordered to be reported favorably by a 13 to 2 vote, with Republicans John Tower, of Texas, and Barry Goldwater, of Arizona, dissenting.

The struggle on the Senate floor was waged between stalwart administration Democrats and party-loyalist Republicans. Swing votes lay with the moderate elements among Southern Democrats and Republicans. The Senate committee bill, as amended, passed 61 to 34 on July 23. There was no attempt to amend Title IV on the floor, although various other provisions were changed. Senator Hubert Humphrey did, however, deliver a speech justifying Title IV in some detail.

Faced with Senate passage of a poverty bill, the House Rules Committee, on July 28, voted on the measure. By an 8 to 7 margin it approved the proposal. After three days of highly partisan debate, the House passed the Senate bill on August 8 with minor amendments. The Senate amendment raising Title IV loans to a maximum of $25,000 was maintained. On August 11, the Senate approved the Economic Opportunity Act by a voice vote, and the SBA, among many agencies, had a new program when the President signed the bill twelve days later.

CONGRESSIONAL OVERSIGHT: SBIC'S

In addition to representing its constituents in their dealings with agencies and considering legislation dealing with agency programs, Congress is responsible for supervising agency operations. Each of the committees with jurisdiction over the SBA carries on this function to a certain extent. The Banking and Currency committees check on the operation of existing programs before giving the SBA new authority. The Appropriations committees scrutinize the uses of funds already allocated before giving more. The Small Business committees carry on a kind of general-purpose, continuing surveillance.

Perhaps the most important committees from the standpoint of investigations, however, are the two Government Operations committees. They have not often investigated the SBA, but in 1966 the Senate Government Operations panel held hearings inquiring into the SBIC program. Some of the results sounded faint echoes of the SBA's precursor agency, the RFC.

It will be remembered that the SBIC program is the newest SBA major division; the Small Business Investment Act was passed in 1958. Its statement of purpose says:

> It is declared to be the policy of the Congress and the purpose of this Act to improve and stimulate the national economy in general and the small-business segment thereof in particular by establishing a program to stimulate and supplement the flow of private equity capital and long-term loan funds which small-business concerns need for the sound financing of their business operations and for their growth, expansion, and modernization, and which are not available in adequate supply.

Under the act, the Small Business Investment Division of SBA is established and authorized to license SBIC's, which are incorporated bodies organized and chartered under state law. Each SBIC has a paid-in capital and surplus of $300,000 or more, and the SBA may purchase an SBIC's debentures in an amount equal to the paid-in capital and surplus or $700,000, whichever is less. The SBA may also lend money, by itself or in cooperation with commercial lending institutions, to individual SBIC's. The agency has various powers under the act to police the operations of SBIC's in order to prevent wrongdoing.

The idea behind the SBIC program was to fill an "equity gap" that existed in the small business community, preventing many existing and prospective entrepreneurs from moving their projects forward. This belief was held by some knowledgeable people at least as far back as the time of the establishment of the SBA in 1953. The idea, however, was controversial: How far should a government agency go in helping prospective small business investors? Senator Sparkman, chairman of the Senate Small Business Committee and a power as well in the Banking and Currency Committee, sponsored the SBIC legislation as a means to fill the equity gap. The bill also provided for longer-term loans than the SBA was empowered to offer in financial assistance under the Small Business Act, which was then its only lending authority.

Over the next few years the program was organized and swung into action. The more conservative policymakers and observers close to SBA affairs thought the agency had no business providing equity capital to small firms. They deemed this function the fundamental responsibility of the entrepreneur himself. Nor did conservatives favor long-term SBA loans, which they considered "soft," or risky. In short, these conservatives—and there were a fair number, even within the SBA itself—considered SBIC's a questionable investment for a government agency.

Many people of a more liberal persuasion—that is, those who favored the SBA's taking greater risks in its investments

—had different criticisms of the SBIC program. Many believed it was too slow in getting under way. A number from the SBIC industry itself complained of delays and red tape in their dealings with the SBA. Still more ominously, quite a few informed persons—inside and outside the SBA, conservatives and liberals alike—began to be concerned over the years about possible improprieties in the workings of the SBIC's.

Slowly Congressional concern grew. In 1959, not long after passage of the Small Business Investment Act, preliminary hearings on the SBIC program were held by the House Small Business Committee. It was too soon, however, for much more than an early interim report to Congress by the SBA and the first SBIC's that had been licensed.

In 1964, the House Small Business Committee again held hearings on the program, the first such sessions of any consequence. The SBA administrator and many spokesmen for individual SBIC's testified at the 1964 hearings. Despite citation of a lengthy *Wall Street Journal* article about conflict of interest problems in the SBIC program, most of the discussion centered upon more technical and less juicy aspects of the program's operations.

For example, an SBIC president, Lee Davis, listed numerous problems of the SBIC's. These included inadequate public understanding and public relations, uncertainty on the part of the SBIC industry about federal rules and regulations, dual regulations and supervision of the industry, excessive attention to the stock market rather than portfolio investments by brokers and directors, overemphasis by some SBIC's on selling securities to the public rather than concern with aid to small business, inadequate capital for SBIC's, and investment in companies that after subsequent merger or acquisition fall above SBA size standards.

Asked specifically about self-dealing in SBIC's, the irregular practice by which an SBIC gives a loan to a company in which an SBIC director has a substantial interest, SBA Deputy Administrator for Investment Richard E. Kelley said, "This has not been a great problem." He added that only seventeen instances of self-dealing had been detected during the preceding year. SBA Administrator Eugene Foley told the House committee that the agency required a semi-annual report from each SBIC, an annual report on each SBIC by an independent public auditor, and in addition had roving examiners to investigate various companies. "We think with these three methods that we have a fairly adequate protection against violation of the [Small Business Investment] Act," he said.

Perhaps because of this kind of confidence, there were no fundamental changes in the SBIC program until 1966. The original legislation had been amended in 1960, 1961, and 1962, but the general thrust of the changes was to alter the scope and general administrative procedure for the program rather than to protect against dubious operations. Principal changes of this nature were the 1961 amendment giving SBA authority to conduct administrative proceedings leading to show-cause orders and cease-and-desist orders and license suspension in cases where wrongdoing was suspected and proved, and the 1963 amendment requiring the agency to adopt formal regulations dealing with the conflict of interest problem.

Hearings on the SBIC program were held in July, 1966, by both the House Small Business Committee and the Small Business Subcommittee of the Senate Banking and Currency Committee. These hearings dealt primarily with the SBA's internal problems in monitoring the investment program. By this time there was fairly widespread recognition that there were problems, perhaps criminal violations, within the SBIC program. There was, in addition, a new SBA administrator, Bernard L. Boutin, and a new deputy administrator for Investment, Howard Greenberg, both of whom had pledged their dedication to tidying up the mess.

In the spring, former Deputy Administrator for Investment Richard Kelley had in an address before the SBIC industry announced that as of April 30, 1966, there were some 232 "problem" SBIC's and estimated that about $15 million in government funds would probably be lost in the 130 most serious of these cases.

Bernard Boutin, who had just become administrator in May, 1966, reviewed with the inquiring Congressional committees the history of the SBIC program, its current status, and his future plans. Senator William Proxmire, chairman of the Banking and Currency subcommittee, invited Boutin to submit draft legislation aimed at correcting the difficulties.

It was the Senate Government Operations Committee, however, that carried on the most detailed investigation of the actual operations of problem SBIC's. The committee had become interested in the SBIC program during the course of its prior investigations into financial institutions. In August, 1965, the subcommittee staff began a preliminary inquiry and reviewed the files of some forty-three SBIC's. Several irregularities were discovered, and the decision was made to proceed with a more formal investigation.

The General Accounting Office, the government agency which customarily performs audits for Congress was called in. It reviewed the files of six SBIC's. Giving a preliminary report to the Government Operations subcommittee, Comptroller General Elmer B. Staats, head of the General Accounting Office, told the senators:

> SBA financial records do not provide accurate, complete, and current information on the status of loans and investments in SBICs or the financial condition of these companies. . . .
>
> Many of the SBICs have been experiencing financial and other difficulties and are considered as problem cases by SBA. The number of these cases have been increasing. . . .
>
> We believe that SBA could improve its administration of the SBIC program by (1) establishing lending criteria for use by the SBIC industry and, (2) strengthening its management con-

trol system. . . . The SBA Administrator [Boutin] has indicated general concurrence with the need for these improvements.

Staats continued that the SBA had failed to exercise appropriate surveillance, and he cited specific sins of omission.

Staats was dispassionate in his testimony; but the upshot of his remarks was that SBIC officials had in many cases been playing fast and loose with the government's money. In each case investigated, there appeared to be loss of a sizable part of the investment in the SBIC, at the expense of the SBA.

There were various sorts of problems in the SBIC effort. SBA Administrator Boutin listed a number in his testimony. First of all, previous licensing standards had allowed unqualified applicants to join the program. Provision for reporting change in control of an SBIC were inadequate to insure close SBA oversight of SBIC's. There were no clear guidelines for SBIC lending policy and practices. Requirements for accounting practices of SBIC's were equally unsatisfactory. Some licensees made little or no attempt to make loans to small business concerns. Conflict of interest regulations were rather laxly enforced by the SBA, as were rules against control of more than one SBIC by the same individuals. Private investment in SBIC's was sometimes inadequate and even juggled in unethical fashion. Some SBIC's were speculating in the real estate market in suspect ways; some were not reporting to the SBA as required. SBA investigations, in turn, were often cursory and shallow, and the agency's accounting system was inadequate. In some instances SBIC's suffered from impairment of their paid-in capital, sustaining losses of 50 per cent or more of capital funds, a violation of SBA regulations. And there were a variety of delays at the SBA in dealing with violators.

Bernard Boutin confessed all these sins of previous SBA administrations to the subcommittee and agreed to cooperate fully with the Senate panel. The Senate investigating staff had conducted its own review of three SBIC's, and all kinds of suspect deals were discovered.

Naturally, disclosures of this sort, particularly those which cited facts and named names, were highly embarrassing to many of the parties concerned. SBA officials and former officials were also on the grill. They were patently on the defensive in attempting to explain why the agency had not exercised closer surveillance over the SBIC's. Richard Kelley, former head of the SBA Investment Division, engaged in the following dialogue with Senator Karl E. Mundt (R-South Dakota):

Mr. Kelley. . . . I might point out, Senator, that Mr. [Eugene] Foley [former SBA Administrator] is responsible for giving me a Superior Service Award for the agency, the highest award in the agency.

Senator Mundt. Say that again.

Mr. Kelley. Mr. Foley gave me the highest award in the agency in 1965, Superior Service Award.

Senator Mundt. I misunderstood you. I thought you said it was under his administration the agency got a high efficiency award.

Mr. Kelley. No.

Senator Mundt. He gave that to you personally?

Mr. Kelley. Yes.

Largely as a result of the hearings investigating the SBIC program, a consensus developed that the program needed to be tightened in specific ways. In a statement at the conclusion of the Government Operations subcommittee hearings, its chairman, Senator Fred R. Harris, expressed dismay and sorrow at the SBA's lax administration of the program and the wheeling and dealing of SBIC officials. He pointed out that in one instance, the SBA had investigated a case at the subcommittee's behest and as a result recouped $400,000. Senator Harris acknowledged SBA Administrator Boutin's cooperation but said the subcommittee staff would continue its own investigation. He added that the subcommittee would recommend remedial legislation and announced that "in view of some brazenly fraudulent activities which were testified to in the hearings, I am asking the staff to forward the transcript to the Department of Justice, the Internal Revenue Service, and the Federal Deposit Insurance Corporation for appropriate action."

Senator Harris ultimately was a cosponsor of a bill introduced by Senator Proxmire, the Small Business Investment Act Amendments of 1966. It provided various procedures for closer SBA monitoring of the SBIC's, civil penalties for failure of SBIC's to report to the SBA as required, civil liability of individual officers and directors of SBIC's in violation of legislation or SBA regulations relating to them, and judicial procedures for prosecuting violators.

In 1967, still more amendments treating the same subject were introduced, with SBA cooperation, by Senator Sparkman. These Small Business Amendments of 1967 provided for a minimum of $1 million private capitalization by each SBIC and more favorable tax treatment for SBIC investments.

The 1966 bill, which was duly enacted, strengthened SBA control over the SBIC industry. The 1967 legislation was designed to strengthen the industry itself. It is unlikely that either measure would have become law without the vigorous exercise by a Congressional committee—indeed, several committees—of the power of legislative oversight over administration.

IX

Relations with the Public

The SBA was founded to serve the public—more specifically, a particular segment of it: entrepreneurs and potential small businessmen. The SBA, therefore, pays particular attention to groups especially concerned with small business affairs. National and local Small Business Advisory Councils offer quasi-official recommendations to SBA officials, and the agency's Office of Public Information is the administrative unit specifically charged with responsibility for liaison with the press and the public at large. Yet, just as relations with Congress are carried on at variety of levels, so, too, SBA officials in many parts of the agency have day-to-day dealings with individuals seeking help. In this chapter, we shall be concerned with both the formal structure and informal dynamics of SBA relations with the public.

Who outside the official world is interested in the SBA? What is the source of their interest? What organized groups have a continuing concern with the SBA? How close is their relationship with the agency, and how effective are they in getting what they want from it? What kind of coverage does the SBA get from the mass media? How is the agency organized in order to cope with requests? What kinds of requests do agency officials most frequently receive? These are the principal questions to be pursued here.

THE PUBLIC OF THE SBA

The philosopher David Hume observed that all government is based on opinion. Following this dictum, each government enterprise draws its clientele and support from a particular segment of the population. For the SBA, "the public" effectively means those people who, for one reason or another, are interested in small business affairs. The intensity of this interest may vary. Some people have a casual or passing concern. This group might include a newspaper reader who spots an unusual feature story about some aspect of the agency's operations, a graduate seeking some kind of job with the federal government, an economist whose study might touch upon some facet of small business, or a person who hears about SBA loans and thinks there might be some way he could qualify for the money.

But the public that matters most to the SBA has a deeper and more continuing interest in the agency. It is what has been called "the attentive public"—those people who always have their antennae attuned to the latest small business developments. Their interest is professional; small business is their job, or part of their job.

This public takes two principal forms: organized interest groups and the working press. Individuals seeking SBA assistance are also vitally interested in the agency's undertakings, but they are generally concerned only with their own cases (this aspect of public relations will be discussed later in this chapter).

BUSINESS GROUPS

Most businessmen pay at least lip service to the virtues of small business. The same is true of most business organizations. Four of the leading voices of American business—the Committee for Economic Development, the American Bankers Association, the National Association of Manufacturers, and the Chamber of Commerce of the United States—have from time to time made themselves heard on small business issues.

The Committee for Economic Development (CED). CED is a nonprofit organization of prominent businessmen and educators established in 1942 to promote economic prosperity. CED publishes periodic statements of national policy on topics of public concern. One of its earliest studies, produced in June, 1947, was "Meeting the Special Problems of Small Business." Noting that as much as 98 per cent of the business population of the United States might be classified as small business, the CED report expressed the hope that the credit and management needs of small firms would be filled by resources of the private sector. Government lending was suggested as only an emergency form of assistance to small business.

CED also sponsors research studies such as A. D. H. Kaplan's definitive scholarly work, *Small Business: Its Place and Problems* (1948). This CED study, completed before the establishment of the SBA, surveys the role and needs of American small business. CED has not published any policy statements on small business from the late 1940's to the present. There has been informal contact between CED members and staff and SBA officials, and some interest in the SBIC program has developed within CED. But it appears that in the main small business has become a matter of relatively minor concern to the tycoons and policy-oriented researchers who are CED.

The American Bankers Association (ABA). Trade association of the banking fraternity, ABA has had a more intimate interest in SBA operations. Finance lies at the heart of both institutions. The SBA, husbanding its own resources and anxious not to appear to compete with private lenders, has long plumped for more loans in participation with banks and bank loans guaranteed by the SBA. The banking community has been fairly responsive. Its lack of greater enthusiasm has resulted from its traditional adherence to strict credit standards. The SBA has taken more lending risks in order to serve its social purposes and has urged bankers to be more flexible. To some extent the agency has succeeded, especially when the social objective has been emphasized.

The ABA has a Small Business Credit Committee which has kept a watchful eye on the SBA. Among its undertakings, the ABA sponsored and, in 1965, published *The Role of Commercial Banks in the SBIC Industry,* by Professor S. J. Flink of the Rutgers University School of Business Administration. The study contained a preface written by Richard E. Kelley, then SBA deputy administrator for Investment. Increased bank participation in the SBIC program was predicted by the ABA study.

During the course of their dialogue about risks and credit standards, SBA relations with individual bankers and the ABA have been reasonably close. It must be emphasized, however, that an organization like ABA concerns itself with many matters it considers to be of greater importance than small business. The relationship might therefore be described as one of mutual adjustment on certain specific matters of common interest.

The National Association of Manufacturers (NAM). The NAM has estimated upon occasion that 83 per cent of its membership consists of small businessmen. NAM members and staff, however, view themselves as the spokesmen not of "the little fellow" but of the manufacturing community as a whole.

The NAM was founded in 1895, essentially by industrialists who sought to offset the growth of the rising labor movement. As labor organized, so did businessmen. In its early days, the NAM was dominated by small manufacturers. By the 1930's, however, big business interests, worried about the New Deal, moved more into leadership positions.

Because it seeks to speak for all manufacturers, the NAM is concerned with a wide spectrum of government policies toward business. The SBA plays only a minor part in this scenario. Accordingly, the NAM has chosen to lend primary attention to broad issues like foreign trade, tax matters, and antitrust policy. Occasionally SBA programs rouse NAM interest. More frequently, SBA officials, when they seek business community involvement, will bring their program to the attention of the NAM. For example, there was some attempt to interest the NAM and similar organizations in the SBA's EOL program during the early days of the War on Poverty. Again, members of organizations like the NAM have been tapped for various SBA management assistance programs. But the general level of NAM involvement in SBA operations has been low.

Chambers of Commerce. The NAM pattern has also been followed on the whole by the U.S. Chamber of Commerce and its local affiliates. Even more than the NAM, the U.S. Chamber is run by prominent big business executives. If anything, the Chamber is perhaps a bit suspicious of a government agency which gives aid to faltering small enterprises. This kind of activity interferes with free operation of the market in which Chamber members profess full faith.

Yet there is a realm of concern shared by the SBA and the Chamber. Both have a stake in the over-all state of the economy, the business population, and the credit situation. The extent to which an attempt is made to foster active cooperation between the Chamber and the SBA depends largely upon the attitudes and interests of Chamber and agency officials. Basically there has been considerable distance between the two at the national level. From time to time, local SBA officials have involved their local chambers of commerce in SBA programs like the Service Corps of Retired Executives (SCORE) or management workshops and conferences.

THE SMALL BUSINESS COMMUNITY

Surely the SBA is of direct importance to the 4.8 million small businessmen of the United States. It is their welfare Congress sought to promote in creating the agency, and they who are eligible for SBA benefits. It is they to whom the SBA must turn for interest-group support. Yet most of the small business organizations are not very effective. The small business community has failed to produce vigorous interest groups because small business, as such, lacks a broadly shared interest and because small businessmen are not very sophisticated politically.

Lack of a Small Business Interest. According to the Small Business Act, a small business is any concern "independently owned and operated . . . which is not dominant in its field." Psychologically, that may entail a meaningful group. Economically, however, the definition is hard to establish. Under SBA size standards, it could mean—depending on the industry —anything from a self-employed bootblack to American Motors. It strains credulity to imagine both being meaningfully represented by the same interest group. Small business is, in fact, a categoric group. That is, it is composed of individuals with a common characteristic but not necessarily a common objective. The organizers of small business associations have difficulty in identifying a meaningful standard to which all honorable small businessmen may repair. Some groups have tried rather successfully to organize on a more narrowly defined interest. Still, attempts to organize groups to speak for the small business community have been relatively unsuccessful. Such groups have been vulnerable to the charge that they do not truly represent that community.

The membership claims of small business groups, therefore, are taken with a grain of salt. SBA and Congressional staffs, doubtless taking a cue from their political bosses, have not been unduly anxious about assignments to prepare replies to complaints or exhortations from such groups. Apparently the organizations are not central to the key policy decisions made about small business. It is not generally believed that the leaders of the groups actually speak for any deeply concerned, far-flung constituency of entrepreneurs.

Lack of Political Sophistication Among Small Businessmen. Another factor tending to discourage formation of effective small business groups is the relative political naïveté of small businessmen. Within government small business circles, there is a faint uncomfortable awareness that many small businessmen have a very strong distaste for the government and very little understanding of it. Most every government official professionally concerned with small business has a favorite story about this phenomenon. One such bureaucrat, shortly after joining the SBA, encountered a small businessman by chance at a social gathering. For quite a while the SBA man listened with mounting impatience to the small businessman's complaints about the great Leviathan in Washington. "The government," the small businessman snorted. "The government doesn't give a damn about me!" The SBA official blurted: "I'm the government, and I care about you." A sudden horrified shock of recognition was evident on the face of the small businessman as he realized that he had met one of the "Feds" face to face.

Scholarship tends to support such anecdotes. The sociologist Martin Trow in a 1958 study found that self-employed persons consistently ranked lower in political tolerance than manual or salaried workers. Trow hypothesized that the reason was "hostility toward . . . industrial capitalism." Trow found, for example, that persons opposing both Big Labor and Big Business were strongest of all groups studied in their support for Senator Joseph R. McCarthy during his heyday of loyalty-security investigations. Trow cautioned that if the factor of education was held constant, small businessmen were no more intolerant than other occupational groups. Yet even if their job was not the direct cause of their attitudes, the upshot of

Trow's study was that many small businessmen were extreme in their views.

This kind of general negativism toward modern society does not provide very useful guidance to those attempting to formulate programs and policies in the small business area. As a result, attempts by rank-and-file small businessmen to influence SBA are of minimal effectiveness unless they concern a very specific problem.

SMALL BUSINESS ORGANIZATIONS

For all the intrinsic problems in creating representative, effective small business groups, associations of small businessmen do exist. The two best-known groups are the National Federation of Independent Business and the National Small Business Association. Other significant groups are restricted to a narrower constituency. This latter category is generally conceded to be more effective in its dealings with the SBA, presumably because a narrow focus tends to obviate the problems of organizing small businessmen.

The National Federation of Independent Business is a fairly widely known group, primarily because of its founder and president, C. Wilson Harder, and its energetic vice president for legislative activities, George Burger. Claiming "the largest individual membership of any business organization in the world," it numbers its clientele at over 239,000. It has some 2,500 local district chapters and a sizable permanent staff that includes legislative representatives in state capitals as well as in Washington. It seeks to defend the small business community generally, particularly from what it considers undue government intervention in the economy and labor union power.

Polling its membership and publicizing the results are key Federation activities. Questions asked in the printed polls deal with business activities of the respondents and their opinions on vital issues of the day. Ballots are tabulated by district chairmen, and the results are sent directly to the district's congressman. National headquarters provides a nationwide summary to all members of Congress. The general idea is to amplify the grass roots' rustle.

The Federation also works with local Chambers of Commerce, testifies on pending legislation, operates speakers programs, and issues publications of various sorts. In 1963, it received a Public Service Award signed by SBA Administrator Eugene P. Foley. The nature of the Federation, however, makes it more suited to dealing with Congress than with the executive branch. It has not been as important in SBA policy councils as, for example, the American Farm Bureau Federation has been in some parts of the Agriculture Department.

The National Small Business Association is smaller than the Federation but quick to point out that it is "the oldest organization in the United States representing small business." One of its own publications describes the group as "a vigorous advocate of free enterprise, frank recognition of the profit motive, the right to private property, individual incentive, and freedom from monopoly either private or governmental."

Its principal functions include testifying before Congressional committees, assisting individual small businessmen, and a community education and information program.

The National Small Business Association has concerned itself with a variety of issues—right-to-work laws and other labor legislation, truth-in-packaging, and fiscal and tax policy. It has not worked hand-in-hand with the SBA in developing the agency's policies and programs.

The National Association of Small Business Investment Companies (NASBIC), trade association of the SBIC industry, is one of the most influential small business groups. It lacks the two stated handicaps of small business organizations: it is composed of businessmen with an intense interest more specific than "small business," and its members are highly sophisticated about the workings of the SBA program in which they take part. NASBIC is thus in a position to deal effectively with SBA officials, and it does.

The NASBIC leadership has been regularly consulted on various aspects of the SBA investment program. SBA officials speak frequently to NASBIC groups and seek the opinions of NASBIC about investment affairs. And when the SBIC program was investigated by Congress, in 1966, NASBIC leaders gave testimony about its operations and possible improvements. NASBIC is a unique segment of the small business community because all the member firms must by law be licensed by the SBA.

Other industry groups, such as the National Association of Retail Druggists and the National Association of Retail Grocers, are similarly effective. Like NASBIC, this type of association finds its common interest in a common occupation. Unlike NASBIC, however, these industries are not in any way regulated by the SBA. Many such single-industry groups deal with the agency constantly on their particular problems.

Bound by common experience and common needs, these groups can speak with a single voice with relative ease. Their national leadership can also boast considerable expertise gained from years of Washington experience in arguing a particular case. And policy-makers at the SBA and elsewhere listen to them as experts.

The National Business League is another specifically focused organization: it represents Negro small businessmen. Founded by Booker T. Washington in 1900, the League came to prominence at the SBA around 1963, when the agency instituted programs aimed at Negro entrepreneurs. The League helps individual Negro businessmen with their problems and speaks for this constituency with a fair degree of effectiveness both on Capitol Hill and at the SBA.

Regional groups provide another basis of a specific small business interest. A notable example is the Smaller Business

Association of New England (SBANE), which has been one of the most effective policy-oriented groups representing small concerns. It has vigorously advocated various policies deemed vital to New England small business. When the possibility of defense spending cutbacks arose, in 1963 and 1964, and many electronics firms located on Boston's Route 128 research and development complex were becoming alarmed, SBANE sponsored a widely publicized conference on the topic. Again, when wide-ranging tariff legislation was being considered by Congress in 1962, SBANE forcefully presented its views—principally protective of New England's textile interests—to members of Congress and executive officials including the White House's special representative for trade negotiations.

The SBA has been another object of SBANE campaigns and a partner in policy discussions. They have cosponsored gatherings, and SBANE has generally had the ear of top agency officials. The SBA's regional director in Boston has worked closely with the group, and SBANE had another strong ally in Washington when Senator Leverett Saltonstall, of Massachusetts, served as a ranking member of the Senate Small Business Committee.

THE PRESS

From time to time, as we have said, the SBA pops into the news. As newspaper copy goes, the SBA is not a glamorous agency like the State or Defense departments or NASA. But it does have a clientele in the press corps. Primarily—and understandably—the SBA is of most interest to reporters who cover business and economic affairs. Coverage of its activities is commonly found on the financial pages of newspapers and magazines and in business publications.

This pattern means that primary attention has been given to SBA lending programs, with relatively scanty coverage of other agency undertakings. As a result, the picture that emerges from a casual perusal of the public prints is not a completely accurate portrait of what the agency does.

There are exceptions to this rule. Some kinds of stories make colorful copy and may have little or nothing to do with the agency's principal functions. These include features of various sorts, juicy gossip, and items about the bureaucracy. While these articles are of minor importance to both the SBA and the public, they serve to put the agency in the public eye.

Wire Services. The two principal nationwide wire services, the Associated Press (AP) and United Press International (UPI), do have some consistent coverage of the SBA. Of the two, AP in its sizable Washington bureau has reporters regularly assigned to the financial beat. AP runs stories about the SBA when they are deemed sufficiently newsworthy. But its financial men are usually fully occupied with covering the Treasury, the Federal Reserve Board, and other pre-eminent financial institutions. Thus AP coverage of SBA tends to be rather sporadic. The story for UPI is much the same.

Daily Newspapers. Coverage of the SBA by daily newspapers is similar to that of the wire services. A principal difference is that more attention is given the agency by reporters for newspapers outside Washington than by their peers at local AP and UPI offices. This is probably because local SBA officials are more interested in seeing their activities described in local papers than in gaining nationwide publicity.

In the nation's capital, *The Washington Post,* biggest of the three daily papers, has several reporters and an editorial writer assigned to financial and economic affairs. The situation is much the same at *The Washington Star.* Both cover the SBA with impressive thoroughness and general approval. Lending programs and the SBIC's get the lion's share of their attention; but there have been numerous stories about other SBA operations, including prominent management programs like SCORE and size standards determinations, as well. The tabloid *Washington Daily News* relies fairly heavily on the wire services and columnists for its news copy, but here and there it, too, runs an item about the SBA.

Outside Washington, coverage of the SBA by daily papers varies. Naturally there is more coverage in cities with local SBA offices. Other factors include the interests and quality of the local newspapers and the interests, activities, and inclinations of local SBA officials.

The EOL program has enjoyed fairly wide coverage in local newspapers. The Philadelphia press gave considerable publicity to the Small Business Opportunities Corporation, a prototype of the EOL program. *The New York Times,* whose mammoth Washington bureau occasionally picks up an SBA item, also covered the EOL program as a local story. Senator Jacob Javits, of New York, who is a member of the Senate Small Business Committee, voiced some criticisms of the EOL effort in Manhattan in late 1966, and *The Times* ran several articles about the controversy. Even Hodding Carter's *Delta Democrat-Times,* of Greenville, Mississippi, got into the EOL act. When two SBA officials visited several Mississippi cities in early 1965 to spread the word about their new program, Carter ran an editorial about their trip. The moral of his story was that not all the "Feds" visiting his state were "outside agitators" from the Justice Department eager to force racial integration on an unwilling South.

Radio and Television. The electronic media have sometimes run programs dealing with the SBA. At the height of interest in the War on Poverty, SBA officials from Washington sent to help organize and publicize the EOL program in the field appeared on radio and TV shows. Other popular or unusual programs, notably assistance to ghetto businessmen and the Service Corps of Retired Executives (SCORE), have been subjects of radio and television coverage. Obviously, TV and radio do not follow the SBA closely. But their demand for material is so enormous that even an agency of modest prominence enjoys occasional attention.

National Magazines. A number of general-interest mass-circulation magazines which maintain Washington bureaus have had occasion to publish stories about the SBA. In general, however, their coverage of the agency has been sporadic and limited to particularly prominent policies and programs.

Business Publications. Inevitably, it is that part of the press corps primarily concerned with business and financial affairs that covers the SBA most closely. The SBA is of greater interest to their readers than to the average man in the street. The business journals generally keep abreast of what the SBA is doing and on the whole have been favorable to its efforts, with the possible exception of *The Wall Street Journal,* which disapproves of government "handouts," and has opposed discrimination either for or against a business soleiy because of its size. As a result, the *Journal* has followed SBA operations with a jaundiced eye ever since the agency's beginning.

Business Week is the magazine that over the years has covered the SBA most fully. It has published dozens of articles involving SBA activities. Most of these have dealt with the lending and investment programs. Others have discussed the SCORE program, the decision to define American Motors as "small" for purposes of government procurement, damage to small businesses as a result of racial riots during the summer of 1967, and an SBA-sponsored study of the future of small business. *Business Week*'s thorough coverage of research and development matters also bears considerable relevance to many small, innovative R&D firms the SBA has been interested in fostering.

The four-page weekly *Kiplinger Letter* represents a different sort of publication concerned with small business problems. The newsletter has a vast subscription list, doubtless including a very large number of small businessmen across the country. It contains information of interest to businessmen about what is happening in Washington, as well as what seems likely to happen. In the course of this survey, the letter includes descriptions of new SBA programs, publications, and other services. It is designed to inform businessmen who cannot afford their own Washington representative, and in so doing it goes far toward bringing agencies like the SBA home to them. Kiplinger's staff follows the SBA quite carefully.

Occasional Coverage of the SBA. From time to time, various media pick up some aspect of the SBA as a special-interest feature story. Although this sort of coverage is irregular, it brings the SBA to the attention of a wider public than the agency would otherwise enjoy.

For example, the SBA now and again is found in the columns of reporters who cover the civil service. A new program in any agency means new jobs, and government workers who follow developments of this sort find items about the SBA in the columns of Jerry Kluttz in *The Washington Post,* Joseph Young in *The Washington Star,* and John Cramer in *The Washington Daily News.* Weekly newspapers circulated to government employees also include this kind of information about the SBA and other agencies.

On rare occasions, the SBA appeals to the newspapers as a juicy tidbit of political gossip. For example, in January, 1968, the press learned that a prominent Alaska Democrat received an SBA disaster loan for $894,000—all he asked—while the state's Republican governor got only half his disaster loan request after a Fairbanks flood had damaged their rival motels.

Similarly, Drew Pearson, one of the most widely read columnists in the United States, charged, in 1966, that the SBA had severely cut back its funds for the EOL program despite the President's reiterated desire to move forward with the War on Poverty.

Newsmen by nature love controversy and scandal; it makes good copy. Unfortunately, extenuating circumstances are not always reported, or reported as prominently as spicier accusations. But at the SBA such stories, whatever their accuracy, are few and far between.

Foreign publications have occasionally picked up SBA as a topic of some interest. For example, the *London Economist* in 1966 ran an article about the agency, with particular attention to the Economic Opportunity Loan program. *Paris-Match*, a popular French magazine, in a 1967 article comparing the French and United States economies included a discussion of SBA operations, much of it based on a lengthy conversation with an SBA economist.

Some stories about the SBA are more whimsical. In June, 1965, the SBA administrator had a brain-storming session with his young professional employees that included a group walk from the SBA offices in the Lafayette Building, a block northwest of the White House, to the Washington Monument. A *Washington Post* reporter made the trip with the hikers, and the story made page one the next day.

The SBA has even made the women's pages of the Washington daily newspapers. Both the *Star* and the *Post* devoted several columns of space in February, 1968, to an account of the SBA-sponsored "Own Your Own Business Show," an exhibition of seventy-five small businesses owner-operated under the franchise system. Top attraction of the show—and basis of the "women's angle" newspaper coverage—was Miss Sally Albert, "guidance counselor" of Puppy Palace Enterprises, Inc., of Philadelphia. Miss Albert's job, according to newspaper reports, was to soothe dogs' psyches, helping them to select an owner and working out any problems that might subsequently arise within their families. Naturally, this kind of coverage was a press officer's dream. Who wouldn't love an agency that helps an attractive young lady be kind to man's best friend?

THE SBA MEETS THE PUBLIC

A rather large number of SBA employees have day-to-day dealings with the public. Formally, the two principal points of contact are the Office of Public Information and the national and local Small Business Advisory Councils. But just as in the case of Congressional relations, interest in particular SBA programs causes members of the public to approach particular officials throughout the agency organization.

The SBA has dealings with the public at large at both the national and the local levels. The SBA loan officer in Fargo, North Dakota, who interviews an applicant for financial assistance, is as much engaged in public relations as the assistant administrator for Congressional and Public Affairs. The principal difference is that at the local level, relations with the public generally come as an offshoot of some sort of program activity, rather than as a professional public relations effort.

This plethora of points of contact may seem confusing. But many people upon occasion want many different sorts of assistance from the SBA—factual information, the opportunity to offer policy and program advice, jobs, loan money, management aid, and so on. For this reason, they take their case to the particular SBA office they think will do the most for them. And thus, although the agency's structure is organized so as to give some officials primary responsibility for dealings with the public, their task is shared by many whose principal duties lie elsewhere.

The Office of Public Information. Like all government agencies, the SBA has always had an office charged with dispensing information to the world outside. At present, SBA's Office of Public Information comes within the general authority of the assistant administrator for Congressional and Public Affairs. Staffed principally by trained newspapermen, this office has about a dozen professional employees.

The job of projecting the SBA's image has numerous facets. Information officers draft speeches and Congressional testimony for delivery by the administrator and other top-ranking officials. They grind out press releases about SBA activities for distribution to the news media. They write and produce television and radio announcements, which dramatize various SBA programs, and are responsible for booklets and pamphlets that describe SBA activities to the general public. And they cheerfully answer inquiries about the SBA from newsmen and strangers who happen to wander by the office.

Speech writing is probably the most important thing the Office of Public Information does. Top officials are very busy men. They are called upon to make remarks about the SBA or small business or related subjects daily, and sometimes more than once a day. Few men are so talented at public speaking as to be able to deliver all or even most of these talks off the cuff. Very few have the time to prepare all their own speeches ahead of the time of delivery. Herein lies the necessity of speech writers. The writer prepares an outline or draft, and the speaker embellishes it.

From time to time, top agency officials may call upon other staff members outside the Office of Public Information to prepare speech drafts. In addition, much of the detailed information about program activities used in speeches is obtained from the economists, the budget office, and the various program offices. But most of the task of preparing public statements falls on the shoulders of the public information officers.

Important speeches are often mimeographed in advance and distributed to the press; more commonly, SBA affairs are described in press releases. Many of these are basically abstracts of major public statements. Others describe specific program developments, such as launching a pilot project or making loans under highly publicized conditions like the War on Poverty or the Hurricane Betsy disaster or the aftermath of a riot. Other SBA press releases contain biographies of newly appointed officials. Most of the day-to-day press coverage of the SBA, such as it is, originates with press releases, generally distributed to a standing list of news media covering the agency on a regular basis.

Recently the SBA has begun to sponsor spot advertisements on television and radio. These briefly describe SBA programs, sometimes in a general review of what the agency has to offer and sometimes in a more detailed summary of a specific program, such as SCORE. These advertisements aim at bringing the SBA to the attention of a wider public. It is difficult to gauge their effectiveness, but common sense suggests that they are useful in gaining public interest and reaching people who do not ordinarily follow the financial page.

Public information officers also write most of the pamphlets and other documents produced by the SBA. The most important of these is the annual report, the preparation of which is coordinated by the Office of Public Information. This document describes SBA activities during the preceding year and is usually published in the spring or summer. In addition, numerous short publications about the SBA and its various programs are written or rewritten each year in the Office of Public Information.

Finally, SBA information officers are responsible for general liaison with the public and the press. They keep in touch with the financial writers who cover the agency regularly. In addition, general inquiries are routinely referred to the public information staff. Some requests come from prospective applicants for program assistance, who are referred to their local SBA offices. Others come from reporters in search of a story who view the SBA as an offbeat item. If the information he wants is detailed or technical, the newsman may be referred to the office in the agency with special responsibility in the area he is investigating. The Office of Public Information remains the central clearinghouse for facts and figures issued to the public.

Small Business Advisory Councils. The SBA has drawn a box for "the public" on its organization chart. The advisory councils are a quasi-official body of prominent small businessmen who offer recommendations to SBA officials. A special assistant to the administrator is responsible for dealings with the advisory councils on a continuing basis. State and local councils are also organized throughout the country. The national group is appointed by the administrator and meets twice a year to offer formal policy and program advice.

While the advisory councils doubtless serve to bring the SBA and the public closer, they do not have any working responsibility for carrying out the SBA's functions as a government agency. They are essentially a ceremonial part of the agency's structure.

Other SBA Offices and the Public. Many of "the public" find it more effective to deal with the SBA through channels other than the Office of Public Information or the advisory councils. Those experienced in dealing with large bureaucratic organizations have found that half the battle consists of locating the right man with whom to do business. Who the right man is depends on what you want. And so SBA officials all over the agency are beseiged with telephone calls, letters, and visits from private citizens.

Many groups have continuing relations with the SBA office of greatest concern to them. For example, the National Association of Small Business Investment Companies works closely with the Investment Division. The machine tool industry has had a long-term interest in financial assistance programs. Size standards for small-business "set-asides" in government procurement have been a concern of business organizations having many members who seek to qualify for such programs. Negro groups like the National Business League have worked closely with officials of programs—notably the EOL program —that are aimed at members of minority groups.

Sometimes the SBA enlists the support of the public, rather than the other way around. For instance, the agency has attempted to interest various trade associations and even big businessmen in its management assistance programs. SBA officials who helped start Small Business Development Centers in the early skirmishes of the War on Poverty also sought a maximum of participation from the local business community.

SBA officials, especially those who wish to innovate programs, would be well advised to try to build an active constituency for their efforts. We have seen that small business interests may be organized effectively for specific purposes. Strong allies within the small business community for particular programs would serve to strengthen the SBA in its dealings with Congress and the Budget Bureau.

At present, there is considerable apathy about the SBA in the public at large and sometimes more apathy than enthusiasm at the SBA about a concerted and continuing effort to enlist public support for agency programs. Yet, where this support exists, it tends to be effective. The attentive public closely interested in a particular program works closely with SBA officials charged with responsibility in that area. Public and private meet in common cause—to persuade each other, to dissuade each other, to work together. The SBA should lend increasing attention to such relations with the public, both sophisticated dealings with reporters and professionals and in its guidance of "the little fellow," who comes hat in hand in search of help.

X

Interagency Relations

The SBA operates within the complex web of the total U.S. Government structure. We have seen how this entails relations with Congress and with the public, but much of what the SBA does also involves working with other agencies of the federal establishment on matters of common concern.

Some of these interagency relationships are more important than others. For the SBA, four executive areas are pre-eminent from a policy and program standpoint. These are the White House, the Bureau of the Budget, the Department of Commerce, and the Department of Defense. The White House, of course, lies at the peak of the executive pyramid. The Budget Bureau, located in the President's executive office, is the central clearinghouse for the principal activities of all agencies and departments, including the SBA. The Commerce Department, which once had an Office of Small Business, is often rumored to covet the SBA's functions; in the meantime, many Commerce activities are carried on in conjunction with the SBA. And the Defense Department, biggest contracting agency of the U.S. Government, is the most important target of SBA procurement programs.

A number of agencies with which the SBA deals on a regular basis have central coordinating responsibilities for activities of all government agencies. In addition to the White

House and the Budget Bureau, these include the Civil Service Commission, which handles personnel matters; the General Services Administration, which provides numerous housekeeping services—e.g., janitors, elevator operators, cars and drivers; the General Accounting Office, which conducts audits of various agencies' programs for Congress, and the agencies concerned with equal employment opportunity.

In addition, many agencies carry on activities particularly pertinent to the SBA. Thus, the Office of Emergency Planning works closely with the SBA in disaster assistance; the Antitrust Division of the Justice Department performs a function of clear interest to the SBA; the Office of Economic Opportunity has had considerable dealings with the SBA during the course of the War on Poverty. And so it goes.

As in architecture, form follows function. Agencies are brought together by related programs. Specialists exchange information across agency boundaries. Lawyers at the SBA talk to lawyers elsewhere in the government; economists talk with other economists. The spider's web of relationships may on first glance appear complex and confusing, it is in fact intricately and rather precisely organized.

The SBA and the Central Coordinating Agencies

The spectrum of SBA relationships with central coordinating agencies within the executive branch of the government ranges from the sublime to the mundane. It starts with the President, who in theory at least supervises the entire executive branch, and runs through the Interdepartmental Savings Bond Committee, which promotes the sale of government bonds to federal employees. Between these two extremes lie agencies charged with specific coordinating responsibilities for all agencies and departments.

The White House. As the head of an independent agency, the SBA administrator formally reports directly to the President. The administrator's Washington status is thus somewhere above a subordinate official of a cabinet department. According to the protocol list used by the State Department, administrators of independent agencies rank just below three-star generals and vice admirals and just above ministers of foreign powers serving in embassies but not accredited. Compared to officials of cabinet departments, heads of independent agencies fall by this standard below assistant secretaries and above deputy assistant secretaries. Among the various independent agencies, the SBA's status also appears to be intermediate, ranking somewhere between the National Aeronautics and Space Administration and the Fine Arts Commission.

Accordingly, the SBA administrator's access to the President is, *ceteris paribus,* genuine but modest. Most frequently, it occurs in connection with the existence of such a semicrisis situation as legislative strategy sessions in which the SBA has a direct interest or the event of a disaster requiring quick SBA aid or the making of a high-level agency appointment or such ceremonial occasions as the annual celebration of National Small Business Week.

Most SBA dealings with the White House take place at the staff level. Generally, there has been a White House policy man or men within whose jurisdiction SBA programs fell. He has consulted most frequently with the SBA administrator, the administrator's chief political assistant, and top SBA program officials.

In addition, the White House Congressional liaison staff is responsible for legislation relevant to the SBA among other agencies. Here again, White House aides deal with the administrator, his political assistant, program officials, the SBA Congressional relations officers.

Recruitment of high-level SBA executives is another matter which brings SBA officials and White House staff together. Over the years, appointment of these so-called super grades have always been cleared by the White House, which generally has one or more aides assigned to screening candidates for such political appointments.

Again, the White House Press Office has sometimes worked closely with the SBA on publicity matters. When an announcement of an SBA activity has been deemed of sufficient importance, the White House itself has made the information public. On other sensitive matters, the press release has sometimes simply been cleared with the White House before being distributed to reporters.

Bureau of the Budget (BOB). The President's strong right arm in the management of the executive branch, the Budget Bureau, was created in 1921 at the behest of the President's Commission on Economy and Efficiency. More than the central federal budget agency, the BOB is the chief executive's staff unit in charge of financial management and accounting, executive branch management and organization, coordination and clearance of legislative proposals and executive orders, development of the Planning-Programing-Budgeting System, and coordination and improvement of governmental statistical activities.

In carrying out these supervisory functions, the Budget Bureau has two primary objectives. It seeks to assure that agencies like the SBA conform to the President's wishes. And it attempts to see to it that they do so with the greatest possible efficiency. In its role as a budgetary unit, the BOB subjects the programs of the SBA to the surveillance of its Commerce and Housing Division. As the federal budget to be presented to Congress is drawn up each year, BOB examiners carefully scrutinize each item proposed by the SBA. Top SBA leadership, agency budget officers, and program officials meet with representatives of the BOB and work out a detailed proposal for SBA activity during the forthcoming year, plus tentative projections for the years to follow.

Over-all, the Budget Bureau has been less than wildly enthusiastic about increased spending plans at the SBA. It will be recalled from Chapter V that the SBA has operated, particularly in recent years, at a chronic deficit. The BOB takes a dim view of such a trend. One of its former top officials has explained its skeptical-critical attitude toward the SBA by pointing to what he terms the failure to develop a sensible rationing device. With a first-come-first-served approach to distributing its loan money, he says, the SBA lacks a system of sorting applications by priority. This, in turn, he adds, has made the perennial SBA crisis inevitable—and animosity at the BOB inescapable, as well.

Because of this attitude, SBA financial management has been a bone of contention. The SBA must seek BOB approval for the means by which it obtains and disburses funds. To this end, SBA leadership and budget men huddle regularly with representatives of the BOB's Office of Financial Management. Deficit problems and means to surmount them are the central topic of conversation. Results of these discussions have included the loan ceilings and moratorium and sale of participation certificates described in Chapter V.

The BOB has also carefully kept watch over the effectiveness of SBA management and organization, principally through the BOB Office of Management and Organization. This has involved conferences of BOB management specialists, SBA management analysts, and the chief program officers affected. For example, when the SBA sets up a new office to man a new program, the BOB works with it in setting forth the organizational guidelines for the new unit. Other requests for increases in SBA personnel have frequently met with resistance at the BOB.

The BOB's Office of Legislative Reference clears all executive agency comments about proposed legislation. This includes both bills drawn up by an agency for submission by a member of Congress and comments on legislation already introduced. The idea is that the incumbent administration should speak with one voice. Here the BOB works primarily with the general counsel and his staff at the SBA.

The Budget Bureau is also the driving force within the executive establishment for one of the outstanding new developments in public administration during the past few years —the Planning-Programing-Budgeting System (PPBS). Joy of the statistically inclined and despair of many others, PPBS represents an attempt at systematic analysis of the relative costs and benefits of government programs. By official edict, program justifications for budgetary purposes throughout the executive branch must be prepared according to PPBS specifications. For the SBA, this has meant that program officers working on these program memoranda must be in constant communication with their own budget officers, the Office of Program Planning and Evaluation, and the Budget Bureau. The result—in addition to grumbling by old SBA hands and their peers all over the government—has been a more thoughtful consideration of the impact and effectiveness of SBA programs.

Finally, the Budget Bureau is the central coordinator and administrator of agency statistical activities. This involves surveillance of the SBA's Office of Budget, the main repository of data concerning SBA program efforts. Since the agency does not have an independent statistical wing of its own like the Commerce Department's Office of Business Economics and Census Bureau or the Labor Department's Bureau of Labor Statistics, this particular Budget control over the SBA has been relatively minor.

Civil Service Commission. The commission has over-all authority for the merit system by which government employees are selected and promoted. Through its Office of Personnel, the SBA like all agencies covered by the merit system has a continuing relationship with the commission. A list of the commission's bureaus suggests the activities involved: Recruiting and Examining; Personnel Investigations; Inspections,

Policies and Standards; Retirement and Insurance; and Executive Manpower.

General Services Administration (GSA). This agency is in charge of managing the property and records of the federal government through construction and operation of buildings, procurement and distribution of supplies, disposal of surplus property, traffic and communications management, stockpiling strategic and critical materials, and record-keeping. It performs these services for the SBA among other departments and agencies. The SBA had a particularly close relationship with the GSA in these housekeeping matters during the tenure of Administrator Bernard L. Boutin; Boutin had previously served as GSA administrator. A number of other officials who had come to the SBA from the GSA with Boutin remained after Boutin's departure and have been able to work effectively with their former colleagues at the GSA.

General Accounting Office (GAO). This unusual agency is a part of the legislative branch of government. Its purpose is to help Congress control public funds, principally through audits, accounting, claims settlement, legal decisions, and records management. The permanent nature of this Congressional watchdog is indicated by the fact that the agency's head, the comptroller general, is appointed for a fifteen-year term with the advice and consent of the Senate.

In the course of its oversight activities, the GAO works at the SBA principally with the assistant administrator for Administration and his staff. One notable instance of GAO auditing of SBA operations came in connection with Congressional investigations of the SBIC program, described in Chapter VIII.

Equal Employment Opportunity. Various administrative units in charge of this surveillance within the federal establishment have also had a continuing liaison with the SBA. Thus, the Equal Employment Opportunity Commission, an independent agency, deals with employment outside the federal government, including employment in small business firms. The Labor Department's U.S. Employment Service attempts to maximize job opportunities for minority group members in government. The Office of Federal Contract Compliance, also located in the Labor Department, administers federal law requiring nondiscrimination in employment by government contractors and subcontractors. At the SBA these agencies have worked principally with the administrator's personal staff, primarily his special assistant for Equal Employment Opportunity.

INTERAGENCY RELATIONS AND PROCUREMENT ASSISTANCE

The SBA's procurement assistance men deal with a number of other agencies, of which the Defense Department is by far the most important. The main mechanism involved is the small business "set-aside" program, under which a certain proportion of an agency's contracts are specifically set aside for exclusive bidding by small business concerns. In interagency relations, the SBA acts principally as a gadfly, compelling contracting agencies to award more contracts to small firms.

Department of Defense. Since Defense commands the lion's share of the government procurement dollar—over 80 per cent—the SBA has concentrated on getting contracts for the small businessman from the Pentagon. The nature of the SBA program has been described more fully in Chapters III and VI.

Administrative arrangements for the defense "set-aside" program have been changing over the years. For many years, the SBA maintained a high-level employee stationed at the Pentagon and numerous procurement center representatives around the country. Their job was to act as liaison officers between the defense establishment and small business contractors. The SBA man at the Pentagon worked with the offices of the assistant secretaries of Defense, Army, Navy, and

Air Force for Installations and Logistics, who are responsible for procurement by their departments.

Then, in an economy move made in 1965, most of these SBA jobs were abolished and the functions transferred to the Defense Department. The change was a controversial one which met with considerable criticism within the SBA and on Capitol Hill. Since then, there has been a gradual shift back to the old system.

Other Contracting Agencies. SBA procurement specialists deal with a variety of other federal units that award contracts for various purposes. To cite a few examples: The Federal Supply Service of the General Services Administration procures personal property and nonpersonal services for all federal agencies. The National Aeronautics and Space Administration has a procurement office that seeks bids for all kinds of sophisticated electronic hardware and other gear. The Atomic Energy Commission administers all of its research and development activities on a contract basis. The Agency for International Development awards contracts for various purposes, most notably for technical assistance projects around the globe. And the Arms Control and Disarmament Agency might be persuaded to offer its research contracts on a small business "set-aside" basis. The SBA maintains contact with these agencies, but mostly it concentrates on where the money is—the Pentagon.

INTERAGENCY RELATIONS AND FINANCIAL ASSISTANCE

The number of agencies with which the SBA works in its various loan programs is legion. The Commerce Department is the most important here, both in broad policy significance and variety of contacts. But there are other agencies involved in the EOL program, the disaster loan program, and other SBA financial undertakings.

Loan Policy. When the SBA was created in 1953, specific provision was made for a Loan Policy Board, to be chaired by the SBA administrator with the secretaries of Commerce and the Treasury as the additional members. It will be remembered that the Eisenhower Administration took a dim view of government "competition" with private business and tried to keep a tight check on the federal purse. The incumbent secretaries of Commerce and the Treasury, Sinclair Weeks and George Humphrey, symbolized the administration viewpoint. It was felt that their involvement in SBA loan policymaking would ensure that this viewpoint, rather than any wild ideas of an RFC ilk, held sway in the new agency. It did. However, on May 27, 1965, the Loan Policy Board was abolished. There was general agreement that after twelve years of experience SBA could run its own house.

Economic Opportunity Loans (EOL's). Authority to make loans under the 1964 Economic Opportunity Act has brought about a host of interagency relationships. By statute, the SBA administrator was made a member of the Economic Opportunity Council—a top-level coordinating group—along with the director of the Office of Economic Opportunity (OEO); the secretaries of Defense, Interior, Agriculture, Commerce, Labor, and Health, Education, and Welfare; the Attorney General; the administrator of the Housing and Home Finance agency (now the Secretary of the Department of Housing and Urban Development), the chairman of the Council of Economic Advisers, and the director of Selective Service. These officials were to act as chiefs of staff in the War on Poverty. Although they did not, they did exchange ideas and information.

Lower-echelon employees of the SBA concerned with the EOL program have also worked with their opposite numbers in these other poverty agencies. In addition, they also conferred with representatives of agencies like the Commission on Civil Rights and the Community Relations Service (then within the Department of Commerce, since transferred to the Department of Justice) on racial aspects of the poverty program. The Commerce Department's Economic Development Administration also took part in the effort by funding some of the Small Business Development Centers (SBDC's) established during the early days of the War on Poverty.

As the EOL program has become routinized, the frequency of the interagency contacts has decreased. In 1966, full responsibility for the program was delegated to the SBA from the Office of Economic Opportunity, which had previously supervised EOL operations and funded most SBDC's. The SBDC's were allowed to expire, at least as federally financed ventures. Staff for the EOL program was cut. Despite all these factors, however, some interagency cooperation on the EOL program has persisted.

Disaster Loans. The Office of Emergency Planning (OEP) in the Office of the President coordinates all emergency preparedness activities of the government, including those caused by nonmilitary disasters. Not until a disaster in a particular community has been officially proclaimed by the SBA administrator can the SBA begin accepting disaster loan applications. The SBA has worked closely with OEP in the wake of such events as the Alaskan earthquake of 1964, Hurricane Betsy (1965), and civil disorders of subsequent summers.

For displaced business disaster loans, the SBA has need to deal with two other agencies—the Urban Renewal Administration of the Department of Housing and Urban Development and the Transportation Department's Federal Highway Administration. Urban renewal and highway construction, of course, account for a large amount of these loans. The SBA keeps in touch with the two agencies in order to learn their plans. This cooperation enables it to help ease the transition for small businessmen whose firms will be affected by a federal project.

Economic Development Administration (EDA) Loans. The SBA also cooperates with EDA in that agency's business loan program, which is for firms in economically distressed areas.

The loan application papers are processed by SBA personnel around the country. Final decision as to whether or not a loan will be made is left to the EDA.

Trade Adjustment Assistance. Under the Trade Expansion Act of 1962, the SBA is empowered to give loans to small business firms damaged as a result of the tariff cuts authorized in the legislation. This program implies SBA liaison with the Bureau of International Commerce in the Commerce Department, the Labor Department, and the Tariff Commission. In reality, there has been little activity of any kind in connection with the SBA trade adjustment authority.

INTERAGENCY RELATIONS AND INVESTMENT ASSISTANCE

Most SBA activities under the SBIC program are carried on either inside the SBA or in direct dealings with the SBIC's themselves. However, occasionally other government agencies become involved.

Securities and Exchange Commission (SEC). Operation of the securities and financial markets is regulated by the SEC. This includes surveillance of the SBIC program as well as the thousands of other small companies whose securities are offered to the public. The SEC requires that all companies putting securities up for public sale make a detailed disclosure of information needed by potential investors. Since SBIC's are licensed and monitored by the SBA, the SEC has relaxed its regulations for SBIC's. There is cooperation between the SBA and SEC in carrying out their respective regulatory responsibilities, but much of their dealings with SBIC's are carried on separately.

Internal Revenue Service (IRS). The SBA from time to time has consulted with the IRS about taxation of SBIC's—and even small business generally. SBA officials involved have been from the agency's Investment Division, lawyers who work closely with the Division, and occasionally economists assigned to investment problems.

INTERAGENCY RELATIONS AND SBA ECONOMISTS

Now working for the most part under the SBA's assistant administrator for Planning, Research, and Analysis, the agency's economists have perhaps the most contacts with other government agencies. They look into all the policy and program activities—with all their interagency implications—carried on by the SBA. They talk regularly with the various data-gathering agencies and handle size matters affecting industries with ties throughout government. And they are responsible for the SBA's research program.

Policy and Programs. Obviously, SBA economists talk with everyone throughout government, from the Council of Economic Advisers on down. If the policy being considered is loans to the poor, the agency called upon may be the Civil Rights Commission or the Office of Economic Opportunity. If the issue concerns the effects of defense cutbacks on small business, SBA economists may confer with Pentagon officials or the arms control agency. If tax policy for small business is under discussion, they will want to talk with the Internal Revenue Service. On tariff matters, SBA economists go to the Bureau of International Commerce and perhaps the State Department or the Tariff Commission. With wide-ranging policy and program interests and responsibilities, the SBA economics corps gets a good look at much of the government.

Data-gathering Agencies. SBA's economists are called upon to produce a great deal of information. They obtain it from four main government sources: The Bureau of the Census (Commerce Department), the Office of Business Economics (Commerce), the Bureau of Labor Statistics (Labor Department), and the Internal Revenue Service (Treasury). If the last source sounds somewhat surprising, recall our discussion in Chapter II of the IRS figures on the business population, which are based on business income tax returns.

Size Standards Cases. Although the size standards staff at the SBA is not currently located in the economic wing of the agency, it consists of working economists. (It has been said that in Washington an economist is any man who calls himself one. In the era of the proliferating Ph.D., this dictum is less true than it once was.) In investigating size cases, the staff frequently works with other government agencies. For example, the SBA economics staff was instrumental in having American Motors declared a small business for purposes of government procurement. The principal purpose of this move was to be able then to persuade the General Services Administration to buy American Motors cars, on a small business "set-aside" basis, for government use.

Research Activities. As an offshoot of their concern with economic research, SBA economists have had occasion to confer with officials of other agencies engaged in the so-called R&D business. These include the National Science Foundation, which sponsors all kinds of scientific research; the Commerce Department's Office of State Technical Services, which supports the dissemination of technical information to the public at designated state universities; and the economic research shops of countless government agencies. In a similar vein, the SBA's chief economist has served as a member of the White House Committee on the Economic Impact of Defense and Disarmament and the Commerce Department's Panel on Invention and Innovation. SBA economists also cooperated with the Federal Reserve Board staff in their pioneering study, *Financing Small Business*.

INTERAGENCY RELATIONS AND SBA LAWYERS

Lawyers are the last of the great generalists, and the SBA Office of General Counsel provides no exception. Although SBA lawyers as individuals specialize in specific SBA program areas, as a group they range far and wide in gathering information upon which to base their legal advice. In addition, lawyers at the SBA deal with regulatory and law-enforcement agencies.

Policies and Programs. Here the story is much the same as for the SBA economists. Legislative drafting, rulings on legal controversies, and so on, very often require consultation with lawyers in other agencies. Much store is set on precedent, and not merely precedent at the SBA. Other agencies have over-lapping jurisdiction, deal with similar problems, and the like. And, fundamentally a lawyer may simply be asked: "What should SBA do about—?" in which case his first instinct is to grab his telephone and call a friend (often a lawyer) in the agency specializing in the subject under discussion. Many policies and programs in Washington come about in such a way.

Regulatory Agencies. The SBA sometimes intercedes for small businessmen before regulatory agencies—the Interstate Commerce Commission, the Federal Trade Commission, the Maritime Commission, or the Civil Aeronautics Board, to name a few. Usually these cases are handled by SBA lawyers because the issues are essentially legal ones. (Perhaps even more often such informal *amicus curiae* briefs are filed on behalf of small businessmen by members of Congressional staffs.)

Law Enforcement: The Justice Department. The Office of General Counsel has had a continuing, if somewhat tenuous, relationship with the Justice Department's Antitrust Division, which is supposed to prevent and break up monopolies. The philosophical kinship with the SBA is evident, but somehow the two have rarely worked in concert.

A second Justice division with which SBA lawyers have dealt is the criminal division, which enforces such laws as those governing SBIC's and other securities transactions. Although some SBIC cases were referred to the Justice Department by the SBA for possible prosecution during and after the 1966 investigations of the industry, it is reassuring to note that interagency relations of this particularly noxious sort have seldom occurred.

XI

Which Way Ahead?

There is a widespread conviction in America that the good society must accord a prominent place to small business. According to this belief, an America in which small businesses succeed and flourish is a better America.

In 1946, two social scientists, interested in the relationship between the distribution of economic power and the good life, undertook a study designed to measure the correlation, if any, between the two. The scholars, sociologist C. Wright Mills and economist Melville J. Ulmer, performed the study for the Smaller War Plants Corporation. They surveyed six U.S. cities, three dominated by big business and three by small business. The two groups of communities were then compared in two respects: the extent to which their economic life was balanced and the general level of civic welfare enjoyed by their citizens. Mills and Ulmer found that the communities dominated by small business had a better-balanced economic life and a higher level of civic welfare, defined as better health, housing, sanitation, distribution of income, education, recreation, economic stability, and so on.

The Mills-Ulmer study is a fascinating document, which unfortunately is almost forgotten today. It provides scholarly verification for the vague belief of many that, when small business thrives, a community is somehow a better place in which to live.

232

Yet small business cannot succeed unaided. Government can help and has done so for many years through such general measures as antitrust policy and tax policy. Such actions have been supported by a broad consensus among policy-makers and the public at large.

The need for more positive action to assist small business has also been widely recognized, and this recognition led to creation of SBA, in 1953, to aid, counsel, and assist small business in a variety of ways. The SBA was not created, however, to lend money to all small business concerns or to procure government contracts for all small business firms. The agency received no blank check from the Congress.

Two problems loom as large today as they did in 1953. Which small businesses should the SBA assist? And how? Many solutions and answers have been posited, but there are no clearly definitive ones.

Perhaps the biggest question concerns whether the banker's approach that has characterized the SBA since its inception should continue to dominate the agency's lending policies and programs.

It will be recalled that the SBA's loss ratio on loans compares favorably with that of America's commercial banks. In the abstract, this performance is highly commendable. The SBA was not established to throw away the taxpayers' money. The extent to which the SBA's loss experience reflects sound credit judgment is, of course, all to the good. But it also reflects something else: an unwillingness to take risks. The SBA is not a commercial bank; it is an arm of the U.S. Government. It was created to make loans that, for one reason or another, the nation's commercial banks would not or could not make to small business concerns.

Any study of the SBA's operations would reveal that, in most of its lending programs, the credit policy is highly conservative. The typical loan applicant must have sufficient collateral, a good balance sheet, and a good profit and loss statement in order to get the loan. Following these strictures, the SBA is hardly different from a commercial bank, and one can well question whether the SBA should exist as presently constituted. A financial institution of the federal government should fill a gap left by the private banking sector. One of the gaps must surely be the innovative firm, which is short on capital but long on ability. Such a firm may not have much collateral or a good balance sheet or a good profit and loss statement. Commercial banks cannot take many flyers on such firms. But society, represented by a government agency like the SBA, should. For when these firms succeed, society benefits.

Another gap is surely that of the disadvantaged in our midst who wish to succeed in business and might do so if given a helping hand by the government. The SBA has done something here with its EOL program, but the effort has been unimaginative and too narrow in scope.

Another indication that the SBA lending policies are highly conservative is the sizable proportion of loans made either in participation with commercial banks or as guarantees of commercial bank loans. On the surface, this policy may seem highly sensible. But a moment's reflection would lead to the conclusion that these are "banker-type" loans, or else the banks would not participate in them. The SBA was not established to minimize risks for the banking community. It was set up to help small businessmen who needed aid.

Still another area where the SBA needs a change of direction is in its small business investment program. As often happens with programs of this sort, much is known about the SBIC's and about the fact that they have not been very profitable as a group, but little is known about the small business firms that they were designed to serve. Are the small businesses that have received assistance from the SBIC's better off than they were previously or better off than small businesses that have had no dealings with the SBIC's? No one really knows about this aspect of the effectiveness of the SBIC program.

It is time that some hard-headed research be undertaken in this area. It may well be that the whole SBIC program is ill conceived and that one of the distinguishing characteristics of small business, as such, is that it has an equity gap. It could well be that the long-term financing needs of small business could be better served by long-term loans from SBA than by the equity-type financings of the SBIC's. Or perhaps not. In either event, we ought to know.

Another area in which small business clearly needs assistance is management. SBA has a variety of programs here, based on the agency's awareness that successful management is as vital to a business firm's prosperity as adequate financing. But the total resources devoted to management assistance by the SBA are quite small; moreover, little is known about which management aids are most effective. More attention to these problems is needed.

Also, innovations in the procurement assistance program are possible. Has the small business set-aside effort been enough? Or are there ways of doing more to help small businesses get a larger share of the government procurement dollar in the future?

All the questions raised here stem from an uncertainty that exists about the essential purpose of the SBA. Sometime soon, the SBA, the White House, the Bureau of the Budget, and Congress must make fundamental decisions about the primary mission of the agency. Should it become more socially oriented? Should it devise a method for allocating its capital and other resources more effectively, not only in the interest of specific small businesses but also in the national interest? Or will the policy continue to be first come, first served? Should the SBA's clientele be more exclusive—that is, should it serve smaller firms than it now does? Or should over 90 per cent of America's businesses continue to be regarded as small?

Change is imperative in all these areas. The SBA should be socially oriented, because the basic rationale for its existence is the improved social welfare believed to result from a thriving small business community. The SBA can truly supplement the efforts of private financial institutions by helping those small firms that would otherwise be unable to obtain aid. Notable among these are innovative firms and those owned and operated by economically disadvantaged persons. Moreover, the SBA must husband its resources so as to aid primarily the most deserving segments of the small business population. The agency must have a clear set of priorities, and these priorities must be consistent over time.

It will not be easy to make decisions of this sort. It will be still more difficult to stand by the decisions as the leadership at the SBA and in the White House and on Capitol Hill changes over the years. But this must be done, in the interests of both common logic and public service. The problems are not insoluble, and the following specific actions would go far toward their solution:

1. The SBA should give increasing attention to the needs of potentially innovative small business firms. Their major problems are usually financial, and, accordingly, the brunt of the SBA assistance should be of this nature.

2. The EOL program should be expanded greatly. Aid to the disadvantaged entrepreneur should be the major mission of the SBA for the next generation or more. In order to make the effort more substantial, the maximum EOL loan should be raised from the current $25,000 to the $350,000 level permitted for the regular SBA business loans.

3. The increased emphasis on EOL's should be accompanied by increased emphasis on management assistance, particularly management counseling for the disadvantaged. This will require additional management personnel at SBA, especially in the field offices, as well as increased emphasis on the SCORE program and the participation of the private business community.

4. A way must be found to make the revolving fund of the SBA truly revolve. The agency must not be permitted to operate in fits and starts, as it has done too often in the past. The most important step in this direction would be to raise the interest rate significantly. At present, the statutory interest rate limit on direct business loans is below the prime rate charged by the commercial banks. This is ludicrous. If the SBA rate were set more in line with the market, much more income could be generated for the SBA revolving fund and the programs that must be financed by it.

5. A complete review of the SBA's size standards should be undertaken. As it now stands, practically all business firms except America's corporate giants are eligible to receive SBA assistance. SBA's size standards must be revised downward substantially if truly small business is to be served by the agency. This will require political courage on the part of all involved. The man whose toe is stepped upon is the one who protests to his congressman.

6. Better statistical tools must be developed for carrying out the agency's procurement programs. We simply do not know enough about the relative efficiencies and capabilities of small and big business in supplying the federal government with the goods and services it requires. Better statistics and more research on these matters would give us the answers we require.

7. Up to now, the SBA's procurement program has been confined to the federal government. It should be extended to state and local governments. This will be particularly important in the future, because all authoritative projections of the national economy for the next decade show that the expenditures of state and local governments will rise at a much faster pace than federal expenditures.

8. Finally, and most importantly, continuity of leadership is essential to the effective operation of any enterprise. This important principle has not been applied with any regularity

to the SBA. During the past five years, there have been no fewer than six administrators at the SBA. Surely this is too much of even a good thing.

Not only has the top man frequently been changed. Each has also brought in "his own people," with their pet prejudices and theories. Usually these are people of considerable ability. Too often, however, they bring to the agency insufficient experience and understanding of the problems of small business. By the time they have gained such insight, they move on.

Most of all, the SBA needs a clearly defined mission and an administrator who serves for three or four years. A man who stays for a shorter period of time may quickly proclaim new SBA policy. But when he leaves, and particularly if he does not relinquish his leadership in favor of a hand-picked successor who has served at the agency with him, he often has made no lasting impact on the SBA. The permanent officials accustomed to the old ways of doing things remain. And a new administrator comes determined to make his mark, which can only be done by changing what his predecessor did. This is a vicious cycle in the extreme. No matter how brilliant the top leadership of the agency, they must be given the time—and must take the time—to implement their objectives. Men of this caliber are rare in Washington, as elsewhere, but surely they can be found.

The SBA is now in its second decade of service to the American small businessman. It has developed from a temporary agency, created almost as an afterthought in the wake of the RFC. It has built up considerable *expertise* and aided many small firms. There are many ways in which the agency's undertakings could be improved, but that is only another way of saying that the SBA faces a challenging future in which its work is more needed than ever before.

APPENDIX I. SBA as a Career

The SBA offers diverse and challenging career opportunities to college graduates. Its programs provide a combination of effective business experience and rewarding public service.

SBA employees are hired in accordance with Civil Service Commission regulations. To be eligible for employment on the professional level, a candidate must successfully compete in the Federal Service Entrance Examination, which is administered by the Commission. The Civil Service Commission announces the results by letter to those who have taken the test.

For an interview at SBA, a candidate should contact the College Placement Officer, 1441 L Street N.W., Room 301, Washington, D.C. 20416. Placement depends upon the needs of the agency as well as the applicant's desires for development in particular career fields.

Starting salaries range from $5,732 (GS-5) to $8,462 (GS-9) per annum, depending on the test score, education, and experience of the applicant. Details regarding eligibility are available in the Civil Service Commission's Federal Service Entrance Examination announcement, #410. More information about the FSEE may be obtained from the nearest local Interagency Board of Civil Service Examiners, the local post office, or by writing to the Civil Service Commission, 1900 E Street, N.W., Washington, D.C. 20415.

SBA has professional positions available in financial assistance; procurement and management assistance; investment analysis; planning, research, and analysis; general legal counsel; electronic data processing; and administrative management.

FINANCIAL ASSISTANCE

SBA's financial assistance personnel perform duties similar to those of bank loan officers. SBA financial assistance staff members should be familiar with the policies and operations of the private lending institutions. They process all types of loans made by the agency—business, disaster, displaced business, economic opportunity, and development company loans.

PROCUREMENT AND MANAGEMENT ASSISTANCE

The SBA procurement assistance effort is designed to ensure that small business gets a fair share of government contracts and sub-contracts. To do this job, the agency needs technical excellence in such areas as procurement law, government contracting and contract administration, industrial production planning and layout, and industrial engineering.

The qualifications for jobs in SBA management assistance programs are less technical. Nonetheless, they require ability to counsel small businessmen and develop public educational programs using SBA publications and training courses.

While experience in the specialized areas is quite useful, SBA welcomes applications from college graduates with a general background and an interest in pursuing careers in which the above skills can be acquired on the job.

INVESTMENT ANALYSIS

In the SBIC program, SBA offers opportunities for college graduates in financial and business management analysis. On-the-job training programs are featured in analysis of financial management, organization, operations, and practices and also in pertinent regulatory provisions, accounting, and legal principles governing the operations of SBIC's.

A comprehensive knowledge of business and financial management is required. Applicants should also have substantial background in credit and financial analysis and money and banking, plus a basic knowledge of accounting and business or corporate financing.

PLANNING, RESEARCH, AND ANALYSIS

SBA has need of staff members trained in fields relevant to economic analysis to study and make recommendations about the agency's policies and programs from an economic standpoint. Not only economists but also college majors in statistics, mathematics, and related fields would have useful backgrounds for this office.

GENERAL COUNSEL

SBA attorneys serve as legal advisors to administrative officials and provide legal assistance for the agency's various programs. Duties of the Washington staff attorneys include advising on the making, servicing, and liquidating of loans; assisting in development of policies and operating procedures; preparing and interpreting regulations and legislative proposals; and maintaining liaison with other agencies. Attorneys in the field serve as house counsel to local SBA officials.

A degree from an accredited law school is required. No competitive examination is necessary. Those who have received a degree but have not yet been admitted to the bar may be hired as a law clerk trainee, GS-7 or GS-9, pending their admission within fourteen months.

ELECTRONIC DATA PROCESSING

Electronic data processing is one of the fastest-growing fields in both government and industry, and SBA too needs people trained in this area. Not only physics and mathematics majors but business majors and graduates with liberal arts backgrounds will be considered for such positions. This work requires a well-rounded person —creative, technically oriented, able to make logical and organized solutions to problems, and cheerful through it all.

ADMINISTRATIVE OFFICES

The administrative activities of SBA—budget, fiscal operations, administrative services, data systems and services, personnel, and management analysis—also offer career opportunities.

Professional positions in these areas are filled through civil service registers developed for those who have passed appropriate examinations. Trainee positions are available for digital computer operators and programers and accountants. In addition, vacancies occasionally exist for mail distributors, library assistants, personnel assistants, supply officers, and graphic and design specialists. Information concerning all types of examinations is available at any Civil Service Commission office.

THE MANAGEMENT INTERN PROGRAM

SBA has recently established a management intern program for highly qualified young people who are seeking executive careers within government. The competition for management internships is keen, since the number of these positions is limited and the standards for eligibility are quite high. However, rewards are commensurate, as the intern is in frequent contact with high-level management and generally advances rapidly.

The management intern training program consists of about one year of rotational assignments in the offices of SBA's headquarters in Washington and in major fields offices. This program exposes the intern to the various administrative functions of SBA as well as to the technical program areas. Most work assignments consist of special projects designed to familiarize the intern with the agency. When the program has been completed, the intern is assigned to a permanent SBA position, usually in an office of his choice.

To be eligible for this program, the college graduate must demonstrate outstanding potential by passing the FSEE and an additional written test, qualifying in a group interview, and receiving personal recommendations. The Civil Service Commission certifies to all government agencies those people who are qualified and eligible for the program.

BENEFITS

All federal employees, including those at SBA, receive thirteen days of vacation and thirteen days of sick leave each year at the start of their careers. After three years of service, annual leave is increased to twenty days a year. After fifteen years, an employee gets twenty-six days of annual leave. Life insurance and health insurance are available at very reasonable rates for all SBA employees.

TRAINING

SBA conducts a comprehensive training program for all its employees. It includes a variety of courses, conferences, or workshops conducted by SBA itself, other federal agencies, professional groups, and universities.

APPENDIX II. Small Business Act

(As Amended)

Citation. SEC. 1. This Act may be cited as the "Small Business Act."

Policy of Congress. 15 U.S.C. 631. SEC. 2. (a) The essence of the American economic system of private enterprise is free competition. Only through full and free competition can free markets, free entry into business, and opportunities for the expression and growth of personal initiative and individual judgment be assured. The preservation and expansion of such competition is basic not only to the economic well-being but to the security of this Nation. Such security and well-being cannot be realized unless the actual and potential capacity of small business is encouraged and developed. It is the declared policy of the Congress that the Government should aid, counsel, assist, and protect, insofar as is possible, the interests of small-business concerns in order to preserve free competitive enterprise, to insure that a fair proportion of the total purchases and contracts or subcontracts for property and services for the Government (including but not limited to contracts or subcontracts for maintenance, repair, and construction) be placed with small-business enterprises, to insure that a fair proportion of the total sales of Government property be made to such enterprises, and to maintain and strengthen the overall economy of the Nation.[1]

[1] The subcontracts of contractors performing work or rendering services under Government procurement contracts were included within the policy statements of this section by sec. 6 of PL 87-305.

(b) Further, it is the declared policy of the Congress that the Government should aid and assist victims of floods and other catastrophes, and small-business concerns which are displaced as a result of federally aided construction programs.[2]

SEC. 3. For the purposes of this Act, a small-business concern shall be deemed to be one which is independently owned and operated and which is not dominant in its field of operation. In addition to the foregoing criteria the Administrator, in making a detailed definition may use these criteria, among others: Number of employees and dollar volume of business. Where the number of employees is used as one of the criteria in making such definition for any of the purposes of this Act, the maximum number of employees which a small-business concern may have under the definition shall vary from industry to industry to the extent necessary to reflect differing characteristics of such industries and to take proper account of other relevant factors. *(Small business defined. 15 U.S.C. 632.)*

SEC. 4. (a) In order to carry out the policies of this Act there is hereby created an agency under the name "Small Business Administration" (herein referred to as the Administration), which Administration shall be under the general direction and supervision of the President and shall not be affiliated with or be within any other agency or department of the Federal Government. The principal office of the Administration shall be located in the District of Columbia. The Administration may establish such branch and regional offices in other places in the United States as may be determined by the Administrator of the Administration. As used in this Act, the term "United States" includes the several States, the Territories and possessions of the United States, the Commonwealth of Puerto Rico, and the District of Columbia. *(Small Business Administration 15 U.S.C. 633. Under President. Independent agency.)*

(b) The management of the Administration shall be vested in an Administrator who shall be appointed from civilian life by the President, by and with the advice and consent of the Senate, and who shall be a person of outstanding qualifications known to be familiar and *(Administrator.)*

[2] The last 15 words of this subsection added by sec. 305(b) of PL 87-70.

sympathetic with small-business needs and problems. The Administrator shall not engage in any other business, vocation, or employment than that of serving as Administrator. The Administrator is authorized to appoint a Deputy Administrator and three Associate Administrators (including the Associate Administrator specified in section 201 of the Small Business Investment Act of 1958) to assist in the execution of the functions vested in the Administration. The Deputy Administrator shall be Acting Administrator of the Administration during the absence or disability of the Administrator or in the event of a vacancy in the office of the Administrator.[3]

(c)[4] (1) There are hereby established in the Treasury the following revolving funds: (A) a disaster loan fund which shall be available for financing functions performed under sections 7(b)(1), 7(b)(2), 7(b)(4), and 7(c)(2) of this Act, including administrative expenses in connection with such functions; and (B) a business loan and investment fund which shall be available for financing functions performed under sections 7(a), 7(b)(3), 7(e), and 8(a) of this Act, titles III and V of the Small Business Investment Act of 1958, and title IV of the Economic Opportunity Act of 1964, including administrative expenses in connection with such functions.

(2) All repayments of loans and debentures, payments of interest and other receipts arising out of transactions heretofore or hereafter entered into by the Administration (A) pursuant to sections 7(b)(1), 7(b)(2), 7(b)(4), and 7(c)(2) of this Act shall be paid into the disaster loan fund; and (B) pursuant to sections 7(a), 7(b)(3), 7(e), and 8(a) of this Act, titles III and V of the Small Business Investment Act of

---

[3] This subsec. 4(b) amended by sec. 8 of PL 89-779 to replace the three Deputy Administrators previously authorized by this subsection and the Deputy Administrator authorized by subsection 201 of the Small Business Investment Act of 1958 with a single Deputy Administrator authorized to be Acting Administrator and three Associate Administrators.

[4] Section 4(c) was substantially amended, effective July 1, 1966, by section 2 of PL 89-409 primarily to establish two revolving funds instead of the former single comingled fund. The amendment also added the requirement for quarterly reports to certain Congressional Committees on the status of the revolving funds and also the provision on preparing Agency budgets according to the Government Corporation Control Act.

1958, and title IV of the Economic Opportunity Act of 1964, shall be paid into the business loan and investment fund.

(3) Unexpended balances of appropriations made to the fund pursuant to this subsection, as in effect immediately prior to the effective date of this paragraph, shall be allocated, together with related assets and liabilities, to the funds established by paragraph (1) in such amounts as the Administrator shall determine. In addition to any sums so allocated, appropriations are hereby authorized to be made to such funds, as capital thereof, in such amounts as may be necessary to carry out the functions of the Administration, which appropriations shall remain available until expended. *Appropriations, unexpended balances.*

(4) The total amount of loans, guarantees, and other obligations or commitments, heretofore or hereafter entered into by the Administration, which are outstanding at any one time (A) under sections 7(a), 7(b)(3), 7(e), and 8(a) of this Act, and title IV of the Economic Opportunity Act of 1964, shall not exceed $1,900,000,000[5]; (B) under title III of the Small Business Investment Act of 1958, shall not exceed $450,-000,000[5]; (C) under title V of the Small Business Investment Act of 1958, shall not exceed $300,000,000[5]; and (D) under title IV of the Economic Opportunity Act of 1964 shall not exceed $200,000,000.[5] *Loans, etc. limitations.*

(5) The Administration shall submit to the Committees on Appropriations and the Committees on Banking and Currency of the Senate and House of Representatives, as soon as possible after the beginning of each calendar quarter, a full and complete report on the status of each of the funds established by paragraph (1). If at the close of the preceding calendar quarter the aggregate amount outstanding or committed by the Administration in carrying out its functions under any of the sections or titles referred to in paragraph (4) exceeded 75 per centum of the total amount authorized to be outstanding or committed under such sections or titles, the Administration's report shall include its rec- *Reports to Congressional committees.*

[5] Current ceiling was established by section 102 of PL 90-104.

Budget preparation.

ommendations for such additional authority as it deems appropriate. Business-type budgets for each of the funds established by paragraph (1) shall be prepared, transmitted to the Congress, considered, and enacted in the manner prescribed by law (sections 102, 103, and 104 of the Government Corporation Control Act (31 U.S.C. 847-849)) for wholly-owned Government corporations.

Interest to Treasury.

(6) The Administration shall pay into miscellaneous receipts of the Treasury, following the close of each fiscal year, interest on the outstanding cash disbursements from each of the funds established by paragraph (1) at rates determined by the Secretary of the Treasury, taking into consideration the current average yields on outstanding interest-bearing marketable public debt obligations of the United States of comparable maturities as calculated for the month of June preceding such fiscal year.

Loan Policy Board.

(d) There is hereby created the Loan Policy Board of the Small Business Administration, which shall consist of the following members, all ex officio: The Administrator, as Chairman, the Secretary of the Treasury, and the Secretary of Commerce. Either of the said Secretaries may designate an officer of his Department, who has been appointed by the President by and with the advice and consent of the Senate, to act in his stead as a member of the Loan Policy Board with respect to any matter or matters. The Loan Policy Board shall establish general policies (particularly with reference to the public interest involved in the granting and denial of applications for financial assistance by the Administration and with reference to the coordination of the functions of the Administration with other activities and policies of the Government), which shall govern the granting and denial of applications for financial assistance by the Administration.[6]

Administrative powers. 15 U.S.C. 634

SEC. 5. (a) The Administration shall have power to adopt, alter, and use a seal, which shall be judicially noticed. The Administrator is authorized, subject to the civil-service and classification laws, to select, employ,

---

[6] The SBA Loan Policy Board was abolished by Reorganization Plan No. 4 of 1965 (effective July 27, 1965; 30 F.R. 9353) and its functions transferred to the SBA Administrator.

appoint, and fix the compensation of such officers, employees, attorneys, and agents as shall be necessary to carry out the provisions of this Act; to define their authority and duties; to provide bonds for them in such amounts as the Administrator shall determine; and to pay the costs of qualification of certain of them as notaries public. The Administration, with the consent of any board, commission, independent establishment or executive department of the Government, may avail itself on a reimbursable or nonreimbursable basis of the use of information, services, facilities (including any field service thereof), officers, and employees thereof, in carrying out the provisions of this Act.[7]

(b) In the performance of, and with respect to, the functions, powers, and duties vested in him by this Act the Administrator may— *Administrator may:*

(1) sue and be sued in any court of record of a State having general jurisdiction, or in any United States district court, and jurisdiction is conferred upon such district court to determine such controversies without regard to the amount in controversy; but no attachment, injunction, garnishment, or other similar process, mesne or final, shall be issued against the Administrator or his property; *Sue and be sued.*

(2) under regulations prescribed by him, assign or sell at public or private sale, or otherwise dispose of for cash or credit, in his discretion and upon such terms and conditions and for such consideration as the Administrator shall determine to be reasonable, any evidence of debt, contract, claim, personal property, or security assigned to or held by him in connection with the payment of loans granted under this Act, and to collect or compromise all obligations assigned to or held by him and all legal or equitable rights accruing to him in connection with the payment of such loans until such time as such obligations may be re- *Dispose of property.*

[7] The last sentence of former sec. 5(a), authorizing 15 positions within SBA to be placed in grades 16, 17, and 18 of the general schedule established by the Classification Act of 1949, was deleted by sec. 103(3) of PL 87-367.

ferred to the Attorney General for suit or collection;

Utilize property.

(3) deal with, complete, renovate, improve, modernize, insure, or rent, or sell for cash or credit upon such terms and conditions and for such consideration as the Administrator shall determine to be reasonable, any real property conveyed to or otherwise acquired by him in connection with the payment of loans granted under this Act;

Collect claims.

(4) pursue to final collection, by way of compromise or otherwise, all claims against third parties assigned to the Administrator in connection with loans made by him. This shall include authority to obtain deficiency judgments or otherwise in the case of mortgages assigned to the Administrator. Section 3709 of the Revised Statutes, as amended (41 U.S.C., sec. 5), shall not be construed to apply to any contract of hazard insurance or to any purchase or contract for services or supplies on account of property obtained by the Administrator as a result of loans made under this Act if the premium therefor or the amount thereof does not exceed $1,000. The power to convey and to execute in the name of the Administrator deeds of conveyance, deeds of release, assignments and satisfactions of mortgages, and any other written instrument relating to real property or any interest therein acquired by the Administrator pursuant to the provisions of this Act may be exercised by the Administrator or by any officer or agent appointed by him without the execution of any express delegation of power or power of attorney. Nothing in this section shall be construed to prevent the Administrator from delegating such power by order or by power of attorney, in his discretion, to any officer or agent he may appoint;

Acquire property.

(5) acquire, in any lawful manner, any property (real, personal, or mixed, tangible or intangible), whenever deemed necessary or appropriate to the conduct of the activities authorized in sections 7(a) and 7(b);

(6) make such rules and regulations as he deems necessary to carry out the authority vested in him by or pursuant to this Act;

Issue regulations.

(7) in addition to any powers, functions, privileges, and immunities otherwise vested in him, take any and all actions, including the procurement of the services of attorneys by contract, determined by him to be necessary or desirable in making, servicing, compromising, modifying, liquidating, or otherwise dealing with or realizing on loans made under the provisions of this Act; but no attorneys' services shall be procured by contract in any office where an attorney or attorneys are or can be economically employed full time to render such services;

Services of attorneys.

(8) pay the transportation expenses and per diem in lieu of subsistence expenses, in accordance with the Travel Expense Act of 1949, for travel of any person employed by the Administration to render temporary services not in excess of six months in connection with any disaster referred to in section 7(b) from place of appointment to, and while at, the disaster area and any other temporary posts of duty and return upon completion of the assignment; and

Employ and reimburse temporary employees.

(9) accept the services and facilities of Federal, State, and local agencies and groups, both public and private, and utilize such gratuitous services and facilities as may, from time to time, be necessary, to further the objectives of section 7(b).

Accept free services.

(c) To such extent as he finds necessary to carry out the provisions of this Act, the Administrator is authorized to procure the temporary (not in excess of one year) or intermittent services of experts or consultants or organizations thereof, including stenographic reporting services, by contract or appointment, and in such cases such services shall be without regard to the civil-service and classification laws and, except in the case of stenographic reporting services by organizations, without regard to section 3709 of the Revised Statutes, as amended (41 U.S.C., sec. 5). Any individual so em-

Employ consultants.

ployed may be compensated at a rate not in excess of $50 per diem, and, while such individual is away from his home or regular place of business, he may be allowed transportation and not to exceed $15 per diem in lieu of subsistence and other expenses.

(d) Section 3648 of the Revised Statutes (31 U.S.C. 529) shall not apply to prepayments of rentals made by the Administration on safety deposit boxes used by the Administration for the safeguarding of instruments held as security for loans or for the safeguarding of other documents.[8]

Safety
deposit
boxes.

Depositaries
of funds.
15 U.S.C.
635.

SEC. 6. (a) All moneys of the Administration not otherwise employed may be deposited with the Treasury of the United States subject to check by authority of the Administration. The Federal Reserve banks are authorized and directed to act as depositaries, custodians, and fiscal agents for the Administration in the general performance of its powers conferred by this Act. Any banks insured by the Federal Deposit Insurance Corporation, when designated by the Secretary of the Treasury, shall act as custodians and financial agents for the Administration. Each Federal Reserve bank, when designated by the Administrator as fiscal agent for the Administration, shall be entitled to be reimbursed for all expenses incurred as such fiscal agent.

Retirement
contribu-
tions.

(b) The Administrator shall contribute to the employees' compensation fund, on the basis of annual billings as determined by the Secretary of Labor, for the benefit payments made from such fund on account of employees engaged in carrying out functions financed by the revolving fund established by section 4(c) of this Act. The annual billings shall also include a statement of the fair portion of the cost of the administration of such fund, which shall be paid by the Administrator into the Treasury as miscellaneous receipts.

Business
loans.
15 U.S.C.
636.

SEC. 7. (a) The Administration is empowered to make loans to enable small-business concerns to finance plant construction, conversion, or expansion, including the acquisition of land; or to finance the acquisition of equipment, facilities, machinery, supplies, or materials;

[8] Subsection 5(d) added by section 4 of PL 87-305.

or to supply such concerns with working capital to be used in the manufacture of articles, equipment, supplies, or materials for war, defense, or civilian production or as may be necessary to insure a well-balanced national economy; and such loans may be made or effected either directly or in cooperation with banks or other lending institutions through agreements to participate on an immediate or deferred basis. The foregoing powers shall be subject, however, to the following restrictions and limitations: *Restrictions on loans.*

(1) No financial assistance shall be extended pursuant to this subsection unless the financial assistance applied for is not otherwise available on reasonable terms. *Not elsewhere available.*

(2) No immediate participation may be purchased unless it is shown that a deferred participation is not available; and no loan may be made unless it is shown that a participation is not available. *Priority on types of loans.*

(3) In agreements to participate in loans on a deferred basis under this subsection, such participation by the Administration shall not be in excess of 90 per centum of the balance of the loan outstanding at the time of disbursement. *90 percent maximum SBA participation.*

(4) Except as provided in paragraph (5)(A), no loan under this subsection shall be made if the total amount outstanding and committed (by participation or otherwise) to the borrower from the revolving fund established by this Act would exceed $350,000; (B) the rate of interest for the Administration's share of any such loan shall be no more than 5½ per centum per annum; and (C) no such loan, including renewals or extensions thereof, may be made for a period or periods exceeding ten years except that such portion of a loan made for the purpose of constructing facilities may have a maturity of fifteen years plus such additional period as is estimated may be required to complete such construction.[9] *$350,000 maximum SBA share.* *5½ percent maximum SBA interest.* *Maximum term.*

[9] The maximum term on the portion of a loan made for constructing facilities was increased from ten to fifteen years by section 103 of PL 90-104.

(5) In the case of any loan made under this subsection to a corporation formed and capitalized by a group of small-business concerns with resources provided by them for the purpose of obtaining for the use of such concerns raw materials, equipment, inventories, supplies or the benefits of research and development, or for establishing facilities for such purpose, (A) the limitation of $350,000 prescribed in paragraph (4) shall not apply, but the limit of such loan shall be $250,000 multiplied by the number of separate small businesses which formed and capitalized such corporation; (B) the rate of interest for the Administration's share of such loan shall be no less than 3 nor more than 5 per centum per annum; and (C) such loan, including renewals and extensions thereof, may not be made for a period or periods exceeding ten years except that if such loan is made for the purpose of constructing facilities it may have a maturity of twenty years plus such additional time as is required to complete such construction.

(6) The Administrator is authorized to consult with representatives of small-business concerns with a view to encouraging the formation by such concerns of the corporation referred to in paragraph (5). No act or omission to act, if requested by the Administrator pursuant to this paragraph, and if found and approved by the Administration as contributing to the needs of small business, shall be construed to be within the prohibitions of the antitrust laws of the Federal Trade Commission Act of the United States. A copy of the statement of any such finding and approval intended to be within the coverage of this section, and any modification or withdrawal thereof, shall be furnished to the Attorney General and the Chairman of the Federal Trade Commission when made, and it shall be published in the Federal Register. The authority granted in this paragraph shall be exercised only (A) by the Administrator, (B) upon the condition that the Administrator consult with Attorney Gen-

---

Marginal notes:

Pool loans: Maximum limit.

Interest between 3 and 5 percent.

Maximum period.

SBA may encourage formation of pools.

Antitrust exemption.

eral and with the Chairman of the Federal Trade Commission, and (C) upon the condition that the Administrator obtain the approval of the Attorney General before exercising such authority. Upon withdrawal of any request or finding hereunder or upon withdrawal by the Attorney General of his approval granted under the preceding sentence, the provisions of this paragraph shall not apply to any subsequent act or omission to act by reason of such finding or request.

(7) All loans made under this subsection shall be of such sound value or so secured as reasonably to assure repayment. *Reasonable assurance of repayment.*

(b) The Administration also is empowered[10]—

(1) to make such loans (either directly or in cooperation with banks or other lending institutions through agreements to participate on an immediate or deferred basis) as the Administration may determine to be necessary or appropriate because of floods or other catastrophes;[11] *Disaster loans.*

(2) to make such loans (either directly or in cooperation with banks or other lending institutions through agreements to participate on an immediate or deferred basis) as the Administration may determine to be necessary or appropriate to any small business concern located in an area affected by a disaster, if the Administration determines that the concern has suffered a substantial economic injury as a result of such disaster and if such disaster constitutes— *Economic injury disaster loans.*

(A) a major disaster, as determined by the President under the Act entitled "An Act to authorize Federal assistance to States and local governments in major disasters, and for other

[10] A number of amendments have been made to subsection 7(b):
PL 87-70 added paragraph (3);
PL 88-264 added paragraph (4) and extended paragraph (2) beyond its former scope relating solely to drought and excessive rainfall disasters;
PL 88-560 added the clause after the word "Government" in paragraph (3); and
PL 89-59 extended the maximum term of disaster loans to thirty years, and provided for suspension of repayments in certain hardship cases.
[11] PL 89-339 provided for partial forgiveness of Hurricane Betsy disaster loans in the States of Florida, Louisiana, and Mississippi.

purposes", approved September 30, 1950, as amended (42 U.S.C. 1855–1855g), or

(B) a natural disaster, as determined by the Secretary of Agriculture pursuant to the Consolidated Farmers Home Administration Act of 1961 (7 U.S.C. 1961);

Displaced business disaster loans.

(3) to make such loans (either directly or in cooperation with banks or other lending institutions through agreements to participate on an immediate or deferred basis) as the Administration may determine to be necessary or appropriate to assist any small business concern in reestablishing its business, if the Administration determines that such concern has suffered substantial economic injury as a result of its displacement by a federally aided urban renewal or highway construction program or by any other construction conducted by or with funds provided by the Federal Government; and the purposes of a loan made pursuant to this paragraph may, in the discretion of the Administrator, include the purchase or construction of other premises whether or not the borrower owned the premises from which it was displaced;

(4) to make such loans (either directly or in cooperation with banks or other lending institutions through agreements to participate on an immediate or deferred basis) as the Administration may determine to be necessary or appropriate to assist any small business concern in reestablishing its business

Product disaster loans.

if the Administration determines that such concern has suffered substantial economic injury as a result of the inability of such concern to process or market a product for human consumption because of disease or toxicity occurring in such product through natural or undetermined causes.

Maximum term 30 years. Interest rates.

No loan under this subsection, including renewals and extensions thereof, may be made for a period or periods exceeding thirty years: *Provided,* That the Administrator may consent to a suspension in the payment of principal and interest charges on, and to an extension in the maturity of, the Federal share of any loan under this subsection for a period of not to exceed five years, if (A) the borrower under such loan is a homeowner or a small-business concern, (B) the loan was made to enable (i) such homeowner to repair or replace his home, or (ii) such concern to repair or replace plant or equipment which was damaged or destroyed as the result of a disaster meeting the requirements of clause (A) or (B) of paragraph (2) of this subsection, and (C) the Administrator determines such action is necessary to avoid severe financial hardship: *Provided further,* That the provisions of paragraph (1) of subsection (c) of this section shall not be applicable to any such loan having a maturity in excess of twenty years. The interest rate on the Administration's share of any loan made under this subsection shall not exceed 3 per centum per annum, except that in the case of a loan made pursuant to paragraph (3), the rate of interest on the Administration's share of such loan shall not be more than the higher of (A) 2¾ per centum per annum; or (B) the average annual interest rate on all interest-bearing obligations of the United States then forming a part of the public debt as computed at the end of the fiscal year next preceding the date of the loan and adjusted to the nearest one-eighth of 1 per centum, plus one-quarter of 1 per centum per annum.[12] In agreements to participate in loans on a deferred basis under this subsection, such participation by the Administration shall not be in excess of 90 per centum of the balance of the loan outstanding at the time of disbursement. Maximum participation 90 percent.

(c)(1) The Administration may further extend the maturity of or renew any loan made pursuant to this section, or any loan transferred to the Administration pursuant to Reorganization Plan Numbered 2 of 1954, or Reorganization Plan Numbered 1 of 1957, for additional periods not to exceed ten years beyond the period Terms may be extended.

[12] The interest rate applicable to loans made pursuant to subsection 7(b)(3) was specified by sec. 305(4) of PL 87-70.

stated therein, if such extension or renewal will aid in the orderly liquidation of such loan.

(2) During any period in which principal and interest charges are suspended on the Federal share of any loan, as provided in subsection (b), the Administrator shall, upon the request of any person, firm, or corporation having a participation in such loan, purchase such participation, or assume the obligation of the borrower, for the balance of such period, to make principal and interest payments on the non-Federal share of such loan: *Provided,* That no such payments shall be made by the Administrator in behalf of any borrower unless (i) the Administrator determines that such action is necessary in order to avoid a default, and (ii) the borrower agrees to make payments to the Administration in an aggregate amount equal to the amount paid in its behalf by the Administrator, in such manner and at such times (during or after the term of the loan) as the Administrator shall determine having due regard to the purposes sought to be achieved by this paragraph.[13]

Research grants.

(d) The Administration also is empowered to make grants to any State government or any agency thereof, any State-chartered development credit or finance corporation, any land-grant college or university, any college or school of business, engineering, commerce, or agriculture, or to any corporation formed by two or more of the entities hereinabove described which are eligible to receive such grants, for studies, research, and counseling concerning the managing, financing, and operation of small business enterprises and technical and statistical information necessary thereto in order to carry out the purposes of section 8(b)(1) by coordinating such information with existing information facilities within the State and by making such information available to State and local agencies. The Administrator may recommend to grant applicants particular studies or research which are to be financed by such grants. The total of all grants (including amendments and modifications thereof) made under this subsection within any one State in any one year shall not

[13] Par. 7(c)(2) added by PL 89-59.

exceed $40,000. The Administration may require, as a condition to any grant (or amendment or modification thereof) made under this subsection, that an additional amount not exceeding the amount of such grant be provided from sources other than the Administration to assist in carrying out the purposes for which such grant is made: *Provided,* That if such grant or any part thereof is to be utilized for the purpose of providing counseling services to individual small business enterprises the Administration shall require that such additional amount be provided and in an amount which is equal to the amount of such grant. What constitutes such additional amount may be defined by the Administration.[14]

(e) The Administration also is empowered to make loans (either directly or in cooperation with banks or other lenders through agreements to participate on an immediate or deferred basis) to assist any firm to adjust to changed economic conditions resulting from increased competition from imported articles, but only if (1) an adjustment proposal of such firm has been certified by the Secretary of Commerce pursuant to the Trade Expansion Act of 1962, (2) the Secretary has referred such proposal to the Administration under that Act and the loan would provide part or all of the financial assistance necessary to carry out such proposal, and (3) the Secretary's certification is in force at the time the Administration makes the loan. With respect to loans made under this subsection the Administration shall apply the provisions of sections 314, 315, 316, 318, 319, and 320 of the Trade Expansion Act of 1962 as though such loans had been made under section 314 of that Act.[15]

Trade adjustment assistance loans.

(f) [16]In the administration of the disaster loan program under subsection (b)(1) of this section, in the case of property loss or damage as a result of a disaster

[14] Former subsec. 7(d) was rewritten by sec. 9 of PL 87-305.
[15] Sec. 7(e), effective July 1, 1966, added by PL 89-409, which simultaneously repealed sec. 2 of PL 87-550 (containing the same authority) and transferred any expended balances of appropriations heretofore appropriated for the purposes of such section to the business loan and investment fund established by sec. 4(c)(1) of the Small Business Act.
[16] Added by PL 89-769, sec. 7(b), which inadvertently used letter (e) for this subsection instead of (f). Designation corrected by sec. 104 of PL 90-104.

which is a "major disaster" as defined in section 2(a) of the Act of September 30, 1950 (42 U.S.C. 1855a(a)), the Small Business Administration, to the extent such loss or damage is not compensated for by insurance or otherwise, may lend to a privately owned college or university without regard to whether the required financial assistance is otherwise available from private sources, and may waive interest payments and defer principal payments on such a loan for the first three years of the term of the loan.

64 Stat. 1109.

SEC. 8. (a) It shall be the duty of the Administration and it is hereby empowered, whenever it determines such action is necessary—

SBA may:

(1) to enter into contracts with the United States Government and any department, agency, or officer thereof having procurement powers obligating the Administration to furnish articles, equipment, supplies, or materials to the Government. In any case in which the Administration certifies to any officer of the Government having procurement powers that the Administration is competent to perform any specific Government procurement contract to be let by any such officer, such officer shall be authorized in his discretion to let such procurement contract to the Administration upon such terms and conditions as may be agreed upon between the Administration and the procurement officer; and

Make contracts.

15 U.S.C. 637.

(2) to arrange for the performance of such contracts by negotiating or otherwise letting subcontracts to small-business concerns or others for the manufacture, supply, or assembly of such articles, equipment, supplies, or materials, or parts thereof, or servicing or processing in connection therewith, or such management services as may be necessary to enable the Administration to perform such contracts.

Let sub-contracts.

(b) It shall also be the duty of the Administration and it is hereby empowered, whenever it determines such action is necessary—

SBA may:

(1)(A) to provide technical and managerial aids to small-business concerns, by advising and counseling on matters in connection with Government procurement and property disposal and on policies, principles, and practices of good management, including but not limited to cost accounting, methods of financing, business insurance, accident control, wage incentives, and methods engineering, by cooperating and advising with voluntary business, professional, educational, and other nonprofit organizations, associations, and institutions and with other Federal and State agencies, by maintaining a clearinghouse for information concerning the managing, financing, and operation of small-business enterprises, by disseminating such information, and by such other activities as are deemed appropriate by the Administration; and

Provide technical and managerial aids.

(B) in the case of any individual or group of persons cooperating with it in furtherance of the purposes of subparagraph (A), (i) to allow such an individual or group such use of the Administration's office facilities and related materials and services as the Administration deems appropriate; and (ii) to pay the transportation expenses and a per diem allowance in accordance with section 5703 of title 5, United States Code, to any such individual for travel and subsistence expenses incurred at the request of the Administration in connection with travel to a point more than fifty miles distant from the home of that individual in providing gratuitous services to small businessmen in furtherance of the purposes of subparagraph (A) or in connection with attendance at meetings sponsored by the Administration;[17]

Volunteer management counselors. Travel expenses, etc.

(2) to make a complete inventory of all productive facilities of small-business concerns or to arrange for such inventory to be made by any other governmental agency which has the facilities. In

Make inventory of small business facilities.

---

[17] This subsec. 8(b)(1)(B) added by Sec. 1017 of PL 89-754; enables SBA to permit members of SCORE and other nonprofit groups use of SBA's available office facilities and services. Section 105 of PL 90-104 added authority to pay travel expenses and per diem.

making any such inventory, the appropriate agencies in the several States may be requested to furnish an inventory of the productive facilities of small-business concerns in each respective State if such an inventory is available or in prospect;

Coordinate utilization of small business.

(3) to coordinate and to ascertain the means by which the productive capacity of small-business concerns can be most effectively utilized;

Consult with Government procurement and disposal officers.

(4) to consult and cooperate with officers of the Government having procurement or property disposal powers, in order to utilize the potential productive capacity of plants operated by small-business concerns;

Obtain information on subcontracting.

(5) to obtain information as to methods and practices which Government prime contractors utilize in letting subcontracts and to take action to encourage the letting of subcontracts by prime contractors to small-business concerns at prices and on conditions and terms which are fair and equitable;

Define what is small within industries.

(6) to determine within any industry the concerns, firms, persons, corporations, partnerships, cooperatives, or other business enterprises which are to be designated "small-business concerns" for the purpose of effectuating the provisions of this Act. To carry out this purpose the Administrator, when requested to do so, shall issue in response to each such request an appropriate certificate certifying an individual concern as a "small-business concern" in accordance with the criteria expressed in this Act. Any such certificate shall be subject to revocation when the concern covered thereby ceases to be a "small-business concern". Offices of the Government having procurement or lending powers, or engaging in the disposal of Federal property or allocating materials or supplies, or promulgating regulations affecting the distribution of materials or supplies, shall accept as conclusive the Administration's determination as to which enterprises are to be designated "small-business concerns", as authorized and directed under this paragraph;

Certify concerns as "small."

(7) to certify to Government procurement offi- Issue certifi-
cates of
cers, and officers engaged in the sale and disposal competency.
of Federal property, with respect to the competency,
as to capacity and credit, of any small-business concern or group of such concerns to perform a specific Government contract. In any case in which a
small-business concern or group of such concerns
has been certified by or under the authority of the
Administration to be a competent Government
contractor with respect to capacity and credit as
to a specific Government contract, the officers of
the Government having procurement or property
disposal powers are directed to accept such certification as conclusive, and are authorized to let such
Government contract to such concern or group of
concerns without requiring it to meet any other
requirement with respect to capacity and credit;

(8) to obtain from any Federal department, Obtain re-
establishment, or agency engaged in procurement ports from Government procurement
or in the financing of procurement or production, agencies.
such reports concerning the letting of contracts
and subcontracts and the making of loans to business concerns as it may deem pertinent in carrying
out its functions under this Act;

(9) to obtain from any Federal department, Obtain re-
establishment, or agency engaged in the disposal ports from Government disposal
of Federal property such reports concerning the agencies.
solicitation of bids, time of sale, or otherwise as
it may deem pertinent in carrying out its functions
under this Act;

(10) to obtain from suppliers of materials in- Obtain infor-
formation pertaining to the method of filling orders mation on allocation of
and the bases for allocating their supply, whenever it materials.
appears that any small business is unable to obtain
materials from its normal sources;

(11) to make studies and recommendations to Study
the appropriate Federal agencies to insure that a procurement and disposal
fair proportion of the total purchases and contracts programs.
for property and services for the Government be
placed with small-business enterprises, to insure
that a fair proportion of Government contracts for

research and development be placed with small-business concerns, to insure that a fair proportion of the total sales of Government property be made to small-business concerns, and to insure a fair and equitable share of materials, supplies, and equipment to small-business concerns;

Insure fair treatment for small business.

(12) to consult and cooperate with all Government agencies for the purpose of insuring that small-business concerns shall receive fair and reasonable treatment from such agencies;

Advisory boards.

(13) to establish such advisory boards and committees as may be necessary to achieve the purposes of this Act and of the Small Business Investment Act of 1958; to call meetings of such boards and committees from time to time; to pay the transportation expenses and a per diem allowance in accordance with section 5703 of title 5, United States Code, to the members of such boards and committees for travel and subsistence expenses incurred at the request of the Administration in connection with travel to points more than fifty miles distant from the homes of such members in attending the meetings of such boards and committees; and to rent temporarily, within the District of Columbia or elsewhere, such hotel or other accommodations as are needed to facilitate the conduct of such meetings;[18]

72 Stat. 689. 15 U.S.C. 661 note.

Assistance to businesses to be displaced by urban renewal.

(14) to provide at the earliest practicable time such information and assistance as may be appropriate, including information concerning eligibility for loans under section 7(b)(3), to local public agencies (as defined in section 110(h) of the Housing Act of 1949) and to small-business concerns to be displaced by federally aided urban renewal projects in order to assist such small-business concerns in reestablishing their operations;[19] and

[18] Section 106 of PL 90-104 added achievement of the purposes of the Small Business Investment Act of 1958 as one of the areas of responsibility of advisory boards; authorizes the payment of travel expenses and per diem; and enables SBA to rent accommodations for advisory board meetings.
[19] Par. 14 of sec. 8(b) was added by PL 88-560.

(15) to disseminate, without regard to the provisions of section 4154 of title 39, United States Code, data and information, in such form as it shall deem appropriate, to public agencies, private organizations, and the general public.[20]

Information, dissemination.
74 Stat. 661.

(c) The Administration shall from time to time make studies of matters materially affecting the competitive strength of small business, and of the effect on small business of Federal laws, programs, and regulations, and shall make recommendations to the appropriate Federal agency or agencies for the adjustment of such programs and regulations to the needs of small business.

Study competitive position of small business.

(d)(1) Within ninety days after the effective date of this subsection, the Administrator, the Secretary of Defense, and the Administrator of General Services shall cooperatively develop a small business subcontracting program which shall contain such provisions as may be appropriate to (A) enable small business concerns to be considered fairly as subcontractors and suppliers to contractors performing work or rendering services as prime contractors or subcontractors under Government procurement contracts, (B) insure that such prime contractors and subcontractors will consult through the appropriate procuring agency with the Administration when requested by the Administration, and (C) enable the Administration to obtain from any Government procurement agency such available or reasonably obtainable information and records concerning subcontracting by its prime contractors and their subcontractors as the Administration may deem necessary: *Provided,* That such program shall not authorize the Administration to (i) prescribe the extent to which any contractor or subcontractor shall subcontract, (ii) specify the business concerns to which subcontracts shall be granted, or (iii) vest in the Administration authority respecting the administration of individual prime contracts or subcontracts: *Provided further,* That such program shall provide that in evaluating bids or in selecting contractors for negotiated contracts, the extensive use of subcontractors by a proposed contractor shall be considered

Small business subcontracting program.

[20] Added by section 107 of PL 90-104.

a favorable factor. The Secretary of Defense and the Administrator of General Services each shall promulgate regulations implementing the program as developed: *Provided,* That prior to the promulgation of such regulations, or any changes therein, the concurrence of the Administration shall be obtained, and if such concurrence cannot be obtained the matter in disagreement shall be submitted to the President who shall make the final determination. In addition, the Administrator of General Services and the Secretary of Defense may issue such other regulations concerning subcontracting not inconsistent with the small business subcontracting program as they each deem necessary or appropriate to effectuate their functions and responsibilities.

Contracts included.
(2) Every contract for property or services (including but not limited to contracts for research and development, maintenance, repair and construction, but excluding contracts to be performed entirely outside of the United States or its territories) in excess of $1,000,000 made by a Government department or agency, which in the opinion of the procuring agency offers substantial subcontracting possibilities, shall require the contractor to conform to the small business subcontracting program promulgated under this subsection, and to insert in all subcontracts and purchase orders in excess of $500,000 which offer substantial possibilities for further subcontracting a provision requiring the subcontractor or supplier to conform to such small business subcontracting program.

SBA report and recommendations.
(3) The Administration shall include in any report filed under section 10(b) of this Act, information and such recommendations as it may deem appropriate, with respect to the administration of the small business subcontracting program established under this subsection.

Proprietary rights protected.
(4) Nothing in this subsection shall be construed to authorize the Administrator, the Secretary of Defense, or the Administrator of General Services to secure and disseminate technical data or processes developed by any business concern at its own expense.[21]

[21] Entire sec. 8(d) was added by sec. 7 of PL 87-305.

(e) It shall be the duty of the Secretary of Commerce, and he is hereby empowered, to obtain notice of all proposed defense procurement actions of $10,000 and above, and all civilian procurement actions of $5,000 and above, from any Federal department, establishment, or agency engaged in procurement of supplies and services in the United States; and to publicize such notices in the daily publication "United States Department of Commerce Synopsis of the United States Government Proposed Procurement, Sales, and Contract Awards," immediately after the necessity for the procurement is established; except that nothing herein shall require publication of such notices with respect to those procurements (1) which for security reasons are of a classified nature, or (2) which involve perishable subsistence supplies, or (3) which are for utility services and the procuring agency in accordance with applicable law has predetermined the utility concern to whom the award will be made, or (4) which are of such unusual and compelling emergency that the Government would be seriously injured if bids or offers were permitted to be made more than 15 days after the issuance of the invitation for bids or solicitation for proposals, or (5) which are made by an order placed under an existing contract, or (6) which are made from another Government department or agency, or a mandatory source of supply, or (7) which are for personal or professional services, or (8) which are for services from educational institutions, or (9) in which only foreign sources are to be solicited, or (10) for which it is determined in writing by the procuring agency, with the concurrence of the Administrator, that advance publicity is not appropriate or reasonable.[22]

> Proposed procurements publicized daily by Secretary of Commerce.

SEC. 9. (a) Research and development are major factors in the growth and progress of industry and the national economy. The expense of carrying on research and development programs is beyond the means of many small-business concerns, and such concerns are handicapped in obtaining the benefits of research and development programs conducted at Government expense.

> Research and development. 15 U.S.C. 638.

[22] Sec. 8(e) was added by sec. 8 of PL 87-305.

These small-business concerns are thereby placed at a competitive disadvantage. This weakens the competitive free enterprise system and prevents the orderly development of the national economy. It is the policy of the Congress that assistance be given to small-business concerns to enable them to undertake and to obtain the benefits of research and development in order to maintain and strengthen the competitive free enterprise system and the national economy.

Policy of Congress.

SBA shall:

(b) It shall be the duty of the Administration, and it is hereby empowered—

Assist in obtaining research contracts.

(1) to assist small-business concerns to obtain Government contracts for research and development;

Assist in obtaining benefits of research.

(2) to assist small-business concerns to obtain the benefits of research and development performed under Government contracts or at Government expense; and

Provide technical assistance.

(3) to provide technical assistance to small-business concerns to accomplish the purposes of this section.

Other agencies to co-operate with SBA.

(c) The Administration is authorized to consult and cooperate with all Government agencies and to make studies and recommendations to such agencies, and such agencies are authorized and directed to cooperate with the Administration in order to carry out and to accomplish the purposes of this section.

(d) (1) The Administrator is authorized to consult with representatives of small-business concerns with a view to assisting and encouraging such firms to undertake joint programs for research and development carried out through such corporate or other mechanism as may be most appropriate for the purpose. Such joint programs may, among other things, include the following purposes:

Joint research and development programs.

Acquisition of facilities.

(A) to construct, acquire, or establish laboratories and other facilities for the conduct of research;

Utilization of applied research. Collection of research information.

(B) to undertake and utilize applied research;
(C) to collect research information related to a particular industry and disseminate it to participating members;

(D) to conduct applied research on a protected, proprietary, and contractual basis with member or nonmember firms, Government agencies, and others; *Applied research programs.*

(E) to prosecute applications for patents and render patent services for participating members; and *Apply for patents.*

(F) to negotiate and grant licenses under patents held under the joint program, and to establish corporations designed to exploit particular patents obtained by it. *Grant licenses.*

(2) The Administrator may, after consultation with the Attorney General and the Chairman of the Federal Trade Commission, and with the prior written approval of the Attorney General, approve any agreement between small-business firms providing for a joint program of research and development, if the Administrator finds that the joint program proposed will maintain and strengthen the free enterprise system and the economy of the Nation. The Administrator or the Attorney General may at any time withdraw his approval of the agreement and the joint program of research and development covered thereby, if he finds that the agreement or the joint program carried on under it is no longer in the best interests of the competitive free enterprise system and the economy of the Nation. A copy of the statement of any such finding and approval intended to be within the coverage of this subsection, and a copy of any modification or withdrawal of approval, shall be published in the Federal Register. The authority conferred by this subsection on the Administrator shall not be delegated by him. *Antitrust exemption.*

(3) No act or omission to act pursuant to and within the scope of any joint program for research and development, under an agreement approved by the Administrator under this subsection, shall be construed to be within the prohibitions of the antitrust laws or the Federal Trade Commission Act. Upon publication in the Federal Register of the notice of withdrawal of his approval of the agreement granted under this subsec-

tion, either by the Administrator or by the Attorney General, the provisions of this subsection shall not apply to any subsequent act or omission to act by reason of such agreement or approval.

Reports:
Operations
under Act.
15 U.S.C.
639

SEC. 10. (a) The Administration shall make a report on December 31 of each year of operations under this Act to the President, the President of the Senate, and the Speaker of the House of Representatives. Such report shall include the names of the business concerns to whom contracts are let and for whom financing is arranged by the Administration, together with the amounts involved, and such report shall include information on the progress of the Administration in liquidating the assets and winding up the affairs of the Reconstruction Finance Corporation, and such other information and such comments and recommendations as the Administration may deem appropriate. The requirement contained in this subsection with respect to the inclusion of information respecting the progress of the Administration in liquidating the assets and winding up the affairs of the Reconstruction Finance Corporation in such report shall be in lieu of any requirement, pursuant to section 106(b) of the Reconstruction Finance Corporation Liquidation Act, and Reorganization Plan Numbered 1 of 1957, that progress reports with respect to such liquidation or winding up of affairs by the Administration be made to the Congress on a quarterly basis.[23]

Expenditure
of funds.
Reports to
Congress
and Small
Business
Committees.

(b) The Administration shall make a report to the President, the President of the Senate, and the Speaker of the House of Representatives, to the Senate Select Committee on Small Business, and to the House Select Committee To Conduct a Study and Investigation of the Problems of Small Business, on December 31 of each year, showing as accurately as possible for each such period the amount of funds appropriated to it that it has expended in the conduct of each of its principal

[23] Former subsec. 10(a) was rewritten and the reporting requirement changed from semiannual to annual by sec. 5(a)(1) of PL 87-305. The report of progress in liquidating the assets and winding up the affairs of the RFC was discontinued by PL 89-348.

activities such as lending, procurement, contracting, and providing technical and managerial aids.[24]

(c)(1) The Attorney General is directed to make, or direct the Federal Trade Commission to make for him, surveys of any activity of the Government which may affect small business, for the purpose of determining any factors which may tend to eliminate competition, create or strengthen monopolies, promote undue concentration of economic power, or otherwise injure small business. *Antitrust reports.*

(2) The Attorney General shall submit to the Congress and the President, at such times as he deems desirable, but not less than once every year, reports setting forth the results of such surveys and including such recommendations as he may deem desirable.[25]

(d) For the purpose of aiding in carrying out the national policy to insure that a fair proportion of the total purchases and contracts for property and services for the Government be placed with small-business enterprises, and to maintain and strengthen the overall economy of the Nation, the Department of Defense shall make a monthly report to the President, the President of the Senate, and the Speaker of the House of Representatives not less than forty-five days after the close of the month, showing the amount of funds appropriated to the Department of Defense, which have been expended, obligated, or contracted to be spent with small-business concerns and the amount of such funds expended, obligated, or contracted to be spent with firms other than small business in the same fields of operation; and such monthly reports shall show separately the funds expended, obligated, or contracted to be spent for basic and applied scientific research and development. *Defense procurement reports.*

(e) The Administration shall retain all correspondence, records of inquiries, memoranda, reports, books, and records, including memoranda as to all investigations conducted by or for the Administration, for a period of at least one year from the date of each there- *Maintenance of records available to Small Business Committees.*

---

[24] The reporting requirements of subsec. 10(b) was changed from semi-annual to annual by sec. 5(a)(2) of PL 87-305.

[25] Former subsec. 10(c) was rewritten and annual reports by the Attorney General made mandatory by sec. 5(a)(3) of PL 87-305.

of, and shall at all times keep the same available for inspection and examination by the Senate Select Committee on Small Business and the House Select Committee To Conduct a Study and Investigation of the Problems of Small Business, or their duly authorized representatives.

Consultation with other Government agencies.

(f) To the extent deemed necessary by the Administrator to protect and preserve small-business interests. the Administration shall consult and cooperate with other departments and agencies of the Federal Government in the formulation by the Administration of policies affecting small-business concerns. When requested by the Administrator, each department and agency of the Federal Government shall consult and cooperate with the Administration in the formulation by such department or agency of policies affecting small-business concerns, in order to insure that small-business interests will be recognized, protected, and preserved. This subsection shall not require any department or agency to consult or cooperate with the Administration in any case where the head of such department or agency determines that such consultation or cooperation would unduly delay action which must be taken by such department or agency to protect the national interest in an emergency.

15 U.S.C. 640.

SEC. 11. (a) The President is authorized to consult with representatives of small-business concerns with a view to encouraging the making by such persons with the approval of the President of voluntary agreements and programs to further the objectives of this Act.

Defense production pools.

(b) No act or omission to act pursuant to this Act which occurs while this Act is in effect, if requested by the President pursuant to a voluntary agreement or program approved under subsection (a) of this section and found by the President to be in the public interest as contributing to the national defense, shall be construed to be within the prohibitions of the antitrust laws or the Federal Trade Commission Act of the United States. A copy of each such request intended to be within the coverage of this section, and any modification or withdrawal thereof, shall be furnished to the Attorney General and the Chairman of the Federal Trade Commission when made, and it shall be published in the Federal Register unless publication thereof would, in the opinion of the President, endanger the national security.

(c) The authority granted in subsection (b) of this section shall be delegated only (1) to an official who shall for the purpose of such delegation be required to be appointed by the President by and with the advice and consent of the Senate, (2) upon the condition that such official consult with the Attorney General and the Chairman of the Federal Trade Commission not less than ten days before making any request or finding thereunder, and (3) upon the condition that such official obtain the approval of the Attorney General to any request thereunder before making the request.[26]

(d) Upon withdrawal of any request or finding hereunder, or upon withdrawal by the Attorney General of his approval of the voluntary agreement or program on which the request or finding is based, the provisions of this section shall not apply to any subsequent act, or omission to act, by reason of such finding or request.

SEC. 12. The President may transfer to the Administration any functions, powers, and duties of any department or agency which relate primarily to small-business problems. In connection with any such transfer, the President may provide for appropriate transfers of records, property, necessary personnel, and unexpended balances of appropriations and other funds available to the department or agency from which the transfer is made.

Transfer of small-business functions. 15 U.S.C. 641.

SEC. 13. No loans shall be made or equipment, facilities, or services furnished by the Administration under this Act to any business enterprise unless the owners, partners, or officers of such business enterprise (1) certify to the Administration the names of any attorneys, agents, or other persons engaged by or on behalf of such business enterprise for the purpose of expediting applications made to the Administration for assistance of any sort, and the fees paid or to be paid to any such per-

Listing of agents and attorneys. 15 U.S.C. 642.

[26] The President delegated this authority to the SBA Administrator by Executive Order 10493, dated Oct. 14, 1953 (18 F.R. 6583).

sons; (2) execute an agreement binding any such business enterprise for a period of two years after any assistance is rendered by the Administration to such business enterprise, to refrain from employing, tendering any office or employment to, or retaining for professional services, any person who, on the date such assistance or any part thereof was rendered, or within one year prior thereto, shall have served as an officer, attorney, agent, or employee of the Administration occupying a position or engaging in activities which the Administration shall have determined involve discretion with respect to the granting of assistance under this Act; and (3) furnish the names of lending institutions to which such business enterprise has applied for loans together with dates, amounts, terms, and proof of refusal.

SEC. 14. To the fullest extent the Administration deems practicable, it shall make a fair charge for the use of Government-owned property and make and let contracts on a basis that will result in a recovery of the direct costs incurred by the Administration.

SEC. 15. To effectuate the purposes of this Act, small business concerns within the meaning of this Act shall receive any award or contract or any part thereof, and be awarded any contract for the sale of Government property, as to which it is determined by the Administration and the contracting procurement or disposal agency (1) to be in the interest of maintaining or mobilizing the Nation's full productive capacity, (2) to be in the interest of war or national defense programs, (3) to be in the interest of assuring that a fair proportion of the total purchases and contracts for property and services for the Government are placed with small-business concerns, or (4) to be in the interest of assuring that a fair proportion of the total sales of Government property be made to small-business concerns; but nothing contained in this Act shall be construed to change any preferences or priorities established by law with respect to the sale of electrical power or other property by the Government or any agency thereof. These determinations may be made for in-

Side notes:

Employment agreement.

Charges for Government-owned property. 15 U.S.C. 643.

Joint-determination program for awarding contracts or selling property. 15 U.S.C. 644.

dividual awards or contracts or for classes of awards or contracts. Whenever the Administration and the contracting procurement agency fail to agree, the matter shall be submitted for determination to the Secretary or the head of the appropriate department or agency by the Administrator.

SEC. 16. (a) Whoever makes any statement know- Penalty for false ing it to be false, or whoever willfully overvalues any statements. security, for the purpose of obtaining for himself or 645. for any applicant any loan, or extension thereof by renewal, deferment of action, or otherwise, or the acceptance, release, or substitution of security therefor, or for the purpose of influencing in any way the action of the Administration, or for the purpose of obtaining money, property, or anything of value, under this Act, shall be punished by a fine of not more than $5,000 or by imprisonment for not more than two years, or both.

(b) Whoever, being connected in any capacity with Penalty for wrongful the Administration, (1) embezzles, abstracts, purloins, conduct. or willfully misapplies any moneys, funds, securities, or other things of value, whether belonging to it or pledged or otherwise entrusted to it, or (2) with intent to defraud the Administration or any other body politic or corporate, or any individual, or to deceive any officer, auditor, or examiner of the Administration, makes any false entry in any book, report, or statement of or to the Administration, or, without being duly authorized, draws any order or issues, puts forth, or assigns any note, debenture, bond, or other obligation, or draft, bill of exchange, mortgage, judgment, or decree thereof, or (3) with intent to defraud participates or shares in or receives directly or indirectly any money, profit, property, or benefit through any transaction, loan, commission, contract, or any other act of the Administration, or (4) gives any unauthorized information concerning any future action or plan of the Administration which might affect the value of securities, or, having such knowledge, invests or speculates, directly or indirectly, in the securities or property of any company or corporation receiving loans or other assistance from the Administration, shall be punished by a fine of not more than $10,000 or by imprisonment for not more than five years, or both.

Penalty for misappropriation of SBA collateral. (c) Whoever, with intent to defraud, knowingly conceals, removes, disposes of, or converts to his own use or to that of another, any property mortgaged or pledged to, or held by, the Administration, shall be fined not more than $5,000 or imprisoned not more than five years, or both; but if the value of such property does not exceed $100, he shall be fined not more than $1,000 or imprisoned not more than one year, or both.[27]

Subordination of SBA collateral.
15 U.S.C. 646. SEC. 17. Any interest held by the Administration in property, as security for a loan, shall be subordinate to any lien on such property for taxes due on the property to a State, or political subdivision thereof, in any case where such lien would, under applicable State law, be superior to such interest if such interest were held by any party other than the United States.

Avoidance of duplication.
15 U.S.C. 647. SEC. 18. The Administration shall not duplicate the work or activity of any other department or agency of the Federal Government and nothing contained in this Act shall be construed to authorize any such duplication unless such work or activity is expressly provided for in this Act.

Separability
15 U.S.C. 648 SEC. 19. If any provision of this Act, or the application thereof to any person or circumstances, is held invalid, the remainder of this Act, and the application of such provision to other persons or circumstances, shall not be affected thereby.

Authorization for appropriations.
15 U.S.C. 649. SEC. 20. There are hereby authorized to be appropriated such sums as may be necessary and appropriate for the carrying out of the provisions and purposes of this Act other than those for which appropriations to the revolving fund are authorized by section 4(c).[28]

Repeal of inconsistent laws.
15 U.S.C. 650. SEC. 21. All laws and parts of laws inconsistent with this Act are hereby repealed to the extent of such inconsistency.

[27] Subsec. (c) of sec. 16 was added by PL 88-264.
[28] The clause excluding the appropriation authority covered by sec. 4(c) was added by sec. 11(h)(2) of PL 87-341.

APPENDIX III.

Small Business Administration Field Office Addresses

(Area, Regional, Branch and Post-of-Duty Stations)

NORTHEASTERN AREA
Boston, Massachusetts 02203
John Fitzgerald Kennedy Federal
  Building
Government Center
  Boston, Massachusetts 02203
  John Fitzgerald Kennedy Federal
    Building
  Government Center
  Augusta, Maine 04330
  Federal Building, U. S. Post Office
  40 Western Ave.
  Concord, New Hampshire 03301
  55 Pleasant Street
  Hartford, Connecticut 06103
  Federal Office Building
  450 Main Street
  Montpelier, Vermont 05601
  Federal Building, P. O. &
    Courthouse
  2nd Floor, 87 State Street
  Providence, Rhode Island 02903
  702 Smith Building, 57 Eddy Street
NEW YORK AREA
New York, New York 10006
61 Broadway, Rm. 2101
  New York, New York 10004
  42 Broadway

Hato Rey, Puerto Rico 00919
255 Ponce De Leon Ave.
P. O. Box 1915
•St. Thomas, U. S. Virgin Islands
  00802
  22 Crystal Gade, P. O. Box 806
Newark, New Jersey 07102
970 Broad Street, Rm. 1636
Syracuse, New York 13202
Hunter Plaza, Fayette & Salina
  Sts.
•Buffalo, New York 14203
  Federal Building, Rm. 9
  121 Ellicott Street
MIDDLE ATLANTIC AREA
Bala Cynwyd, Pennsylvania 19004
1 Decker Square, East Lobby
  Philadelphia, Pennsylvania 19107
  1317 Filbert Street
•Dover, Delaware 19901
  21 the Green
Baltimore, Maryland 21201
1113 Federal Building
31 Hopkins Plaza
Clarksburg, West Va. 26301
Lowndes Bank Building
119 N. 3rd Street

277

•Charleston, West Va. 25301
3000 U. S. Courthouse & Fed.
   Bldg.
500 Quarrier Street, Rm. 3000
Cleveland, Ohio 44113
Standard Building, 1370 Ontario
   St.
•Toledo, Ohio 43602
Federal Office Building
234 Summit Street
Columbus, Ohio 43215
Beacon Bldg., 50 West Gay Street
•Cincinnati, Ohio 45202
4515 Federal Building
Louisville, Kentucky 40202
1900 Commonwealth Building
Fourth and Broadway
Pittsburgh, Pennsylvania 15222
Federal Bldg., 1000 Liberty Ave.
Richmond, Virginia 23226
P. O. Box 8565, 1904 Byrd Ave.
Washington, D. C. 20417
1321 H St., N. W. (Mezzanine)
SOUTHEASTERN AREA
Atlanta, Georgia 30309
1401 Peachtree Street, N. E.
Atlanta, Georgia 30303
52 Fairlie Street, N. W.
Birmingham, Alabama 35205
S. 20th Building, 908 S. 20th St.
Charlotte, North Carolina 28202
American Bldg., 201 S. Tryon St.
Columbia, South Carolina 29201
1801 Assembly Street
Jackson, Mississippi 39201
322 U. S. Post Office &
   Courthouse Bldg.
Capital & West Streets
Jacksonville, Florida 32202
Federal Office Building
400 W. Bay St., P. O. Box 35067
Miami, Florida 33130
912 Federal Office Building
51 S. W. 1st Avenue
*Tampa, Florida 33602
Federal Office Building, Rm. 208
500 Zack Street
Nashville, Tennessee 37219
Security Federal Savings & Loan
   Bldg.
500 Union Street

•Knoxville, Tennessee 37902
Room 122
301 West Cumberland Avenue
MIDWESTERN AREA
Chicago, Illinois 60604
Federal Office Building, Rm. 437
219 South Dearborn Street
Chicago, Illinois 60604
Federal Office Building, Rm. 437
219 South Dearborn Street
Des Moines, Iowa 50309
New Federal Building, Rm. 749
210 Walnut Street
Detroit, Michigan 48226
1200 Book Bldg., 1249 Wash. Blvd.
•Marquette, Michigan 49855
502 West Kaye Avenue
Indianapolis, Indiana 46204
Century Building
36 South Pennsylvania Street
Kansas City, Missouri 64106
911 Walnut Street
Madison, Wisconsin 53703
25 West Main
•Milwaukee, Wisconsin 53203
Straus Building, 238 W.
   Wisconsin Ave.
Minneapolis, Minnesota 55402
Reimann Bldg., 816 2nd Ave.
   South
St. Louis, Missouri 63102
Federal Bldg., 208 N. Broadway
SOUTHWESTERN AREA
Dallas, Texas 75202
1309 Main Street
Dallas, Texas 75201
Mayflower Bldg., 411 N. Akard St.
Albuquerque, New Mexico 87101
Federal Bldg., & U. S. Court
   House
Suite 3509, 500 Gold Ave. S. W.
Houston, Texas 77002
Niels Esperson Building
808 Travis Street
Little Rock, Arkansas 72201
377 Post Office & Court House
   Bldg.
600 W. Capitol Avenue
Lubbock, Texas 79401
204 Federal Office Building
1616 19th Street

Marshall, Texas 75670
201 Travis Terrace Bldg.,
P. O. Box 1349
505 East Travis Street
New Orleans, Louisiana 70130
Gateway Bldg., 124 Camp Street
Oklahoma City, Oklahoma 73102
Rm. 511, Oklahoma Mortgage
Bldg.
324 North Robinson Street
San Antonio, Texas 78205
301 Broadway, 300 Manion Bldg.
•Harlingen, Texas 78550
219 E. Jackson Street
ROCKY MOUNTAIN AREA
Denver, Colorado 80202
721 19th Street
Denver, Colorado 80202
Federal Office Building
1961 Stout Street
Casper, Wyoming 82601
Western Bldg., 300 North Center
St.
Fargo, North Dakota 58102
300 American Life Bldg.
207 North Fifth Street
Helena, Montana 59601
P. O. Box 1690, 205 Power Block
Corner Main & 6th Avenue
Omaha, Nebraska 68102
7425 Federal Building
215 North 17th Street
Salt Lake City, Utah 84111
2237 Federal Building
125 State Street
Sioux Falls, South Dakota 57102
402 Nat'l Bank of South Dakota
Bldg.
8th and Main Avenue
Wichita, Kansas 67202
302 - 120 Building
120 South Market Street

PACIFIC COASTAL AREA
San Francisco, California 94102
Federal Building
450 Golden Gate Ave., Box 36044
San Francisco, California 94102
Federal Building
450 Golden Gate Ave., Box 36044
Anchorage, Alaska 99501
632 Sixth Avenue, Suite 450
•Fairbanks, Alaska 99701
510 Second Avenue
Boise, Idaho 83702
Room 408, Idaho Building
216 North 8th Street
Honolulu, Hawaii 96813
1149 Bethel Street, Rm. 402
•Agana, Guam 96910
Ada Plaza Center Building
P. O. Box 927
Los Angeles, California 90014
849 South Broadway
•Las Vegas, Nevada 89101
300 Las Vegas Blvd., South
Room 4-104
Phoenix, Arizona 85004
Central Towers Building
2727 North Central Avenue
*Tucson, Arizona 85701
155 E. Alameda
Portland, Oregon 97205
700 Pittock Block
921 S. W. Washington Street
San Diego, California 92101
110 West C Street
Seattle, Washington 98104
1206 Smith Tower, 506 Second
Ave.
Spokane, Washington 99210
651 U. S. Court House
P. O. Box 2167

•Branch Office
8 Area Offices
62 Regional Offices
*Post-of-Duty Station
13 Branch Offices
2 Post-of-duty Stations

Bibliography

BOOKS

ABELS, JULES. *The Truman Scandals*. Chicago: Henry Regnery, 1956.

AMERICAN ASSEMBLY. *The Federal Government Service*. Englewood Cliffs, N.J.: Prentice Hall, 1965.

BUNZEL, JOHN H. *The American Small Businessman*. New York: Random House, 1962.

CAVES, RICHARD E. *American Industry: Structure, Conduct, Performance*. Englewood Cliffs, N.J.: Prentice Hall, 1964.

CHEIT, EARL F., ed. *The Business Establishment*. New York: John Wiley & Sons, 1964.

CLARK, COLIN. *The Conditions of Economic Progress*. London: Macmillan, 1960.

COMMISSION ON MONEY AND CREDIT. *Fiscal and Debt Management Policies*. Englewood Cliffs, N.J.: Prentice Hall, 1963.

COMMITTEE FOR ECONOMIC DEVELOPMENT. *Meeting the Special Needs of Small Business*. New York: Committee for Economic Development, 1948.

FLINK, S. J. *Equity Financing for Small Business*. New York: Simmons-Boardman, 1962.

————. *The Role of Commercial Banks in the SBIC Industry*. New York: American Bankers Association, 1965.

FOLEY, EUGENE P. *The Achieving Ghetto*. Washington, D.C.: National Press, 1968.

FREEMAN, J. LEIPER. *The Political Process: Executive Bureau–Congressional Committee Relationships*. New York: Random House, 1955.

GALBRAITH, JOHN KENNETH. *The New Industrial State*. Boston: Houghton Mifflin, 1967.

GRIFFITH, ERNEST S. *The Impasse of Democracy*. New York: Harrison-Hilton Books, 1939.

HAMBERG, DANIEL. *R & D: Essays on the Economics of Research and Development*. New York: Random House, 1966.

281

HOLLANDER, EDWARD D., and others. *The Future of Small Business*. New York: Frederick A. Praeger, 1967.

JEWKES, JOHN, SAWERS, DAVID, and STILLERMAN, RICHARD. *The Sources of Invention*. London: Macmillan, 1961.

JONES, JESSE H., with ANGLY, EDWARD. *Fifty Billion Dollars*. New York: Macmillan, 1951.

KAPLAN, A. D. H. *Small Business: Its Place and Problems*. New York: McGraw-Hill, 1949.

MARCH, JAMES G., and SIMON, HERBERT A. *Organizations*. New York: John Wiley & Sons, 1958.

MASON, EDWARD S. *Economic Concentration and Monopoly Problems*. Cambridge: Harvard University Press, 1957.

MASSEL, MARK S. *Competition and Monopoly*. Washington: The Brookings Institution, 1962.

PRESTHUS, ROBERT. *The Organizational Society*. (Vintage ed.) New York: Random House, 1962.

PROXMIRE, WILLIAM. *Can Small Business Survive?* Chicago: Henry Regnery, 1964.

ROBINSON, E. A. G. *The Structure of Competitive Industry*. Cambridge Economic Handbooks Series. London: Nisbet, 1931.

SIMON, HERBERT A. *Administrative Behavior*. (2d ed.) New York: Macmillan, 1957.

SMITHIES, ARTHUR. *The Budgetary Process in the United States*. New York: McGraw-Hill, 1955.

THOMPSON, VICTOR A. *Modern Organization*. New York: Alfred A. Knopf, 1961.

WILDAVSKY, AARON. *The Politics of the Budgetary Process*. Boston: Little, Brown, 1964.

ZEIGLER, HARMON. *The Politics of Small Business*. Washington: Public Affairs Press, 1961.

ARTICLES

BACH, G. L., and HUIZENGA, C. J. "The Differential Effects of Tight Money," *American Economic Review*, March 1961, pp. 52–80.

BENSTON, GEORGE J. "Commercial Bank Price Discrimination Against Small Loans: An Empirical Study," *Journal of Finance*, December 1964, pp. 631–43.

FOLEY, EUGENE P. "The Negro Businessman: In Search of A Tradition," *Daedalus*, Winter 1966, pp. 107–44.

HAYES, SAMUEL L., and WOODS, DONALD H. "Are SBICs Doing Their Job?" *Harvard Business Review*, March-April 1963, pp. 6–19 ff.

Law and Contemporary Problems. Special issue on small business. Winter 1959.

LEES, HANNAH. "The Making of A Negro Middle Class," *The Reporter*, October 8, 1964, pp. 41–44.

LINDBLOM, CHARLES E. "The Science of 'Muddling Through,' " *Public Administration Review*, XXIV (1959), pp. 79–88.

TROW, MARTIN. "Small Businessmen, Political Tolerance, and Support for McCarthy," *American Journal of Sociology*, November 1958, 270–81.

ULMER, MELVILLE J., and NEILSON, ALICE. "Business Turnover and Causes of Failure," *Survey of Current Business*, April 1947, pp. 10–16.

VINYARD, DALE. "Congressional Committees on Small Business," *Midwest Journal of Political Science*, August 1966, pp. 364–77.

WEINTRAUB, DAVID, and MAGDOFF, HARRY. "The Service Industries in Relation to Employment Trends," *Econometrica*, October 1940, pp. 289–311.

GOVERNMENT DOCUMENTS

MAYER, KURT B., and GOLDSTEIN, SIDNEY. *The First Two Years: Problems of Small Firm Growth and Survival*. Washington: Small Business Administration, 1961.

MILLS, C. WRIGHT, and ULMER, MELVILLE J. *Small Business and Civic Welfare*. Report of the Smaller War Plants Corporation to the Special Committee to Study Problems of American Small Business, United States Senate. Washington: Government Printing Office, 1946.

U.S. FEDERAL RESERVE BOARD. *Financing Small Business*. Three parts. Washington: Government Printing Office, 1958.

U.S. HOUSE. APPROPRIATIONS COMMITTEE. *Departments of State, Justice, Commerce, the Judiciary, and Related Agencies*. Hearings. Washington: Government Printing Office, annual.

U.S. HOUSE. BANKING AND CURRENCY COMMITTEE. *Creation of Small Business Administration*. Hearings on H.R. 5141, 83rd Cong., 1st Sess. Washington: Government Printing Office, 1953.

―――. *Report on H.R. 5141*. 83rd Cong., 1st Sess. Washington: Government Printing Office, 1953.

U.S. HOUSE. EDUCATION AND LABOR COMMITTEE. *Economic Opportunity Act of 1964*. Hearings on H.R. 10440, 88th Cong., 2d Sess. Washington: Government Printing Office, 1964.

―――. *Poverty in the United States*. Washington: Government Printing Office, 1964.

―――. *Report on H.R. 11337*, 88th Cong., 2d Sess. Washington: Government Printing Office, 1964.

U.S. HOUSE. SELECT COMMITTEE ON SMALL BUSINESS. *Small Business in Urban Areas*. Six parts. Washington: Government Printing Office, 1965, 1966.

U.S. SENATE. BANKING AND CURRENCY COMMITTEE. *Government Lending Agencies.* Hearings on S. 892 *et al.,* 83rd Cong., 1st Sess. Washington: Government Printing Office, 1953.

———. *Study of the Reconstruction Finance Corporation.* Hearings, 81st Cong., 2d Sess. Four parts. Washington: Government Printing Office, 1950.

———. *Study of the Reconstruction Finance Corporation.* Interim Reports. Five parts. Washington: Government Printing Office, 1950, 1951.

U.S. SENATE. GOVERNMENT OPERATIONS COMMITTEE. *Investigation Into Small Business Investment Companies.* Two parts. Washington: Government Printing Office, 1966, 1967.

U.S. SENATE. SELECT COMMITTEE ON SMALL BUSINESS. *Annual Report.* Washington: Government Printing Office, annual.

———. *Organization and Operation of the Small Business Administration, 1966.* Report. Washington: Government Printing Office, 1966.

———. *Review of Small Business Administration Financial Assistance Programs.* Report. Washington: Government Printing Office, 1967.

———. *Small Business Administration—1965.* Hearings, 89th Cong., 1st Sess. Washington: Government Printing Office, 1965.

———. *Small Business Administration Lending Programs.* Hearings, 89th Cong., 1st Sess. Washington: Government Printing Office, 1966.

———. *SBA's Financial Assistance Programs.* Hearing, 89th Cong., 1st Sess., Washington: Government Printing Office, 1967.

———. *Status and Future of Small Business.* Hearings, 90th Cong., 1st Sess. Three parts. Washington: Government Printing Office, 1967.

U.S. SMALL BUSINESS ADMINISTRATION. *Annual Report.* Washington: Government Printing Office, annual.

U.S. TEMPORARY NATIONAL ECONOMIC COMMITTEE. *Problems of Small Business.* Monograph No. 17. Washington: Government Printing Office, 1941.

UNPUBLISHED MATERIAL

HEIMLICH, JUDITH ANN. "The Business of Poverty." Unpublished doctoral dissertation, Department of Public Law and Government, Columbia University, 1967.

MILLS, JAMES IRA. "A Study of Small Business and Federal Government Programs to Assist Small Business." Unpublished doctoral dissertation, Department of Business Administration, George Washington University, 1965.

Index

National income, 47, 49; and persons engaged in production, 28
National Planning Association, 39
National Science Foundation, 230
National Small Business Administration, 203–4
National Small Business Advisory Council, 83
National Small Business Week, 219
Neighborhood Youth Corps, 62
Neilson, Alice, 51*n.*
Nelson, Richard R., 140
New Deal, 9, 13
New York Times, The, 208
News coverage of SBA, 206–11

OEO (Office of Economic Opportunity), 113, 114, 115, 227
OEP (Office of Emergency Planning), 227

Panel on Invention and Innovation of Commerce Department, 140–41
Paris-Match, 211
Participation certificates, 122–26
Patman, Wright, 21, 22, 24, 29, 32–33, 153, 169, 173
Pearson, Drew, 210
Philadelphia Small Business Opportunities Corporation, 181
Planning, Research and Analysis: assistant administrator for, 86, 178; as SBA career, 241
Planning-Programing-Budgeting System, 82, 85, 220, 222
Powell, Adam Clayton, 115, 184
President and SBA, 217, 218–20
Presthus, Robert, 79
Principles of Scientific Management, The (Taylor), 78
Procurement, 66–69, 127–49; and interagency relations, 224–25; as SBA career, 240
Procurement and Management Assistance Division of SBA, 32; associate administrator of, 88
Program Advisory Council, 85
Property, sale of surplus, 69
Proxmire, William, 161, 169, 173, 192, 195

Public Affairs, Office of (of SBA), 177
Public Information, Office of (of SBA), 196, 212–14
Public Inquiry and Analysis, Office of (of SBA), 177
Publications of SBA, 146

R & D: Essays on the Economics of Research and Development (Hamberg), 137*n.*
Reconstruction Finance Corporation (RFC), 6–7, 8–18, 22–23, 81; formation of, 9; hearings on, 17; loans by, 18
Reconversion, 12–13
Research and development: economics of, 139–42; government role in, 138–39; growth of, in U.S. economy, 136–38; increased share of, for small business, 142–43
Retail trades, business size standards for, 32, 33
Revolving funds, 117–26
RFC (*see* Reconstruction Finance Corporation)
Robertson, A. Willis, 155
Role of Commercial Banks in the SBIC Industry, The (Flink), 199
Rooney, John J., 169–70
Roosevelt, Franklin D., 9, 10, 11–12
Rostow, Walt W., 46
Rubber Reserve Company, 11

Saltonstall, Leverett, 173, 206
SBA (*see* Small Business Administration)
SBANE (*see* Smaller Business Association of New England)
SBDC's (*see* Small Business Development Centers)
SBI Act (*see* Small Business Investment Act)
SBIC's (*see* Small Business Investment Centers)
Science and Astronautics, House Committee on, 141
SCORE (*see* Service Corps of Retired Executives)